THE
TO HEAVEN

THE SECRET KEY
TO HEAVEN

THE VITAL IMPORTANCE
OF PRIVATE PRAYER

Thomas Brooks

THE BANNER OF TRUTH TRUST

THE BANNER OF TRUTH TRUST
3 Murrayfield Road, Edinburgh EH12 6EL, UK
P.O. Box 621, Carlisle, PA 17013, USA

*

First published in London as
The Privie Key of Heaven, 1665

First Banner of Truth edition, 2006
© Banner of Truth Trust, 2006

ISBN-10: 0 85151 924 5
ISBN-13: 978 0 85151 924 1

*

Typeset in 10.5/13.5 pt Sabon at the
Banner of Truth Trust, Edinburgh
Printed in the USA by
Versa Press, Inc.,
East Peoria, IL

Contents

PART FIVE
Eleven Instructions (continued)

PART SIX
Means, Rules, and Directions for Faithful
Private Prayer

PART SIX

Means, Rules, and Directions (continued)

Closing Advice

Publisher's Note

SINGULARLY LITTLE is known about Thomas Brooks as a man, other than can be ascertained from his many writings. Born, probably of well-to-do parents, in 1608, Brooks entered Emmanuel College, Cambridge, in 1625, where he was preceded by such men as Thomas Hooker, John Cotton, and Thomas Shepard. He was licensed as a preacher of the gospel by 1640 at the latest. Before that date he seems to have spent a number of years at sea, probably as a chaplain with the fleet. He is thus able to speak of his numerous friends abroad, and of the scenes and happenings he had 'observed in other nations and countries'. Mention, too, is made of 'some terrible storms'. 'I have been some years at sea', he tells us, 'and through grace I can say that I would not exchange my sea experiences for England's riches.' 'Troubles, trials, temptations, dangers, and deaths' were all encountered during his experiences on board ship.

The Civil War over, Brooks became minister of the Word at Thomas Apostle's, London, and was sufficiently renowned to be chosen as preacher before the House of Commons on 26 December, 1648. Three or four years later he moved to St Margaret's, Fish-street Hill, London, but encountered considerable opposition as he refused baptism and the Lord's Supper to those clearly 'unworthy' of such privileges. The following years were filled with written as well as spoken ministry.

In 1662 he fell victim to the notorious Act of Uniformity, but he appears to have remained in his parish and to have preached the Word as opportunity offered. Treatises continued to flow from his agile pen. In 1677 or 1678 he married for the second time, 'she spring-young, he winter-old'. Two years later he went home to his Lord. No portrait of him survives.

The Privie Key of Heaven, was originally published during the awful Plague of London in 1665. It is less well known than any of Brooks' other writings and does not seem to have remained in print for very long after it first appeared. A. B. Grosart reported in the early 1860s that he had 'not been able to trace a reprint until a modern date'.

The complete and unabridged edition that appears here has been taken from vol. 2 of *The Works of Thomas Brooks*.[1] The text has been lightly and sympathetically edited: the material has been more clearly set out in its various parts and sections, errata have been corrected, and archaic words have been updated, where it was thought necessary, for the sake of clarity.

---

[1] Also published by the Banner of Truth Trust in a six-volume, cloth-bound set (ISBN 0 85151 302 6).

Author's Preface

CHRISTIAN READER,

THE EPISTLE DEDICATORY being occasionally[1] so large, I shall do little more than give you the grounds and reasons of sending forth this little piece into the world, especially in such a day as this is. Now, my reasons are these:

1. *First,* Because God by his present dispensations calls more loudly for closet prayer now than he hath done in those last twenty years that are now passed over our heads. See more of this in the sixteenth argument for closet prayer.

2. *Secondly,* Because I have several reasons to fear that many Christians do not clearly nor fully understand the necessity, excellency, and usefulness of this subject, and that many (oh, that I could not say 'any'), live in too great a neglect of this indispensable duty, and that more than a few, for want of light, err in the very practice of it.

---

[1] Because of the occasion, the great Plague of London in 1665. The epistle dedicatory, an exposition and application of Micah 6:9, 'Hear ye the rod and who hath appointed it', is not included in this edition.

3. *Thirdly,* For the refreshing, support, and encouragement of all those churches of Christ that walk in the fear of the Lord, and in the comforts of the Holy Ghost, etc., especially that particular church to whom I stand related.

4. *Fourthly,* To preserve and keep up the power of religion and godliness both in men's houses, hearts, and lives. The power of religion and godliness lives, thrives, or dies, as closet prayer lives, thrives, or dies. Godliness never rises to a higher pitch than when men keep closest to their closets.

5. *Fifthly,* Because closet prayer is a most sovereign remedy, a most precious antidote of God's own prescribing, against the plague that now rages in the midst of us (*1 Kings* 8:37–39).

6. *Sixthly,* Because every man is that really which he is secretly. Never tell me, how handsomely, how purely, how bravely, this or that man acts his part before others but tell me, if you can, how he acts his part before God in his closet; for the man is that certainly, that he is secretly. There are many that sweat upon the stage that are key-cold[1] in their closets.

7. *Seventhly,* Though many worthies have done worthily upon all other parts of prayer, yet there are none either of a former or later date, that have fallen under my eye, that have written any treatise on this subject. I have not a little wondered that so many eminent writers should

---

[1] Cold as a metal key, stone cold.

pass over this great and princely duty of closet prayer, either with a few brief touches, or else in a very great silence. If several Bodies of Divinity are consulted, you will find that all they say clearly and distinctly as to closet prayer may be brought into a very narrow compass, if not into a nutshell.

I have also inquired of several old disciples, whether among all the thousand sermons that they have heard in their days, that ever they have heard one sermon on closet prayer? And they have answered, No. I have also inquired of them, whether ever they had read any treatise on that subject? And they have answered, No.

And truly this has been no small encouragement to me, to make an offer of my mite; and if this small attempt of mine shall be so blessed as to provoke others that have better heads, and hearts, and hands, than any I have to do Christ and his people more service, in the handling of this choice point in a more copious way than what I have been able to reach unto, I shall therein rejoice.

8. *Eighthly*, and lastly, That favour, that good acceptance and fair quarter that my other poor labours have found, not only in this nation, but in other countries also, has put me upon putting pen to paper once more; and I hope that the good will of him that 'dwelt in the bush', will rest upon this, as it has to the glory of free grace rested upon my former endeavours. I could add other reasons, but let these suffice.

Good reader, when you are in your closet, pray hard for a poor, weak, worthless worm, that I may be found faithful and fruitful to the death, that so at last I may receive a crown of life.

So wishing you all happiness, both in this lower and in that upper world, I rest,

Yours in our dear Lord Jesus,
THOMAS BROOKS

PART 1

THE DOCTRINE OF THE TEXT STATED AND PROVED

But thou, when thou prayest, enter into thy closet, and when thou hast shut thy door, pray to thy Father which is in secret; and thy Father, which seeth in secret, shall reward thee openly (Matt. 6:6)

THESE WORDS of our Saviour are plain, and to be taken literally, and not allegorically, for he speaks of shutting the door of the chamber. In this chapter there is a clear opposition between the Pharisees praying in the synagogues and corners of the streets, and others praying in secret.

In the text you have a positive precept for every Christian to pray alone: 'But thou, when thou prayest.' He does not say, when *you* [plural] pray, but *thou*, 'when thou prayest, enter into thy closet', etc., as speaking not so much of a joint duty of many praying together, as of a duty which each person is to do alone. The command in the text sends us as well to the closet as to the church; and he is a real hypocrite that chooses the one and neglects the other; for thereby he tells the world he cares for neither, he makes conscience of neither. He that puts on a religious habit abroad to gain himself a great name among men, and at the same time lives like an atheist at home, shall at the last be uncovered by God, and presented before all the world for a most outrageous hypocrite.

Bellarmine[1] and some others turn the text into an allegory. They say that in these words there are two allegories. First, the chamber door is the senses, 'shut the door', that is, they say, your senses, lest vain imaginations and worldly thoughts distract your mind in praying. Secondly, the door, they say, is our mouth, 'shut your door', that is, your lips, they say, and let your prayer be like the prayer of Hannah, conceived in your mind, but not uttered with your mouth. It is usual with papists and other monastic men that lie in wait to deceive, to turn the blessed Scriptures into a nose of wax, under pretence of allegories and mysteries. Origen was a great admirer of allegories.[2] By the strength of his faculties and undisciplined mind, he turned most of the Scriptures into allegories, and by the just judgment of God upon him, he foolishly understood and absurdly applied Matthew 19:12 literally, 'Some have made themselves eunuchs for the kingdom of heaven', and so gelded himself. And indeed he might as well have plucked out one of his eyes upon the same account, because Christ says, 'It is better to go to heaven with one eye, than having two eyes to be cast into hell fire' (*Matt.* 18:9). In all ages heretics

---

[1] Robert Bellarmine (1542–1621), *De Sanct.*, lib. iii. cap. iv, etc.
[2] Eusebius (c. 260–341), *Ecclesiastical History,* lib. vi. cap. viii

have commonly defended their heresies by the translating of Scriptures into allegories. The apostle speaks of such as, denying the resurrection of the body, turn all the testimonies of the resurrection into an allegory, meaning thereby only the spiritual resurrection of the soul from sin, of which sort was Hymenaeus and Philetus, who destroyed the faith of some, saying, 'the resurrection is past already' (2 *Tim.* 2:17, 18). And are there not many among us that turn the whole history of the Bible, into an allegory and that turn Christ, and sin, and death, and the soul, and hell, and heaven, and all into an allegory? Many have and many do miserably pervert the Scriptures by turning them into vain and groundless allegories. Some undisciplined wits[1] have expounded paradise to be the soul, man to be the mind, the woman to be the sense, the serpent to be delight, the tree of knowledge of good and evil to be wisdom, and the rest of the trees to be the virtues and endowments of the mind. Oh friends! it is dangerous to bring in allegories where the Scripture does not clearly and plainly warrant them, and to take those words figuratively which should be taken properly.

The word ταμιειον, that is in the text rendered *closet*, has only three most usual significations amongst Greek authors. First, it may be taken for a secret chamber, or closed and locked parlour; secondly, for a safe or cupboard to lay victuals in; thirdly, for a locked chest or cupboard wherein treasure usually is reserved.

The best and most judicious interpreters that I have cast mine eye upon, both of a former and later date, do all

---

[1] Philo Judaeus, and others of a later date.

expound my text of private prayer in retired places; and with them I concur; and so the main doctrine that I shall gather from the words is this:

> *That closet prayer or private prayer is an indispensable duty that Christ himself has laid upon all that are not willing to lie under the woeful brand of being hypocrites.*

THE DOCTRINE OF THE TEXT PROVED

I beseech you seriously to lay to heart these five things:

SECRET PRAYER A DUTY

1.*First, If any prayer be a duty, then secret prayer must necessarily be a duty;* for secret prayer is as much prayer as any other prayer is prayer; and secret prayer prepares and fits the soul for family prayer, and for public prayer. Secret prayer sweetly inclines and strongly disposes a Christian to all other religious duties and services.

THE WITNESS OF CONSCIENCE

2. *Secondly,* If secret prayer be not an indispensable duty that lies upon you, *by what authority does conscience so upbraid you, and so accuse you, and so condemn you, and so terrify you, as it often does for the neglect of this duty?*

GOD'S PROMISE OF A REWARD

3. *Thirdly, Was it ever the way or method of God to promise again and again a reward, an open reward, for that work or service which he himself never commanded?*

Surely no. Now, to this duty of secret prayer, the Lord has again and again promised an open reward (*Matt.* 6:6, 18). And therefore, without any question, this is a duty incumbent upon all Christians.

THE LORD'S EXPECTATION

4. *Fourthly,* Our Saviour in the text *takes it for granted that every child of God will be frequent in praying to his heavenly Father;* and therefore he encourages them so much the more in the work of secret prayer. 'When you pray'; as if he had said, I know you can as well hear without ears, and live without food, and fight without hands, and walk without feet, as you are able to live without prayer. And therefore when you go to wait on God, or to give your heavenly Father a visit, 'Enter into your closet, and shut your doors', etc.

THE OPPOSITION OF SATAN

5. *Fifthly,* If closet prayer be not an indispensable duty that Christ has laid upon all his people, *why does Satan so much oppose it? Why does he so industriously and so unweariedly labour to discourage Christians in it, and to take off Christians from it?* Certainly, Satan would never make such a fierce and constant war as he does upon private prayer, were it not a necessary duty, a real duty, and a soul-enriching duty. But more of this you will find in the following discourse; and therefore let this touch suffice for the present.

Now, these five things do very clearly and evidently demonstrate that to hold intercourse with God, secretly

THE SECRET KEY TO HEAVEN

and solitarily is the undoubted duty of every Christian. But for a more full opening and confirmation of this great and important point, I shall lay down the following twenty arguments or considerations.

PART 2

TWENTY ARGUMENTS
FOR PRIVATE PRAYER

1: The Most Eminent Saints
Engaged in Private Prayer

THE FIRST argument is that the most eminent saints in both the Old Testament and the New applied themselves to private prayer. Moses was alone in the mount with God forty days and forty nights (*Exod.* 34:28). Similarly, Abraham fills his mouth with arguments, and reasons the case out alone with God in prayer, to prevent Sodom's desolation and destruction, and never leaves off pleading and praying till he had brought God down from fifty to ten (*Gen.* 18:22–32); and in Genesis 21:33, you have Abraham again at his private prayers: 'And Abraham planted a grove in Beersheba, and called there on the name of the LORD, the everlasting God.' Why did Abraham plant a grove, but that he might have a most private place to pray and pour out his soul before the Lord in?

So Isaac: *Gen.* 24:63, 'And Isaac went out to meditate in the field at even-tide.' The Hebrew word *lasuach*, that is here rendered *meditate*, signifies to pray as well as to meditate, and so it is often used. It is a comprehensive word, that takes in both prayer and meditation. So you shall find Jacob at his private prayer: *Gen.* 32:24–28, 'And Jacob was left alone; and there wrestled a man with him until the breaking of the day.' When Jacob was all alone, and in a dark night, and when his joints were out of joint, he so wrestles and weeps, and weeps and wrestles in private prayer, that as a prince at last he prevails with God (*Hos.* 12:3, 4). So David, *Psa.* 55:16, 17, 'As for me, I will call upon God; and the LORD shall save me. Evening, and morning, and at noon, will I pray, and cry aloud; and he shall hear my voice.'

So Daniel was three times a day in private prayer: *Dan.* 6:10, 'Now when Daniel knew that the writing was signed, he went into his house; and, his windows being open in his chamber toward Jerusalem, he kneeled upon his knees three times a day, and prayed, and gave thanks before his God, as he did aforetime.' Daniel had accustomed himself to private prayer; he went to his closet before he went to his public employment and state affairs; and at his return to dinner, he turned first into his chamber to serve his God and refresh his soul before he sat down to feast his body; and at the end of the day, when he had despatched his business with men, he made it his business to wait upon God in his chamber.

So Jonah keeps up private prayer when he was in the fish's belly, yes, when he was in the belly of hell (*Jon.* 2:1, 2, etc). So we have Elijah at prayer under the juniper tree (*1 Kings* 19:4; so Hannah (*1 Sam.* 1:13). Now, Hannah speaks in her heart; only her lips moved, but her voice was not heard. The very soul of prayer lies in the pouring out of the soul before God, as Hannah did, verse 15. Neither was Rebekah a stranger to this duty, who, upon the babe's struggling in her womb, went to inquire of the Lord (*Gen.* 25:22); that is, she went to some secret place to pray, says Calvin, Musculus, Mercerus, and others.

So Saul is no sooner converted, but presently he falls upon private prayer: *Acts* 9:11, 'And the Lord said unto him, Arise, and go into the street which is called Straight, and inquire in the house of Judas for one called Saul of Tarsus: for, behold, he prayeth.' Though he was a strict Pharisee, yet he never prayed properly before, and never prayed in private before. The Pharisees used to pray in the corners of the streets, and not in the corners of their houses. And after his conversion he was frequently in private prayer, as you may see by comparing of these Scriptures together: *Rom.* 1:9; *Eph.* 1:15, 16; *Phil.*. 1:3, 4; 2 *Tim.* 1:3.

So Epaphras was a warm man in closet prayer (*Phil.* 4:12, 13; so Cornelius had devoted himself to private prayer (*Acts* 10:2, 4); and so Peter gets up to the housetop to pray: verse 9, 'On the morrow, as they went on their journey, and drew nigh unto the city, Peter went up upon the house top to pray, about the sixth hour.' Peter got up upon the roof, not only to avoid distraction, but that he might be the more secret in his private devotion. Eusebius tells us of James called Justus, that his knees were grown hard and brawny with kneeling, so much in private prayer.[1] And Nazianzen reports of his sister Gorgonia,

---

[1] *Ecclesiastical History*, ii.

that her knees seemed to cleave to the earth by her often praying in private. And Gregory says of his aunt Trucilla, that her elbows were as hard as horn by often leaning upon her desk at private prayer. I have read of a devout person, who, when the set time for his private devotion was come, whatever company he was in, he would break from them with this neat and handsome come-off, 'I have a friend that stays for me; farewell.' And there was once a great lady of this land, who would frequently 'withdraw from the company of lords and ladies of great quality, who came to visit her, rather than she would lose her set times of waiting upon God in her closet; she would, as they called it, rudely take her leave of them, that so she might in private attend the Lord of lords. She would spare what time she could to express her favours, civilities, and courtesies among her relations and friends; but she would never suffer them to rob God of his time, nor her soul of that comfort and communion which she used to enjoy when she was with God in her closet.[1] And indeed, one hour's communion with God in one's closet, is to be preferred before the greatest and best company in the world.

And there was a child of a Christian gentlewoman, that was so given to prayer from its infancy, that before it could well speak, it would use to get alone and go to prayer; and as it grew, it was more frequent in prayer and retiring of itself from company; and he would ask his mother very strange questions, far above the capacity of one of his years; but at last, when this child was but five

---

[1] Lady Brooke, the friend of Richard Sibbes. See Parkhurst's 'Sermon' on her death.

years old and whipping of his top, on a sudden he flung away his scourge-stick and top, and ran to his mother, and with great joy said unto her, 'Mother, I must go to God; will you go with me?' She answered, 'My dear child, how do you know you shall go to God? He answered, 'God has told me so, for I love God, and God loves me.' She answered, 'Dear child, I must go when God pleases. But why will you not stay with me?' The child answered, 'I will not stay; I must go to God.' And the child did not live above a month after, but never cared for play more; but falling sick, he would always be saying that he must go to God, he must go to God; and this sometimes 'out of the mouths of babes and sucklings God hath perfected praise,' (*Matt.* 21:16). Certainly such persons will be ripe for heaven early who begin early to seek God in a closet, in a corner.

And Eusebius reports of Constantine the emperor, that every day he used to shut up himself in some secret place in his palace, and there, on bended knees, did make his devout prayers and soliloquies to God. 'My God and I are good company', said famous Dr Sibbes. A man whose soul is conversant with God in a closet, in a hole, behind the door, or in a desert, a den, a dungeon, shall find more real pleasure, more choice delight, and more full content, than in the palace of a prince. By all these famous instances, you see that the people of God in all ages have addicted themselves to private prayer.

Oh friends! These pious examples should be very awakening, very convincing, and very encouraging to you. Certainly it is as much your duty as it is your glory to follow these pious patterns that are now set before you. Witness these following Scriptures: *Prov.* 2:20, 'That thou mayest walk in the way of good men, and keep the paths of the righteous'; *1 Cor.* 11:1, 'Be ye followers of me, even as I also am of Christ;' *Phil.* 3:17, 'Brethren, be followers together of me, and mark them which walk so, as ye have us for an ensample'; *Phil.* 4:9, 'Those things which ye have both learned, and received, and heard, and seen in me, do; and the God of peace shall be with you'; *1 Thess.* 1:6, 'And ye became followers of us, and of the Lord, having received the word in much affliction'; *Heb.* 6:12, 'That ye be not slothful, but followers of them who through faith and patience inherit the promises.' So *2 Tim.* 3:10–12, 14; *Titus* 2:7.

It was an excellent law that the Ephesians made, viz., that men should propound to themselves the best patterns, and ever bear in mind some eminent man.[1] Bad men are wonderfully in love with bad examples (*Jer.* 44:16, 17). An Indian, hearing that his ancestors were gone to hell, said that then he would go thither too. Some men have a mind to go to hell for company's sake. Oh, that we were as much in love with the examples of good men as others are in love with the examples of bad men; and then we should be oftener in our closets than now we are! Oh, that our eyes were more fixed on the pious examples of all that have in them *aliquid Christi*, anything of Christ, as Bucer spake! Shall we love to look upon the pictures of our friends; and shall we not love to

---

[1] *Praecepta docent, exempla movent* (precepts teach, but examples move).

look upon the pious examples of those that are the lively and lovely picture of Christ? The pious examples of others should be the mirrors by which we should dress ourselves. He is the best and wisest Christian that writes after the fairest Scripture copy, that imitates those Christians that are most eminent in grace, and that have been most exercised in closet prayer, and in the most secret duties of religion.

Jerome having read the life and death of Hilarion, one that lived most Christianly, and died most comfortably, folded up the book, saying, 'Well, Hilarion shall be the champion that I will follow; his good life shall be my example, and his godly death my precedent.' It is noble to live and die by the examples of the most eminent saints.

2: Christ Engaged in Secret Prayer

CONSIDER, next, that *when Christ was on earth, he did much exercise himself in secret prayer;* he was often with God alone, as you may see in many well-known Scriptures: *Matt.* 14:23, 'And when he had sent the multitudes away, he went up into a mountain apart to pray; and when the evening was come, he was there alone.'

Christ's choosing solitudes for private prayer, does not only hint to us the danger of distraction and deviation of thoughts in prayer, but how necessary it is for us to choose the most convenient places we can for private prayers. Our own fickleness and Satan's restlessness call upon us to get into such corners, where we may most freely pour out our souls into the bosom of God: *Mark* 1:35, 'And in the morning, rising up a great while before day, he went out, and departed into a solitary place, and there prayed.' As the morning time is the fittest time for prayer, so solitary places are the fittest places for prayer: *Mark* 6:46, 'And when he had sent them away, he departed into a mountain to pray.' He that would pray to purpose, had need be quiet when he is alone: *Luke* 5:16, 'And he withdrew himself into the wilderness and prayed' (Greek: 'He was departing and praying', to give us to understand that he did thus often. When Christ was neither exercised in teaching nor in working of miracles, he was then very intent on private prayer: *Luke* 6:12, 'And it came to pass in those days that he went out into a mountain to pray, and continued all night in prayer to God.' Did Christ spend whole nights in private prayer to save our souls; and shall we think it much to spend an hour or two in the day for the furtherance of the internal and eternal welfare of our souls? *Luke* 21:37, 'And in the day-time he was teaching in the temple, and at night he went out, and abode in the mount that is called the mount of Olives.'

Christ frequently joins praying and preaching together, and what Christ has joined together, let no man presume to put asunder: *Luke* 22:39, 41, 44, 45, 'And he came out, and went as he was wont to the mount of Olives, and his disciples also followed him. And he was withdrawn from them about a stone's cast, and kneeled down and prayed. And being in an agony, he prayed more earnestly, and his sweat was as it were great drops of blood [clotted or congealed blood] falling down to the ground [never was garden watered before or since with blood as this was]. And when he rose up from prayer, and was come to his disciples, he found them sleeping for sorrow.' Ah! what sad pieces of vanity are the best of men in an hour of trial and temptation! These very men, that a little before did stoutly profess and promise that they would never leave him nor forsake him, and that they would go to prison for Christ, and die for Christ, yet when the day of trial came, they could not so much as watch with him one hour; they had neither eyes to see nor hands to wipe off Christ's bloody sweat; so *John* 6:15–17.

Thus you see, by all these famous instances, that Christ was frequent in private prayer. Oh, that we would daily propound to ourselves this noble pattern for our imitation, and make it our business, our work, our heaven, to write after this blessed copy that Christ hath set us, viz. to be much with God alone. Certainly Christianity is nothing else but an imitation of the divine nature, a reducing of a man's self to the image of God, in which he was created 'in righteousness and true holiness'. A Christian's whole life should be nothing but a visible representation of Christ.

The heathens had this notion amongst them, as Lactantius reports, that the way to honour their gods was to be like them. Sure I am that the highest way of honouring Christ is to be like to Christ: *1 John* 2:6, 'He that saith he abideth in him, ought himself also to walk even as he walked.' Oh, that this blessed Scripture might always lie warm upon our hearts. Christ is the sun, and all the watches of our lives should be set by the dial of his motion. Christ is a pattern of patterns; his example should be to us instead of a thousand examples. It is not only our liberty, but our duty and glory, to follow Christ in all his moral virtues absolutely. Other patterns are imperfect and defective, but Christ is a perfect pattern; and of all his children, they are the happiest that come nearest to this perfect pattern.

Heliogabalus loved his children the better for resembling him in sin. But Christ loves his children the more for resembling him in sanctity. I have read of some springs that change the colour of the cattle that drink of them into the colour of their own waters, as Du Bartas[1] sings:

> Cerona, Xanth, and Cephisus do make
> The thirsty flocks, that of their waters take,
> Black, red, and white; and near the crimson deep,
> The Arabian fountain maketh crimson sheep.

Certainly, Jesus Christ is such a fountain, in which whosoever bathes, and of which whosoever drinks, shall be changed into the same likeness (2 *Cor.* 3:18).

QUESTION: But why was our Lord Jesus so much in private prayer? Why was he so often with God alone?

ANSWER 1: *First, It was to put a very high honour and value upon private prayer;* it was to enhance and raise the price of this duty.

Men naturally are very apt and prone to have low and undervaluing thoughts of secret prayer. But Christ, by exercising himself so frequently in it, has put an everlasting honour and an inestimable value upon it. But,

---

[1] Guillaume du Bartas (1544–90), French Huguenot poet.

ANSWER 2: *Secondly,* He was much in private prayer, he was often with God alone, *that he might not be seen of men, and that he might avoid all shows and appearances of ostentation and popular applause.*

He that has commanded us to abstain from all appearances of evil (*1 Thess.* 5:22), would not himself, when he was in this world, venture upon the least appearance of evil. Christ was very shy of every thing that did but look like sin; he was very shy of the very show and shadow of pride or vain-glory.

ANSWER 3: *Thirdly, To avoid interruptions in the duty.*

Secrecy is no small advantage to the serious and lively carrying on of a private duty. Interruptions and disturbances from without are oftentimes quench-coals to private prayer. The best Christians do but bungle when they meet with interruptions in their private devotions.

ANSWER 4: *Fourthly, To set us such a blessed pattern and gracious example that we should never please nor content ourselves with public prayers only, nor with family prayers only, but that we should also apply ourselves to secret prayer, to closet prayer.*

Christ was not always in public, nor always in his family, but he was often in private with God alone, that by his own example he might encourage us to be often with God in secret; and happy are they that tread in his steps, and that write after his copy.

ANSWER. 5: *Fifthly, That he might approve himself to our understandings and consciences to be a most just and faithful High Priest* (*Heb.* 2:17; *John* 17).

Christ was wonderfully faithful and careful in both parts of his priestly office, viz., satisfaction and intercession; he was his people's only spokesman.

Ah! how earnest, how frequent was he in pouring out prayers, and tears, and sighs, and groans for his people in secret, when he was in this world (*Heb.* 5:7). And now he is in heaven, he is still making intercession for them (*Heb.* 7:25).

ANSWER 6: *Sixthly, Christ was much in private prayer to convince us that his Father hears and observes our private prayers, and bottles up all our secret tears,* and that he is not a stranger to our closet desires, wrestlings, breathings, hungerings, and thirstings.

3: Secret Prayer Distinguishes Sincerity from Hypocrisy

CONSIDER, next, *that the ordinary exercising of your selves in secret prayer, is that which will distinguish you from hypocrites, who do all they do to be seen of men.*[1] Matt. 6:2, 'Take heed that you do not your alms before men, to be seen of them; otherwise ye have no reward of your Father which is in heaven. Therefore, when thou doest thine alms, do not sound a trumpet before thee, as the hypocrites do in the synagogues, and in the streets, that they may have glory of men. Verily, I say unto you, they have their reward.'

[1] They say of the nightingale, that when she is solitary in the woods, she is careless of her notes, but composes herself more quaintly and elegantly, if she conceives there be any auditors, or if she be near houses. Just so it is with hypocrites in religious duties.

Self is the only oil that makes the chariot-wheels of the hypocrite move in all religious concerns. Verse 5, 'And when thou prayest, thou shalt not be as the hypocrites are; for they love to stand praying in the synagogues, and in the corners of the streets, that they may be seen of men. Verily, I say unto you, they have their reward.' Verse 16, 'Moreover, when ye fast, be not as the hypocrites, of a sad countenance: for they disfigure their faces, that they may appear unto men to fast. Verily, I say unto you, they have their reward.' Thus you see that these hypocrites look more at men than at God in all their duties. When they give alms, the trumpet must sound; when they pray, it must be in the synagogues and in the corners of the streets. And when they fasted, they disfigured their faces that they might appear to men to fast. Hypocrites live upon the praises and applauses of men. Naturalists report of the Chelydonian stone,[1] that it will retain its virtue no longer than it is enclosed in gold. So hypocrites will keep up their duties no longer than they are fed, and encouraged, and enclosed with the golden praises and applauses of men. Hypocrites are like blazing stars, which, so long as they are fed with gases, shine as if they were fixed stars; but let the gases dry up, and presently they vanish and disappear.

Closet duty speaks out most sincerity. He prays with a witness that prays without a witness. The more sincere the soul is, the more in closet duty the soul will be (*Job* 31:33). Where do you read in all the Scripture, that Pharaoh, or Saul, or Judas, or Demas, or Simon Magus, or the

---

[1] That is, from *Chelidoniae Insulae*, Swallow Islands – *Pliny*, v. 33.

scribes and Pharisees, did ever use to pour out their souls before the Lord in secret? Secret prayer is not the hypocrite's ordinary walk, his ordinary work or trade.

There is great cause to fear that his heart was never right with God, whose whole devotion is spent among men, or among many; or else our Saviour, in drawing the hypocrite's picture, would never have made this to be the very cast of his countenance, as he does in Matthew 6:5. It is very observable, that Christ commands his disciples, that they should not be as the hypocrites. It is one thing to *be* hypocrites, and it is another thing to be *as* the hypocrites. Christ would not have his people to look like hypocrites, nor to be like to hypocrites. It is only sincerity that will enable a man to make a trade of private prayer. In praying with many, there are many things that may bribe and provoke a carnal heart, as pride, vainglory, love of applause, or to get a name. An hypocrite, in all his duties, trades more for a good name than for a good life, for a good report than for a good conscience; like fiddlers, that are more careful in tuning their instruments, than in composing their lives. But in private prayer there is no such trade to be driven.

4: Secret Prayer Lets Us Unbosom Ourselves before God

CONSIDER, fourthly, *that in secret we may more freely and fully, and safely unbosom our souls to God than we can in the presence of many or a few.* Hence the husband is to mourn apart, and the wife apart (*Zech.*

12:12–14), not only to show the soundness of their sorrow, but also to show their sincerity by their secrecy. They must mourn apart, that their sins may not be disclosed nor discovered one to another. Here they are severed to show that they wept not for company's sake, but for their own particular sins, by which they had pierced and crucified the Lord of glory.

In secret, a Christian may descend into such particulars, as in public or before others he will not, he may not, he ought not, to mention. Ah! how many Christians are there who would blush and be ashamed to walk in the streets, and to converse with sinners or saints, should but those infirmities, enormities, and wickednesses be written in their foreheads, or known to others, which they freely and fully lay open to God in secret.

There are many sins which men have fallen into before conversion and since conversion, should they be known to the world, would make themselves to stink, and religion to stink, and their profession to stink in the nostrils of all that know them. Yes, should those weaknesses and wickednesses be published upon the housetops, which many are guilty of before grace received, or since grace received, how would weak Christians be staggered, young beginners in the ways of God discouraged, and many mouths of blasphemy opened, and many sinners' hearts hardened against the Lord, his ways, reproofs, and the things of their own peace; yes, how would Satan's banner be displayed, and his kingdom strengthened, and himself infinitely pleased and delighted! It is an infinite mercy and condescension in God to lay a law of restraint upon

Satan, who else would be the greatest blab in all the world. It would be mirth and music to him to be continually laying open the follies and weaknesses of the saints.

Ambrose brings in the devil boasting against Christ, and challenging Judas as his own. 'He is not yours, Lord Jesus, he is mine: his thoughts beat for me; he eats with you, but is fed by me; he takes bread from you, but money from me; he drinks with you, and sells your blood to me.' There is not a sin that a saint commits, but Satan would trumpet it out to all the world, if God would but give him permission. No man that is in his right mind, will lay open to every one his bodily infirmities, weaknesses, diseases, ailments, griefs, etc., but to some near relation, or choice friend, or able physician. So no man that is in his right mind will lay open to every one his soul-infirmities, weaknesses, diseases, ailments, griefs, etc., but to the Lord, or to some particular person that is wise, faithful, and able to contribute something to his soul's relief.

Should a Christian but lay open or rip up all his follies and vanities to the world, how sadly would some deride him and scorn him! and how severely and bitterly would others censure him and judge him!

When David was alone in the cave, then he poured out his complaint to God, and showed before him his trouble (*Psa.* 142:2). And when Job was all alone, then his eyes poured out tears to God (*Job* 16:20). There is no hazard, no danger in the ripping up of all before God in a corner, but there may be a great deal of hazard and danger in the ripping up of all before men.

5: Secret Duties Shall Have Open Rewards

FIFTHLY, *Secret duties shall have open rewards.*[1] *Matt.* 6:6, 'And thy Father, which seeth in secret, shall reward thee openly.' So, verse 18, God will reward his people here in part, and hereafter in all perfection. He is a rewarder of them that diligently seek him in a corner. They that sow in tears secretly, shall reap in joy openly. Private prayer shall be rewarded before men and angels publicly.

How openly did God reward Daniel for his secret prayer! (*Dan.* 6:10, 23–28). Mordecai privately discovered a plot of treason against the person of King Ahasuerus, and he is rewarded openly (*Esther* 2:21–23, with chap 6). Darius, before he came to the kingdom, received privately a garment for a gift of one Syloson; and when he came to be a king, he rewarded him openly with the command of his country Samos.[12] God, in the great day, will recompense his people before all the world, for every secret prayer, and secret tear, and secret sigh, and secret groan that has come from his people. God, in the great day, will declare to men and angels, how often his people have been in pouring out their souls before him in such and such holes, corners, and secret places; and accordingly he will reward them.

Ah, Christians! did you really believe this, and seriously dwell on this, you would,

---

[1] *Eccles.* 12:14; 2 *Cor.* 5:10; *Rev.* 22:12; *Psa.* 126:5; *Luke* 14:14; *Matt.* 25:34, 37.

[2] Told by Herodotus, iii, 29, 139–49, vi. 13; Strabo, xiv.

1. Walk more thankfully.
2. Work more cheerfully.
3. Suffer more patiently.
4. Fight against the world, the flesh, and the devil, more courageously.
5. Lay out yourselves for God, his interest and glory, more freely.
6. Live with what providence has cut out for your portion, more quietly and contentedly. And,
7. You would be in private prayer more frequently, more abundantly.

6: God Most Manifests Himself in Secret

Sixthly, consider *that God has usually let out himself most to his people when they have been in secret, when they have been alone at the throne of grace.*[1]

Oh, the sweet meltings, the heavenly warmings, the blessed cheerings, the glorious manifestations, and the choice communion with God, that Christians have found when they have been alone with God in a corner, in a closet, behind the door! When had Daniel that vision and comfortable message, that blessed news, by the angel, that he was 'greatly beloved', but when he was all alone at prayer?

Dan. 9:20–23: 'And while I was speaking, and praying, and confessing my sin, and the sin of my people Israel, and presenting my supplication before the Lord my God, for the holy mountain of my God, yea, while I was speak-

---

[1] 'O Lord, I never come to you but by you; I never go from you without you' (*Bernard*).

ing in prayer, even the man Gabriel, whom I had seen in the vision at the beginning, being caused to fly swiftly, touched me about the time of the evening oblation; and he informed me, and talked with me, and said, O Daniel, I am now come forth to give thee skill and understanding. At the beginning of thy supplications the commandment came forth, and I am come to show thee; for thou art greatly beloved. Therefore understand the matter, and consider the vision.' Whilst Daniel was at private prayer, God, by the angel Gabriel, reveals to him the secret of his counsel, concerning the restoration of Jerusalem, and the duration thereof, even to the Messiah; and whilst Daniel was at private prayer, the Lord appears to him, and in an extraordinary way assures him that he was 'a man greatly beloved', or as the Hebrew *chumudoth* has it, a man of 'desires', that is, a man whom God's desires are towards, a man singularly beloved of God, and highly in favour with God, a man who is very pleasing and delightful to God. God loves to load the wings of private prayer with the sweetest, choicest, and chiefest blessings.

Ah! how often has God kissed a poor Christian at the beginning of private prayer, and spoke peace to him in, the midst of private prayer, and filled him with light and joy and assurance upon the close of private prayer! And so Cornelius is highly commanded and graciously rewarded upon the account of his private prayer: *Acts* 10:1–4, 'There was a certain man in Caesarea called Cornelius, a centurion of the band called the Italian band, a devout man, and one that feared God with all his house; which gave much alms to the people, and prayed to God always: he saw in a vision evidently, about the ninth hour of the day, an angel of God coming in to him, and saying unto him, Cornelius. And when he looked on him, he was afraid, and said, What is it, Lord? and he said unto him, Thy prayers and thine alms are come up for a memorial before God.' Verse 30, 31, 'And Cornelius said, Four days ago I was fasting until this hour' (that is, until three o'clock in the afternoon, verse 3), 'and at the ninth hour I prayed in my house, and, behold, a man stood before me in bright clothing, and said, Thy prayer is heard, and thine alms are had in remembrance in the sight of God.' Mark, as he was praying in his house, namely, 'by himself alone, a man in bright clothing – that was an angel in man's shape, verse 3 – appeared to him, and said, 'Cornelius, thy prayer is heard.' He does not mean only that prayer which he made when he fasted and humbled himself before the Lord, verses. 30, 31; but, as verses 2, 3, 4 show, his prayers, his prayers which he made alone. For it seems none else were with him then, for he only saw that man in bright clothing; and to him alone the angel addressed his present speech, saying, 'Cornelius, Thy prayers are heard, verses. 4, 31.

Here you see that Cornelius' private prayers are not only heard, but kindly remembered, and graciously accepted, and gloriously rewarded. Praying Cornelius is not only remembered by God, but he is also visited, sensibly and evidently, by an angel, and assured that his private prayers and good deeds are an odour, a sweet smell, a sacrifice acceptable and well pleasing to God. And so, when did Peter have his vision but when he was praying alone on the housetop? *Acts* 10:9–13, 'On the morrow, as they went on their journey, and drew near unto the city, Peter went up unto the housetop to pray, about the sixth hour. And he became very hungry and would have eaten; but while they made ready, he fell into a trance, and saw heaven opened, and a certain vessel descending unto him, as it had been a great sheet, knit at the four corners, and let down to the earth, wherein were all manner of four-footed beasts of the earth, and wild beasts, and creeping things, and fowls of the air. And there came a voice to him, Rise, Peter; kill, and eat.' When Peter was upon the housetop at prayer alone, then he fell into a trance, and he saw heaven opened; and then he had his spirit raised, his mind elevated, and all the faculties of his soul filled with a divine revelation.

And so when Paul was at prayer alone (*Acts* 9:12), he saw in a vision a man named Ananias coming in and putting his hand on him that he might receive his sight. Paul had not been long at private prayer before it was revealed to him that he was a chosen vessel, and before he was filled with the gifts, graces, and comforts of the Holy Ghost.

And when John was alone in the isle of Patmos, 'for the word of God, and for the testimony of Jesus Christ' – to which place he was banished by Domitian, a most cruel emperor[1] – then he had a glorious sight of the Son of man, and then the Lord revealed to him most deep and profound mysteries, both concerning the present and future state of the church, to the end of the world. And when

[1] Eusebius, iii. 18; *Rev.* 1:9ff; 5:1–9.

[27]

John was weeping, in private prayer doubtless, then the sealed book was opened to him. So when Daniel was at private prayer, God despatches a heavenly messenger to him, and his errand was to open more clearly and fully the blessed Scripture to him. Some comfortable and encouraging knowledge this holy man of God had attained to before by his frequent and constant study in the Word, and this eggs him on to private prayer, and private prayer sends an angel from heaven to give him a clearer and fuller light.[1]

Private prayer is a golden key to unlock the mysteries of the Word to us. The knowledge of many choice and blessed truths is but the outcome of private prayer. The Word most dwells richly in their hearts who are most in pouring out their hearts before God in their closets. When Bonaventura, that seraphical doctor, as some call him, was asked by Aquinas from what books and helps he derived such holy and divine expressions and contemplations, he pointed to a crucifix, and said, '*Iste est liber*', etc., 'Prostrate in prayer at the feet of this image, my soul receiveth greater light from heaven than from all study and disputation.' Though this be a monastic tradition and superstitious fiction, yet some improvement may be made of it. Certainly that Christian or that minister that in private prayer lies most at the feet of Jesus Christ, he shall understand most of the mind of Christ in the gospel, and he shall have most of heaven and the things of his own peace brought down into his heart.

---

[1] Dr [William] Ames [1576–1633] got his learning by private prayer; and so did Solomon his wisdom.

There is no service in which Christians have such a near, familiar, and friendly intercourse with God as in this of private prayer; neither is there any service in which God doth more delight to make known his truth and faithfulness, his grace and goodness, his mercy and bounty, his beauty and glory to poor souls, than this of private prayer. Luther professes, 'That he profited more in the knowledge of the Scripture by private prayer in a short space, than he did by study in a longer space',[1] as John by weeping in a corner got the sealed book opened. Private prayer crowns God with the honour and glory that is due to his name; and God crowns private prayer with a discovery of those blessed weighty truths to his servants that are a sealed book to others.

Certainly the soul usually enjoys most communion with God in secret. When a Christian is in a wilderness, which is a very solitary place, then God delights to speak friendly and comfortably to him: *Hos.* 2:14, 'Behold, I will allure her, and bring her into the wilderness, and speak friendly, or comfortably, to her', or as the Hebrew has it, 'I will speak to her heart.' When I have her alone, says God, in a solitary wilderness, I will speak such things to her heart, as shall exceedingly cheer her, and comfort her, and even make her heart leap and dance within her.[2]

A husband imparts his mind most freely and fully to his wife when she is alone; and so does Christ to the believ-

---

[1] *Bene orasse, est bene studuisse* [to have prayed well is to have studied well] (Luther).

[2] *Nunquam minus solus, quam cum solus;* 'Never less alone, than when alone', said the heathen [attributed to Scipio, 185–129 BC]. And may not a saint say so much more who has communion with God?

THE SECRET KEY TO HEAVEN

ing soul. Oh, the secret kisses, the secret embraces, the secret visits, the secret whispers, the secret cheerings, the secret sealings, the secret discoveries, etc., that God gives to his people when alone, when in a hole, when under the stairs, when behind the door, when in a dungeon! When Jeremiah was calling upon God alone in his dark dungeon, he had great and wonderful things shown him that he knew nothing of (*Jer.* 33:1–3).

Ambrose frequently said, 'I am never less alone, than when I am alone; for then I can enjoy the presence of my God most freely, fully, and sweetly, without interruption.'

And it was a most sweet and divine saying of Bernard, 'O saint, do you not know,' he says, 'that your husband Christ is bashful, and will not be familiar in company? Withdraw yourself therefore by prayer and meditation into your closet or the fields, and there you shall have Christ's embraces.'

A gentlewoman being at private prayer and meditation in her parlour, had such sweet, choice, and full enjoyments of God, that she cried out, 'Oh, that I might ever enjoy this sweet communion with God!' etc.

Christ loves to embrace his spouse, not so much in the open street, as in a closet; and certainly the gracious soul never has sweeter views of glory, than when it is most out of the view of the world.

Wise men give their best, their choicest, and their richest gifts in secret; and so does Christ give to his the best of the best, when they are in a corner, when they are all alone. But as for such as cannot spare time to seek God in a closet, to serve him in secret, they sufficiently show that

[30]

they have little fellowship or friendship with God, whom they so seldom come to.

7: This Life is the Only Time for Private Prayer

S EVENTHLY, consider that *the time of this life is the only time for private prayer.* There will be no secret prayer in heaven.

In heaven there will be no secret sins to trouble us, no secret needs to pinch us, no secret temptations to betray us, no secret snares to entangle us, no secret enemies to supplant us.

We ought to live much in the practice of that duty here on earth that we shall never be exercised in after death. Some duties that are incumbent upon us now, as praising of God, admiring of God, exalting and lifting up of God, joying and delighting in God, etc., will be forever incumbent upon us in heaven; but this duty of private prayer, we must say good-bye to when we come to lay our heads in the dust.

8: Private Prayer's Prevailing Power

E IGHTHLY, consider *the great prevalency of secret prayer.* Private prayer is *porta coeli, clavis paradisi,* the gate of heaven, a key to let us into paradise. Oh, the great things that private prayer has done with God! (*Psa.* 31:22). Oh, the great mercies that have been obtained by private prayer! (*Psa.* 38:8, 9). And oh, the great threatenings that have been diverted by private prayer! And oh, the great judgments that have been removed by private

prayer! And oh, the great judgments that have been prevented by private prayer! I have read of a malicious
woman who gave herself to the devil, provided that he
would do a mischief to such a neighbour, whom she mor-
tally hated: the devil went again and again to do his
errand, but at last he returns and tells her, that he could
do no hurt to that man, for whenever he came, he found
him either reading the Scriptures, or at private prayer.

Private prayers pierce the heavens, and are commonly
blessed and loaded with gracious and glorious returns
from there. Whilst Hezekiah was praying and weeping in
private, God sent the prophet Isaiah to him, to assure him
that his prayer was heard, and that his tears were seen,
and that he would add unto his days fifteen years (*Isa.*
38:5). So when Isaac was all alone meditating and praying, and treating with God for a good wife in the fields, he
meets Rebekah (*Gen.* 24:63, 64). So Jacob: *Gen.* 32:24–
28, 'And Jacob was left alone; and there wrestled a man
with him until the breaking of the day. And when he saw
that he prevailed not against him, he touched the hollow
of his thigh; and the hollow of Jacob's thigh was out of
joint, as he wrestled with him. And he said, Let me go, for
the day breaketh. And he said, I will not let thee go, except thou bless me. And he said unto him, What is thy
name? and he said, Jacob. And he said, Thy name shall be
called no more Jacob, but Israel; for as a prince hast thou
power with God and with men, and hast prevailed.' In
this Scripture we have an elegant description of a duel
fought between the Almighty and Jacob; and in it there
are these things most observable:

Six Observations on Jacob's Wrestling with God in Prayer

First, We have the *combatants or duellists,* Jacob and God, who appeared in the shape or appearance of a man. He that is here said to be a man was the Son of God in human shape, as it appears by the whole narrative, and by Hosea 12:3–5. Now, that this man that wrestled with Jacob was indeed God, and not really man, is most evident by these reasons:

1. *First, Jacob desires a blessing from him,* verse 26. Now, it is God's prerogative-royal to bless, and not angels', nor men's.

2. *Secondly, He calls him by the name of God,* 'thou hast power with God', verse 28. And Jacob says, 'I have seen God face to face', verse 30. Not that he saw the majesty and essence of God: for no man can see the essential glory of God and live (*Exod.* 33:20, 23); but he saw God more apparently, more manifestly, more gloriously than ever he had done before. Some created shape, some glimpse of glory, Jacob saw, whereby God was pleased for the present to testify his more immediate presence, but not himself.

3. *Thirdly, The same person that here Jacob wrestles with is he whom Jacob remembers in his benediction as his deliverer from all evil* (*Gen.* 48:16). It was that same God that appeared to him at Bethel when he fled from the face of his brother (*Gen.* 35:7).

4. *Fourthly, Jacob is reproved for his curious inquiring or asking after the angel's name,* verse 29, which is a clear argument or demonstration of his majesty and glory, God

being above all notion and name. God is a super-substantial substance, an understanding not to be understood, a word never to be spoken. One who was asked what God was, answered, 'That he must be God himself, before he could know God fully.'[1] We are as well able to comprehend the sea in a cockle-shell, as we are able to comprehend the Almighty, or that *nomen Majestativum*, as Tertullian phrases it. 'In searching after God', says Chrysostom, 'I am like a man digging in a deep spring: I stand here, and the water rises upon me; and I stand there, and still the water rises upon me.'

In this conflict you have not one man wrestling with another, nor one man wrestling with a created angel, but a poor, weak, mortal man wrestling with an immortal God; weakness wrestling with strength, and a finite being with an infinite being. Though Jacob had no second, though he was all alone, though he was wonderfully overmatched, yet he wrestles and keeps his hold, and all in the strength of him he wrestles with.

Secondly, You have *the place where they combated*, and that was beside the ford Jabbok, verse 22. This is the name of a brook or river springing by Rabbath, or Rabbah, the metropolis of the Ammonites, and issuing into Jordan beneath the Sea of Galilee (*Num.* 21:24; *Deut.* 2:37; *Judg.* 11:13, 15; *Deut.* 3:16).

Jacob did never enjoy so much of the presence of God as when he had left the company of men. Oh! the sweet communion that Jacob had with God when he withdrew from his family, and was all alone with his God by the

[1] Dionys. Areop., *De Divin. Nom.*, cap. i

ford Jabbok! Certainly Jacob was never less alone than at this time, when he was so alone. Saints often meet with the best wine and with the strongest cordials when they are all alone with God.

Thirdly, You have *the time of the combat,* and that was the night. At what time of the night this wrestling, this duel began, we nowhere read; but it lasted till break of day, it lasted till Jacob had the better of the angel. How many hours of the night this conflict lasted, no mortal man can tell. God's design was that none should be spectators nor witnesses of this combat but Jacob only; and therefore Jacob must be wrestling when others were sleeping.

4. *Fourthly,* You have *the ground of the quarrel,* and that was Jacob's fear of Esau, and his importunate desire for a blessing. Jacob flies to God, that he might not fall before man; he flies to God, that he might not fly before men. In a storm, there is no shelter like the wing of God. He is safest, and happiest, and wisest, that lays himself under divine protection. This Jacob knew, and therefore he runs to God, as to his only city of refuge. In this conflict, God would have given out: 'Let me go, for the day breaketh', verse 26; but Jacob keeps his hold, and tells him boldly to his very face that he would not let him go unless he would bless him.

Oh, the power of private prayer! It hath a kind of omnipotency in it; it takes God captive; it holds him as a prisoner; it binds the hands of the Almighty; yea, it will wring a mercy, a blessing, out of the hand of heaven itself.

Oh, the power of that prayer that makes a man victorious over the greatest, the highest power! Jacob, though a man, a single man, a travelling man, a tired man, yea, though a worm, that is easily crushed and trodden under foot, and no man (*Isa.* 41:14), yet in private prayer he is so potent, that he overcomes the omnipotent God; he is so mighty, that he overcomes the Almighty.

5. *Fifthly,* You have *the nature or manner of the combat,* and that was both outward and inward, both corporal and spiritual. It was by might and flight; it was as well by the strength of his body as it was by the force of his faith. He wrestled not only with spiritual strugglings, tears, and prayers (*Hos.* 12:4), but with corporal also, wherein God assailed him with one hand, and upheld him with the other. In this conflict, Jacob and the angel of the covenant did really lay arm on arm, and set shoulder to shoulder, and put foot to foot, and used all other sleights and ways as men do that wrestle one with another.

The Hebrew word *abaq* that is here rendered wrestled, signifies the raising of the dust; because those which did wrestle of old did not only wrestle naked, as the manner then was, but did also use to cast dust one upon another, that so they might take more sure hold one of another. Some, from this word *abaq* do conclude that Jacob and the angel did tug, and strive, and turn each other, till they sweat again; for so much the word imports. Jacob and the angel did not wrestle for fun, but in all seriousness; they wrestled with their might, as it were, for the trophy; they strove for victory as for life.

But as this wrestling was corporal, so it was spiritual also. Jacob's soul takes hold of God, and Jacob's faith takes hold of God, and Jacob's prayers take hold of God, and Jacob's tears take hold of God (*Hos* 12:4–5). Certainly Jacob's weapons in this warfare were mainly spiritual, and so 'mighty through God'.

There is no overcoming of God but in his own strength. Jacob did more by his royal faith than he did by his noble hands, and more by weeping than he did by sweating, and more by praying than he did by all his bodily strivings.

6. *Sixthly and lastly,* You have *the issue of the* combat, and that is, victory over the angel, verse 28. Jacob wrestles in the angel's arms and armour, and so overcomes him. As a prince, he overpowers the angel by that very power he had from the angel. The angel was as freely and fully willing to be conquered by Jacob, as Jacob was willing to be conqueror. When lovers wrestle, the strongest is willing enough to take a fall from the weakest; and so it was here. The father, in wrestling with his child, is willing enough, for his child's comfort and encouragement, to take a fall now and then; and so it was between the angel and Jacob in the present case. Now in this blessed story, as in a crystal glass, you may see the great power and prevalency of private prayer; it conquers the great conqueror; it is so omnipotent that it overcomes an omnipotent God.

Now this you may see more fully and sweetly cleared up in Hosea 12:3–4, 'He took his brother by the heel in the womb, and by his strength he had power with God: yea, he had power over the angel, and prevailed; he wept, and made supplication unto him: he found him in Bethel, and there he spake with us.' When Jacob was all alone and in a dark night, and but on one leg, yet then he 'played the prince with God', as the Hebrew has it. Jacob by prayers and tears did so prince it with God as that he carried the blessing. Jacob's wrestling was by weeping, and his prevailing by praying. Prayers and tears are not only very pleasing to God, but also very prevalent with God. And thus you see that this great instance of Jacob speaks out aloud the prevalency of private prayer.

See another instance of this in David: *Psa.* 6:6, 'I am weary with my groanings: all the night make I my bed to swim; I water my couch with my tears.' These are all excessive figurative speeches, to set forth the greatness of his sorrow, and the multitude of his tears. David in his retirement makes the place of his sin, viz. his bed, to be the place of his repentance. David sins privately upon his bed, and David mourns privately upon his bed. Every place which we have polluted by sin, we should sanctify and water with our tears: verse 8, 'Depart from me, all ye workers of iniquity; for the Lord hath heard the voice of my weeping.'

As blood has a voice, and as the rod has a voice, so tears have a voice. Tears have tongues, and tears can speak. There is no noise like that which tears in secret make in the ears of God. A prudent and indulgent father can better pick out the desires and necessities of his children by their secret tears than by their loud complaints, by their weeping than by their words: and do you think that God can't do as much? Tears are not always mutes: *Lam.* 2:18. 'Cry aloud,' says one, 'not with your tongue, but with your eyes; not with your words, but with your tears; for that is the prayer that makes the most forcible entry into the ears of the great God of heaven.' Penitent tears are undeniable ambassadors that never return from the throne of grace without a gracious answer. Tears are a kind of silent prayer, which, though they say nothing, yet they obtain pardon; and though they plead not a man's cause, yet they obtain mercy at the hands of God. As you see in that great instance of Peter, who, though he said nothing that we read of, yet, weeping bitterly, he obtained mercy (*Matt.* 26:75). I have read of Augustine, who, coming as a visitant to the house of a sick man, he saw the room full of friends and family, who were all silent, yet all weeping: the wife sobbing, the children sighing, the family lamenting, all mourning; whereupon Augustine uttered this short spontaneous prayer, 'Lord, what prayer do you hear, if not these?'

Psa. 6:9, 'The LORD hath heard my supplication; the LORD will receive my prayer.' God sometimes answers his people before they pray: *Isa.* 65:24, 'And it shall come to pass, that before they call, I will answer.' And sometimes while they are praying; so it follows in the same verse, 'And while they are yet speaking, I will hear.' So *Isa.* 30:19, 'He will be very gracious unto thee at the voice of thy cry; when he shall hear it, he will answer thee.' And sometimes after they have prayed, as the experiences of all Christians can testify. Sometimes God neither hears nor receives a prayer; and this is the common case and lot of the wicked (*Prov.* 1:28; *Job* 27:9; *Isa* 1:15). Sometimes God hears the prayers of his people, but does not presently answer them, as in that case of Paul (2 *Cor.* 12:7–9); and sometimes God both hears and receives the prayers of his people, as here he did David's. Now in this instance of David, as in a mirror, you may run and read the prevalency of private prayer and of secret tears.

You may take another instance of this in Jonah chap. 2:1, 2, 3, 5, 7, 10, 'Then Jonah prayed unto the LORD his God out of the fish's belly, and said, I cried by reason of my affliction unto the LORD, and he heard me; out of the belly of hell cried I, and thou heardest my voice. For thou hadst cast me into the deep, into the midst of the seas, and the floods compassed me about: all thy billows and thy waves passed over me . . . The waters compassed me about, even to the soul: the depth closed me round about, the weeds were wrapped about my head . . . When my soul fainted within me, I remembered the LORD; and my prayer came in unto thee, into thy holy temple . . . And the LORD spake unto the fish, and it vomited out Jonah upon the dry land.'

When Jonah was all alone, and in the midst of many dangers and deaths, when he was in the whale's belly, yea, in the belly of hell – so called because horrid and hideous, deep and dismal – yet then private prayer fetches him from there. Let a man's dangers be never so many, nor never so great, yet secret prayer has a certain omnipotency in it that will deliver him out of them all. In multiplied afflictions, private prayer is most prevalent with God. In the very midst of drowning, secret prayer will keep both head and heart above water. Upon Jonah's private prayer, God sends forth his *mandamus*[1], and the fish serves Jonah for a ship to sail safe to shore. When the case is even desperate, yet then private prayer can do much with God. Private prayer is of that power that it can open the doors of leviathan, as you see in this great instance, which yet is reckoned as a thing not feasible (*Job* 41:14).

Another instance of the prevalency of private prayer you have in 2 Kings 4:32–35, 'And when Elisha was come into the house, behold, the child was dead, and laid upon his bed. He went in therefore, and shut the door upon them twain, and prayed unto the LORD.' Privacy is a good help to fervency in prayer. 'And he went up, and lay upon the child, and put his mouth upon his mouth, and his eyes upon his eyes, and his hands upon his hands; and he stretched himself upon the child, and the flesh of the child waxed warm. Then he returned, and walked in the house to and fro; and went up, and stretched himself upon him: and the child sneezed seven times, and the child opened his eyes.'

Oh, the power, the prevalency, the omnipotency of private prayer, that raises the dead to life! And the same effect had the private prayer of Elijah in raising the widow's son of Zarephath to life (*1 Kings* 17:20–23). The great prevalency of Moses' private prayers you may read of in the following Scriptures: *Num.* 11:1, 2, 'And when the people complained, it displeased the LORD: and the LORD heard it: and his anger was kindled: and the fire of the LORD burnt among them, and consumed them that

[1] A writ or command from a higher court: 'We command . . .'.

were in the uttermost parts of the camp. And the people cried unto Moses; and when Moses prayed unto the LORD, the fire was quenched.' Moses by private prayer rules and overrules with God; he was so potent with God in private prayer that he could have what he would of God. So *Num.* 21:7-9; *Psa.* 106:23; *Exod.* 32:9-14; *Exod.* 14:15-17. The same you may see in Nehemiah, chap. 1:11, compared with chap. 2:4-8.

So Luther, perceiving the cause of God and the work of reformation to be greatly strained and in danger, he went into his closet, and never left wrestling with God till he had received a gracious answer from heaven; upon which he comes out of his closet to his friends leaping and triumphing with *Vicimus, vicimus*, 'We have overcome, we have overcome', in his mouth. At which time it is observed that there came out a proclamation from Charles V, that none should be further molested for the profession of the gospel. At another time, Luther being in private prayer for a sick friend of his, who was very comfortable and useful to him, had a particular answer for his recovery; whereupon he was so confident, that he sent word to his friend that he should certainly recover; and so it fell out accordingly.

And so Latimer prayed with great zeal for three things:

1. That Queen Elizabeth might come to the crown;

2. That he might seal the truth with his heart blood;

3. That the gospel might be restored once again, which he expressed with great vehemency of spirit: all which three God heard him in.[1]

[1] Foxe, *Acts & Monuments*; Sibbes refers to this, *Works*, vol. 1, p. 250.

Constantine commanded that his effigies should be engraved, not as other emperors in their armour leaning, but as in a posture of prayer, kneeling to show to the world that he won more by secret prayer than by open battles.

Mr Dod[1] reports that when many good people had often sought the Lord in the behalf of a woman that was possessed with the devil, and yet could not prevail, at last they appointed a day for fasting and prayer; at which time there came a poor woman to the chamber door where the exercise was begun and craved entrance, but she being poor they would not admit her in; upon that, the poor woman kneeled down behind the door and sought God by prayer. But she had not prayed long before the evil spirit raged, roared, and cried out in the possessed woman, 'Take away the old woman behind the door, for I must be gone; take away the old woman behind the door, for I must be gone.' And so by the old woman's prayers behind the door he was cast out. Oh, the prevalency of prayer behind the door! And thus you see by all these great instances the great prevalency of private prayer.

Private prayer, like Saul's sword and Jonathan's bow, when duly qualified as to the person and act, never returns empty; it hits the mark, it carries the day with God; it pierces the walls of heaven, though, like those of Gaza, made of brass and iron (*Isa.* 45:2). Oh, who can express the powerful oratory of private prayer!

---

[1] John Dod (c. 1555–1645), an early Puritan minister.

9: Private Prayer Is the Most Soul-Enriching of Duties

NINTHLY, consider, *that secret duties are the most soul-enriching duties.*

Consider that, as secret meals make fat bodies, so secret duties make fat souls; and as secret trades bring in great earthly riches, so secret prayers make many rich in spiritual blessings, and in heavenly riches.

Private prayer is that privy key of heaven that unlocks all the treasures of glory to the soul. The best riches and the sweetest mercies God usually gives to his people when they are in their closets upon their knees. Just as the warmth the chickens find by sitting close under the hen's wings cherishes them, so the graces of the saints are enlivened, and cherished, and strengthened by the sweet secret influences which their souls fall under when they are in their closet-communion with God.

Private prayer conscientiously performed is the privy key of heaven, that has unlocked such treasures and such secrets as has passed the skill of the most cunning devil to find out.

Private prayer midwifes the choicest mercies and the chiefest riches in upon us. Certainly there are none so rich in gracious experiences as those that are most exercised in closet duties. *Psa.* 34:6: 'This poor man cried', says David, 'and the LORD heard him, and saved him out of all his troubles.' David, pointing to himself, tells us that he 'cried', that is, silently and secretly, as Moses did at the Red Sea, and as Nehemiah did in the presence of the king of Persia; 'and the LORD saved him out of all his troubles' (*Exod.* 14:15; *Neh.* 1:11; and 2:4). And, oh, what additions were these deliverances to his experiences!

O my friends, look, as the tender dew that falls in the silent night makes the grass and herbs and flowers to flourish and grow more abundantly than great showers of rain that fall in the day, so secret prayer will more abundantly cause the sweet herbs of grace and holiness to grow and flourish in the soul, than all those more open, public, and visible duties of religion, which too, too often are mingled and mixed with the sun and wind of pride and hypocrisy.

Beloved! you know that many times a favourite at court gets more by one secret approach, by one private request to his prince, than a tradesman or a merchant gets in twenty years' labour and pains. So a Christian many times gets more by one secret approach, by one private request to the King of kings, than many others do by trading long in the more public duties of religion.

O sirs! remember that in private prayer we have a far greater advantage as to the exercise of our own gifts and graces and parts, than we have in public; for in public we only hear others exercise their parts and gifts, etc.; in public duties we are more passive, but in private duties we are more active. Now, the more our gifts and parts and graces are exercised, the more they are strengthened and increased. All acts strengthen habits. The more sin is acted, the more it is strengthened. And so it is with our gifts and graces; the more they are acted, the more they are strengthened.

10: Secret Prayer and Secret Sins

Tenthly, all Christians have their secret sins. *Psa.* 19:12: 'Who can understand his errors? cleanse thou me from secret faults.' Secret not only to other men, but himself; even such secret sins as grew from errors which he did not understand. It naturally belongs to every man to err, and then to be ignorant of his errors. Many sins I see in myself, he says, and more there are which I cannot see, which I cannot find out; no, I think, he says, that every man's sins go beyond his reckoning. There is not the best, the wisest, nor the holiest man in the world, that can give a full and entire list of his sins.

'Who can understand his errors?' This question has the force of an affirmation: 'Who can?' No man! no, not the most perfect and innocent man in the world. O friends! who can reckon up the secret sinful imaginations, the secret sinful inclinations, or the secret pride, the secret blasphemies, the secret hypocrisies, the secret atheistical risings, the secret murmurings, the secret repinings, the secret discontentments, the secret insolencies, the secret filthinesses, the secret unbelievings, etc., that God might every day charge upon his soul! Should the best and holiest man on earth have but his secret sins every day written on his forehead, it would not only make him blush, but it would make him pull his hat over his eyes, or cover his face with a double scarf. So *1 Kings* 8:38: 'What prayer and supplication soever be made by any man, or by all thy people Israel, which shall know every man the plague of his own heart,' etc. Sin is the greatest plague in the world, but never more dangerous than when it reaches the heart. Now, secret sins commonly lie nearest the heart, the fountain from whence they take a quick, immediate, and continual supply. Secret sins are as near to original sin as the first droppings are to the fountain-head. And as every secret sin lies nearest the heart, so every secret sin is the plague of the heart.

Now, as secret diseases are not to be laid open to every one, but only to the prudent physician, so our secret sins, which are the secret plagues, the secret diseases of our souls, are not to be laid open to every one, but only to the physician of souls, who alone is able not only to cure them but to pardon then.

And as all Christians have their secret sins, so all Christians have their secret temptations, 2 *Cor.* 12:8, 9. And as they have their secret temptations, so they have their secret needs; yea, often they have such particular and personal needs that there is not one in the congregation, nor one in the family, that has the same. And as they have their secret needs, so they have their secret fears, and secret snares, and secret trials, and secret troubles, and secret doubts, and secret jealousies, etc. And how do all these things call aloud upon every Christian to be frequent and constant in secret prayer!

11: Secret Prayer Delights Christ

ELEVENTHLY, consider, *Christ is very much affected and delighted in the secret prayers of his people. Song of Sol.* 2:14, 'O my dove that art in the clefts of the rock, in the secret places of the stairs, let me see thy countenance, let me hear thy voice; for sweet is thy voice, and thy countenance is comely.' Christ observes his spouse when she is in the clefts of the rock; when she is gotten into a corner and is praying, he looks upon her with singular delight, and with special intimations of his love. Nothing is more sweet, delightful, and welcome to Christ than the secret services of his people. Their secret breathings are like lovely songs to him (*Mal.* 3:4); their secret prayers in the clefts of the rock, or under the stairs, are as sweet incense to Jesus. The spouse retires to the secret places of the stairs not only for security, but also for secrecy, that so she might the more freely, without suspicion of hypocrisy, pour out her soul into the bosom of her beloved.

The great delight that parents take in the secret lispings and whisperings of their children, cannot be compared to the delight which Christ takes in the secret prayers of his people. And therefore, as you would be friends and promoters of Christ's delight, be much in secret prayer.

12: Only Believers Share God's Secrets

TWELFTHLY, consider *you are the only persons in all the world that God has made choice of to reveal his secrets to.* 'Henceforth I call you not servants, for the servant knoweth not what his lord doth; but I have called you friends, for all things that I have heard of my Father I have made known unto you' (*John* 15:15). Everything that God the Father had communicated to Christ as mediator to be revealed to his servants, he did make known to his disciples as to his closest, dearest friends. Christ loves his people as friends, and he treats them as friends, and he opens his heart to them as friends.

There is nothing in the heart of Christ that concerns the internal and eternal welfare of his friends, but he reveals it to them: he reveals himself, his love, his eternal good will, the mysteries of faith, and the secrets of his covenant, to his friends.[1] Christ loves not to entertain his friends with things that are commonly and vulgarly known. Christ will reveal the secrets of his mind, the secrets of his love, the secrets of his thoughts, the secrets of his heart, and the secrets of his purposes, to all his dearest friends. Samson could not hide his mind, his secrets, from Delilah, though it cost him his life (*Judg.* 16:15–17); and do you think that Christ can hide his mind, his secrets, from them for whom he hath laid down his life? Surely not. O sirs! Christ is:

1. A universal friend.
2. An omnipotent friend, an almighty friend. He is no less than thirty times called Almighty in that book of Job; he can do above all expressions and beyond all apprehensions.
3. An omniscient friend.
4. An omnipresent friend.
5. An indeficient [complete and perfect] friend.
6. An independent friend.
7. An unchangeable friend.
8. A watchful friend.
9. A tender and compassionate friend.
10. A close and faithful friend.

[1] *1 Cor.* 2:10–11; *John* 1:9; *Rom.* 16:25; *1 Cor.* 2:7; *Eph.* 3:3, 4, 9.

Therefore he cannot but open and unburden his heart to all his dearest friends. To be reserved and close is against the very law of friendship. Faithful friends are very free in imparting their thoughts, their minds, their secrets, one to another. A real friend considers nothing worth knowing unless he makes it known to his friends. He rips up his greatest and most inward secrets to his friends. Job calls his friends 'inward friends', or the men of his secrets (*Job* 19:19). All Christ's friends are inward friends; they are the men of his secrets: *Prov.* 3:32, 'His secrets are with the righteous', that is, his covenant and fatherly affection, which is hid and secret from the world. He that is righteous in secret, where no man sees him, he is the righteous man, to whom God will communicate his closest secrets, as to his dearest, closest friend. It is only a close friend to whom we will open our hearts. So Psalm 25:14, 'The secret of the LORD is with them that fear him; and he will shew them his covenant.'

Now, there are three sorts of divine secrets.

1. *First, there are secrets of providence,* and these he reveals to the righteous, and to them that fear him (*Psa.* 107:43; *Hos.* 14:9). The prophet Amos speaks of these secrets of providence: *Amos* 3:7, 'Surely the Lord GOD will do nothing, but he revealeth his secrets unto his servants and prophets.' Micaiah knew the secret of the Lord touching Ahab, which neither Zedekiah nor any other of the false prophets knew. So *Gen.* 18:17, 'And the LORD said, Shall I hide from Abraham that thing, which I do?' The destruction of Sodom was a secret that lay in the heart of God; but Abraham being a dear friend, God

communicates this secret to him, verses 19–21. Abraham was a friend, a faithful friend, a special friend (*James* 2:23); and therefore God makes him a member both of his court and counsel. Oh, how greatly God condescends to his people. He speaks to them as a man would speak to his friend; and there are no secrets of providence, which may be for their advantage, but he will reveal them to his faithful servants. As all faithful friends have the same friends and the same enemies, so they are mutual in the communication of their secrets one to another; and so it was between God and Abraham.

2. Secondly, *there are the secrets of his kingdom;* and these he reveals to his people: *Matt.* 13:11, 'Unto you it is given to know the mysteries of the kingdom of heaven, but unto them it is not given.' So *Matt.* 11:25, 'At that time Jesus answered and said, I thank thee, O Father, Lord of heaven and earth, because thou hast hid these things from the wise and prudent, and hast revealed them unto babes.' 'Let us not think', says Jerome,[1] 'that the gospel is in the words of Scripture, but in the sense; not in the outside, but in the marrow; not in the leaves of words, but in the root of reason.' Augustine humbly begged of God, that if it were his pleasure, he would send Moses to him to interpret some more abstruse and intricate passages in his book of Genesis.[2]

There are many choice, secret, hidden, and mysterious truths and doctrines in the gospel which Christ reveals to his people, that this poor, blind, ignorant world are

---

[1] Jerome, *Ad Eph*. lib. i.
[2] Augustine on Genesis.

strangers to.[1] There are many secrets wrapped up in the plainest truths and doctrines of the gospel, which none can effectually open and reveal but the Spirit of the Lord, who searches all things, yes, the deep things of God. There are many secrets and mysteries in the gospel, that all the learning and labour in the world can never give a man insight into. There are many that know the doctrine of the gospel, the history of the gospel, that are mere strangers to the secrets of the gospel. There is a secret power, a secret authority, a secret efficacy, a secret prevalency, a secret goodness, a secret sweetness in the gospel, that none experience but those to whom the Lord is pleased to impart gospel secrets to: *Isa.* 8:16, 'Seal the law among my disciples.' The law of God to wicked men is a sealed book that they cannot understand (*Dan.* 12:9, 10). It is like blotted paper that they cannot read. As a private letter to a friend contains secret matter that no one else may read because it is sealed, so the law of grace is sealed up under the privy-seal of heaven, so that no man can open it or read it, but Christ's faithful friends to whom it is sent. The whole Scripture, says Gregory, is but one entire letter despatched from the Lord Christ to his beloved spouse on earth.

The Rabbis say that there are four keys that God has under his girdle: 1, the key of the clouds; 2, the key of the womb; 3, the key of the grave; 4, the key of food; and I may add a fifth key that is under his girdle, and that is the key of the Word, the key of the Scripture; which key none can turn but he who 'hath the key of David, that opens,

---

[1] *Joel* 2:28; *1 Tim.* 3:9, 16; *Col.* 1:26-27; *1 Cor.* 2:9-12; *Eph.* 4:21.

and no man shuts; and that shuts and no man opens' (*Rev.* 3:7). O sirs! God reveals himself, and his mind, and will, and truth, to his people, in a more friendly and familiar way than he does to others: *Mark* 4:11, 'And he said unto them, Unto you it is given to know the mysteries of the kingdom of God: but unto them that are without, all these things are done in parables'; *Luke* 8:10, 'And he said, Unto you it is given to know the mystery of the kingdom of God: but to others in parables; that seeing they might not see, and hearing they might not understand.' Though great doctors, and profound clerks, and deep-studied but unsanctified divines may know much of the doctrines of the gospel, and highly commend the doctrines of the gospel, and often dispute for the doctrines of the gospel, and frequently glory in the doctrines of the gospel, and take a great deal of effort to dress and trim up the doctrines of the gospel, with the flowers of rhetoric or eloquence – though it be much better to present truth in her native plainness, than to hang her ears with counterfeit pearls; the Word, without human adornments, is like the stone *garamantides*, that has drops of gold in itself, sufficient to enrich the believing soul – yet the special, spiritual, powerful, and saving knowledge of the doctrines of the gospel, is a secret, a mystery, yes, a hidden mystery to them (*Rom.* 16:25; *1 Cor.* 2:7).

Chrysostom compares the mysteries of Christ, in regard of the wicked, to a written book, that the ignorant can neither read nor spell; he sees the cover, the leaves, and the letters, but cannot understand the meaning of what he sees. He compares the mystery of grace to a written letter, which an unskilful idiot[1] viewing, cannot read it, cannot understand; he knows it is paper and ink, but the sense, the matter, he does not know, he does not understand. So unsanctified persons, though they are never so well-educated, and though they may perceive the bark of the mystery of Christ, yet they do not perceive, they do not understand, the mystery of grace, the inward sense of the Spirit, in the blessed Scriptures. Though the devil be the greatest scholar in the world, and though he has more learning than all the men in the world have, yet there are many thousands of secrets and mysteries in the gospel of grace, that he doesn't know, really, spiritually, feelingly, efficaciously, powerfully, thoroughly, savingly, etc.

Oh, but now Christ makes known himself, his mind, his grace, his truth, to his people, in a more clear, full, familiar, and friendly way: 2 *Sam.* 7:27, 'For thou, O LORD of hosts, God of Israel, hast revealed to thy servant'; so you read it in your books; but in the Hebrew it is thus: 'LORD, you have revealed this to the ear of your servant.' Now, the emphasis lies in that word, *to the ear,* which is left out in your books.

When God makes himself known to his people, he reveals things to their ears, as we use to do to a friend who is intimate with us: we speak a thing in his ear. There is many a secret which Jesus Christ speaks in the ears of his servants, which others never come to be acquainted with: 2 *Cor.* 4:6, 'God, who commanded the light to shine out of darkness, hath shined in our hearts, to give the light of the knowledge of the glory of God in the face of Jesus Christ.'

[1] That is, the unlearned (ιδιωτης, *1 Cor.* 14:24).

The six several gradations that are in this Scripture are worthy of our most serious consideration. Here is,

First, Knowledge; and,

Secondly, The knowledge of the glory of God; and,

Thirdly, The light of the knowledge of the glory of God; and,

Fourthly, Shining; and,

Fifthly, Shining into our hearts; and,

Sixthly, Shining into our hearts in the face of Jesus Christ.

And thus you see that the Lord reveals the secrets of himself, his kingdom, his truth, his grace, his glory, to the saints.

3. *Thirdly, There are the secrets of his favour, the secrets of his special love, that he bears to them; the secret purposes of his heart to save them;* and these are those great secrets, those 'deep things of God', which none can reveal 'but the Spirit of God'. Now these great secrets, these deep things of God, God reveals to his people by his Spirit: *1 Cor.* 2:10–12, 'But God hath revealed them unto us by his Spirit: for the Spirit searcheth all things, yea, the deep things of God. For what man knoweth the things of a man, save the spirit of man which is in him? Even so the things of God knoweth no man, but the Spirit of God. Now we have received, not the spirit of the world, but the Spirit which is of God, that we might know the things that are freely given to us of God.'

Now what are the things that are freely given to us of God, but our election, vocation, justification, sanctification, and glorification? And why has God given us his

Spirit, but that we should know 'the things that are freely given to us of God.' Some by *secret* in that 25th Psalm, do understand a particular assurance of God's favours, whereby happiness is secured to us, both for the present and for the future. They understand by secret, the sealing of the Spirit, the hidden manna, the white stone, and the new name in it, 'which none knoweth but he that hath it'. And so much those words, 'He will shew them his covenant', seems to import: for what greater secret can God impart to his people, than that of opening the covenant of grace to them in its freeness, fullness, sureness, sweetness, suitableness, everlastingness, and in sealing up his good pleasure, and all the spiritual and eternal blessings of the covenant to them? Such as love and serve the Lord shall be of his cabinet-council, they shall know his soul-secrets, and be admitted into a very gracious familiarity and friendship with himself: *John* 14:21–2.3, 'He that hath my commandments, and keepeth them, he it is that loveth me; and he that loveth me shall be loved of my Father, and I will love him, and manifest myself unto him. Judas saith unto him (not Iscariot), Lord! how is it that thou wilt manifest thyself unto us, and not unto the world? Jesus answered and said unto him, If any man love me, he will keep my words: and my Father will love him, and we will come unto him, and make our abode with him.'

God and Christ will keep house with them, and manifest the secrets of their love to them that are observant of their commands. And thus you see that the saints are the only persons to whom God will reveal the secrets of his providence, the secrets of his kingdom, and the secrets of his love unto. Christ came out of the bosom of his Father, and he opens all the secrets of his Father only to his bosom-friends. Now what an exceeding high honour is it for God to open the secrets of his love, the secrets of his promises, the secrets of his providences, the secrets of his counsels, and the secrets of his covenant, to his people!

Tiberius Caesar thought no man fit to know his secrets. And among the Persians none but noblemen, lords, and dukes, might be made partakers of state secrets; they esteeming secrecy a god, a divine thing, as Ammianus Marcellinus affirms. But now such honour God has put upon all his saints, as to make them lords and nobles, and the only privy statesmen in the court of heaven. The highest honour and glory that earthly princes can put upon their subjects is to communicate to them their greatest secrets. Now this high honour and glory the King of kings has put upon his people; 'For his secrets are with them that fear him, and he will shew them his covenant.' It was a high honour to Elisha (2 *Kings* 6:12), that he could tell the secrets that were spoken in the king's bedchamber. Oh! what an honour must it then be for the saints to know the secrets that are spoken in the presence-chamber of the King of kings!

Now I appeal to the very consciences of all that fear the Lord, whether it be not a just, equal, righteous, and necessary thing, that the people of God should freely and fully lay open all the secrets of their hearts before the Lord, who has thus highly honoured them, as to reveal the secrets of his providence, kingdom, and favour to them?

Yea, I appeal to all serious and ingenuous Christians, whether it is not against the light and law of nature, and against the law of love, and law of friendship, to be reserved and close, yes, to hide our secrets from him who reveals his greatest and our choicest secrets to us? And if it is, why then do not you in secret lay open all your secret sins, and secret needs, and secret desires, secret fears, etc., to him who sees in secret? You know all secrets are to be communicated only in secret. None but very foolish people will communicate secrets upon a stage, or before many.

13: Private Prayer the Christian's Refuge in Trouble

THIRTEENTHLY, consider that *in times of great straits and trials, in times of great afflictions and persecutions, private prayer is the Christian's meat and drink*; it is his chief city of refuge; it is his shelter and hiding-place in a stormy day. When the saints have been driven by violent persecutions into holes, and caves, and dens, and deserts, and howling wildernesses, private prayer has been their meat and drink, and under Christ their only refuge.[1] When Esau came forth with hostile intentions against Jacob, secret prayer was Jacob's refuge: *Gen.* 32:6-9, 11, 'And the messengers returned to Jacob, saying, We came to thy brother Esau, and also he cometh to meet thee, and four hundred men with him': all cut-throats. 'Then Jacob was greatly afraid and distressed: and he divided the

---

[1] *Heb.* 11:37-38; *Rev.* 12:6; *Psa.* 102:6-14.

people that was with him, and the flocks, and herds, and the camels, into two bands; and said, If Esau come to the one company and smite it, then the other company which is left shall escape.' When all is at stake, it is Christian prudence to save what we can, though we cannot save what we would. 'And Jacob said, O God of my father Abraham, and God of my father Isaac, the LORD which saidst unto me, Return unto thy country, and to thy kindred, and I will deal well with thee.' Promises in private must be prayed over. God loves to be sued upon his own bond, when he and his people are alone. 'Deliver me, I pray thee, from the hand of my brother, from the hand of Esau: for I fear him, lest he will come and smite me, and the mother with the children'; or upon the children, meaning he will put all to death. Some look upon the words to be a metaphor taken from fowlers, who kill and take away the young and the dams together, contrary to that old law (*Deut.* 22:6). Others say it is a phrase that most lively represents the tenderness of a mother, who, seeing her children in distress, spares not her own body nor life, to hazard the same for her children's preservation, by interposing herself, even to be massacred together with and upon them (*Hos.* 10:14).

When Jacob, and all that was near and dear unto him, were in eminent danger of being cut off by Esau, and those men of blood who were with him, he turns to private prayer as his only city of refuge against the rage and malice of the mighty. And so when Jeremiah was in a solitary and loathsome dungeon, private prayer was his meat and drink, it was his only city of refuge: *Jer.* 33:1-3,

'Moreover, the word of the LORD came unto Jeremiah the second time, while he was yet shut up in the court of the prison, saying, Thus saith the LORD, the maker thereof, the LORD that formed it, to establish it; the LORD is his name: call unto me, and I will answer thee, and I will shew thee great and mighty', or hidden [margin] 'things, which thou knowest not.' When Jeremiah was in a lonesome, loathsome prison, God encouraged him by private prayer, to seek for further discoveries and revelations of those choice and singular favours, which in future times he purposed to confer upon his people: so 2 *Chron.* 33:11–13, 'Wherefore the LORD brought upon them the captains of the host of the king of Assyria, which took Manasseh among the thorns, and bound him with fetters', or chains, 'and carried him to Babylon. And when he was in affliction, he besought the LORD his God, and humbled himself greatly before the God of his fathers, and prayed unto him: and he was entreated of him, and heard his supplication, and brought him again to Jerusalem into his kingdom. Then Manasseh knew that the LORD he was God.' When Manasseh was in fetters in his enemy's country, when he was stripped of all his princely glory, and led captive into Babylon, he turns to private prayer as his only city of refuge; and by this means he prevails with God for his restoration to his crown and kingdom.

Private prayer is a city of refuge that no power nor policy, no craft nor cruelty, no violence nor force, is ever able to surprise. Though the joint prayers of the people of God together were often obstructed and hindered in the times of the ten persecutions, yet they were never able to obstruct or hinder secret prayer, private prayer. When iron and devils have done their worst, every Christian will be able to maintain his private trade with heaven. Private prayer will shelter a Christian against all the national, domestic, and personal storms and tempests that may threaten him. When a man is lying upon a sick-bed alone, or when a man is in prison alone, or when a man is with Job left upon the dunghill alone, or when a man is with John banished for the testimony of Jesus into this or that island alone, oh, then private prayer will be his meat and drink, his shelter, his hiding-place, his heaven. When all other trades fail, this trade of private prayer will hold good.

14: God Is Omnipresent

FOURTEENTHLY, consider *that God is omnipresent.*[1] We cannot get into any blind hole, or dark corner, or secret place, but the Lord has an eye there, the Lord will keep us company there: *Matt.* 6:6, 'And thy Father, which seeth in secret, shall reward thee openly.' So verse 18. There is not the darkest, dirtiest hole in the world into which a saint creeps, but God has a favourable eye there. God never lacks an eye to see our secret tears, nor an ear to hear our secret cries and groans, nor a heart to grant our secret requests, and therefore we ought to pour out our souls to him in secret: *Psa.* 38:9, 'Lord, all my desire is before thee; and my groaning is not hid from thee.'

[1] *Jer.* 16:17; *Job* 34:21; *Prov.* 5:21; *Jer.* 32:19; *Rev.* 2:23; *Lam.* 3:56.

Though our private desires are never so confused, though our private requests are never so broken, and though our private groanings are never so much hidden from men, yet God eyes them all, God records them all, and God puts them all upon the file of heaven, and will one day crown them with glorious answers and returns. We cannot sigh out a prayer in secret, but he sees us; we cannot lift up our eyes to him at midnight, but he observes us. The eye that God has upon his people when they are in secret is such a special tender eye of love as opens his ear, his heart, and his hand, for their good: *1 Pet.* 3:12, 'For the eyes of the Lord are over the righteous, and, his ears are open unto their prayers'; or, as the Greek has it, 'his ears are unto their prayers'. If their prayers are so faint, that they cannot reach up as high as heaven, then God will bow the heavens and come down to their prayers.[1]

God's eye is upon every secret sigh, and every secret groan, and every secret desire, and every secret pant of love, and every secret breathing of soul, and every secret melting and working of heart; all which should encourage us to be much in secret duties, in closet services. As a Christian is never out of the reach of God's hand, so he is never out of the view of God's eye.

If a Christian cannot hide himself from the sun, which is God's minister of light, how impossible will it be to hide himself from him whose eyes are ten thousand times brighter than the sun? In every private duty, a Christian is still under the eye of God's omnisciency. When we are in

[1] God is *totus occulus*, all eye.

the darkest hole, God has windows into our hearts, and observes all the secret actings of our inward man (*1 Tim.* 2:8).

The eye of God is not confined to this place or that, to this company or that; God has an eye upon his people as well when they are alone, as when they are among a multitude; as well when they are in a corner, as when they are in a crowd. Diana's temple was burnt down when she was busy at Alexander's birth, and could not be at two places together,¹ But God is present both in paradise and in the wilderness, both in the family and in the closet, both in public and in private at the same time. God is an omnipresent God; he is everywhere. *Non est ubi, ubi non est Deus* [there is nowhere where God is not]. As he is included in no place, so he is excluded from no place: *Jer.* 23:24, 'Can any man hide himself in secret places, that I shall not see him, saith the Lord?' *Prov.* 15:3, 'The eyes of the Lord are in every place, beholding the evil and the good', or, 'contemplating the evil and the good', as the Hebrew may be read. Now, to *contemplate*, is more than simply to *behold*; for contemplation adds to a simple apprehension a deeper degree of knowledge, entering into the very inside of a matter; and so indeed doth God discern the very inward intentions of the heart, and the most secret motions of the spirit.

God is an infinite and immense being, whose centre is everywhere, and whose circumference is nowhere. Now, if

¹ This remark was ascribed to Hegesias the Magnesian, but by Cicero to Timaeus of Tauromenium. Plutarch, *Alexander,* 3. Cicero, *De Natura Deorum*, ii. 27.

our God be omnipresent, then, wherever we are, our God is present with us: if we are in prison alone like Joseph, our God is present with us there; or if we are in exile alone like David, our God is present with us there; or if we are alone in our closets, our God is present with us there. God sees us in secret; and therefore let us seek his face in secret. Though heaven be God's palace, yet it is not his prison.

15: If We Neglect Private Prayer, God Will Not Hear Our Public Prayers

FIFTEENTHLY, *he that willingly neglects private prayer shall certainly be neglected in his public prayer;* he that will not call upon God in secret shall find by sad experience that God will neither hear him nor regard him in public. The absence of private duties is the great reason why the hearts of many are so dead and dull, so formal and carnal, so barren and unfruitful under public ordinances.

Oh, that Christians would seriously lay this to heart! Certainly, that man or woman's heart is best in public who is most frequent in private. They make most yearnings in public ordinances that are most conscientiously exercised in closet duties. No man's graces rise so high, nor no man's experiences rise so high, nor no man's communion with God rises so high, nor no man's divine enjoyments rise so high, nor no man's springs of comfort rise so high, nor no man's hopes rise so high, nor no man's parts and gifts rise so high, etc., as theirs do, who conscientiously wait upon God in their closets before they wait upon him in the assembly of his people; and who when they return from public ordinances retire into their closets and look up to heaven for a blessing upon the public means. It is certain that private duties fit the soul for public ordinances. He who conscientiously waits upon God in private, shall find by experience that God will wonderfully bless public ordinances to him (*Mic.* 2:7). My design is not to set up one ordinance of God above another, nor to cause one ordinance of God to clash with another – the public with the private, or the private with the public – but that every ordinance may have its proper place and right, the desires of my soul being to prize every ordinance, and to praise every ordinance, and to practise every ordinance, and to improve every ordinance, and to bless the Lord for every ordinance. But as ever you would see the beauty and glory of God in his sanctuary, as ever you would have public ordinances to be lovely and lively to your souls, as ever you would have your drooping spirits revived, and your languishing souls refreshed, and your weak graces strengthened, and your strong corruptions weakened under public ordinances, be more careful and conscientious in the performance of closet duties (*Psa.* 63:1–3).

Oh, how strong in grace! Oh, how victorious over sin! Oh, how dead to the world! Oh, how alive to Christ! Oh, how fit to live! Oh, how prepared to die! – might many a Christian have been, had they been but more frequent, serious, and conscientious in the discharge of closet duties. Not but that I think there is a truth in that saying of Bede – the word *church* being rightly understood – viz.,

THE SECRET KEY TO HEAVEN

that he that comes not willingly to church shall one day
go unwillingly to hell.

16: The Times Call for Private Prayer

Sᴛ IXTEENTHLY, consider, *the times in which we live call
aloud for secret prayer.* Hell seems to have broken
loose, and men turned into incarnate devils: land-
destroying and soul-damning wickednesses walk up and
down the streets with a whore's forehead, without the
least check or control: *Jer.* 3:3, 'Thou hast a whore's forehead, thou refusest to be ashamed.' *Jer.* 6:15, 'Were they
ashamed when they had committed abomination? nay,
they were not at all ashamed, neither could they blush.'[1]

They had sinned away shame, instead of being ashamed
of sin. Custom in sin had quite banished all sense of sin
and all shame for sin, so that they would not suffer nature
to draw her veil of blushing before their great abominations. They were like to Caligula, a wicked emperor,
who used to say of himself, that he loved nothing better
in himself than that he could not be ashamed. The same
words are repeated in *Jer.* 8:12. How applicable these
Scriptures are to the present time I will leave the prudent
reader to judge. But what does the prophet do, now they
were as bold in sin and as shameless as so many harlots?
That you may see in *Jer.* 42:17: 'But if ye will not hear it,
my soul shall weep in secret places', or *secrecies*, 'for your
pride; and mine eye shall weep sore' (Hebrew, 'weeping,
weep', or 'shedding tears, shed tears'; the doubling of the

---

[1] Curtius, a heathen, said that the man was undone who knew no
shame.

[66]

verb notes the bitter and grievous lamentation that he should make for them), 'and run down with tears.' Now they were grown up to that height of sin and wickedness, that they were above all shame and blushing; now they were grown so proud, so hardened, so obstinate, so rebellious, so mad upon mischief, that no mercies could melt them or allure them, nor no threatenings nor judgments could any ways terrify them or stop them. The prophet goes into a corner, he retires himself into the most secret places, and there he weeps bitterly, there he weeps as if he were resolved to drown himself in his own tears.

When the springs of sorrow rise high, a Christian turns his back upon company, and retires himself into places of greatest privacy, so that he may the more freely and the more fully vent his sorrow and grief before the Lord.

Ah, England, England! what pride, luxury, lasciviousness, licentiousness, wantonness, drunkenness, cruelties, injustice, oppressions, fornications, adulteries, falsehoods, hypocrisy, bribery, atheism, horrid blasphemies, and hellish impieties, are now to be found rampant in your midst! Ah, England! England! how are the Lord's Sabbaths profaned, pure ordinances despised, Scriptures rejected, the Spirit resisted and derided, the righteous reviled, wickedness countenanced, and Christ many thousand times in a day by these cursed practices afresh crucified! Ah, England! England! were our forefathers alive, how sadly would they blush to see such a horrid degenerate posterity as is to be found in our midst! How is our forefathers' hospitality converted into riot and luxury, their frugality into pride and prodigality, their simplicity into subtlety, their sincerity into hypocrisy, their charity into cruelty, their chastity into chambering and wantonness, their sobriety into drunkenness, their plain-dealing into dissembling, their works of compassion into works of oppression, and their love to the people of God into an utter enmity against the people of God! etc.

And what is the voice of all these crying abominations, but every Christian to his closet, every Christian to his closet, and there weep, with weeping Jeremiah, bitterly, for all these great abominations whereby God is dishonoured openly. Oh, weep in secret for their sins who openly glory in their sins, which should be their greatest shame. Oh, blush in secret for them that are past all blushing for their sins; for who knows but that the whole land may fare the better for the sakes of a few who are mourners in secret?

But however it goes with the nation, such as mourn in secret for the abominations of the times, may be confident that when sweeping judgments shall come upon the land, the Lord will hide them in the secret chambers of his providence, he will set a secret mark of deliverance upon their foreheads, who mourn in secret for the crying sins of the present day, as he did upon theirs in Ezekiel 9:4–6.

17: Those Near to the Lord Should Engage in Secret Prayer

SEVENTEENTHLY, consider that *the near and dear relation that you stand in to the Lord calls aloud for secret prayer, John* 15:14–15. You are his friends. Now, a true friend loves to visit his friend when he may find him alone, and enjoy privacy with him. A true friend loves to pour out his heart into the heart of his friend when he has him in a corner, or in the field, or under a hedge. You are his favourites; and what favourite is there that hides his secret from his prince? Do not all favourites open their hearts to their princes when they are alone? You are his children; and what ingenuous child is there that does not delight to be much with his father when he is alone, when nobody is by? Oh, how free and open are children when they have their parents alone, beyond what they are when company is present. You are the spouse of Christ; and what spouse, what wife is there that does not love to be much with her husband when he is alone?

True lovers are always best when they are most alone: *Song of Sol.* 7:10–12, 'I am my beloved's, and his desire is towards me. Come, my beloved, let us go forth into the field; let us lodge in the villages. Let us get up early to the vineyards; let us see if the vines flourish, whether the tender grape appear, and the pomegranates bud forth: there will I give thee my loves.' The spouse of Christ is very desirous to enjoy his company in the fields, that so, having her beloved alone, she might the more freely and the more secretly open her heart to him. As wives, when they are walking alone with their husbands in the fields, are more free to open their minds and the secrets of their hearts, than they are when in their houses with their children and servants about them, so it was with the spouse.

Without a doubt, they have very great cause to question whether they are Christ's real friends, favourites, children, spouse, who seldom or never converse with Christ in their closets, who are shy of Christ when they are alone, who never accustom themselves to give Christ secret visits.

What Delilah said to Samson, *Judg.* 16:15, 'How canst thou say, I love thee, when thou hast not told me wherein thy great strength lieth' (the discovery of which secret at last cost him his life), that Christ may say to very many in our days: How can you say you love me, when you never acquaint me with your secrets? How can you say you love me, when you never bestow any private visits upon me? How can you say that you are my friends, my faithful friends, my dearest friends, when you never in private unburden yourselves to me? How can you say that you are my favourites, when you can spend one month after another, and one quarter of a year after another, and yet not let me know one of all your secrets, when every day you might have my ear in secret if you pleased? How can you say that you are my children, and yet be so close and reserved as you are? How can you say you are my spouse, and that you lie in my bosom, and yet never take any delight to open your hearts, your secrets, to me when I am alone?

What Alexander said to one that was of his name, but a coward, 'Either lay down the name of Alexander, or fight like Alexander',[1] that I say to you, Either be frequent in closet duties, as becomes a Christian, or else lay down the name of a Christian; either open yourselves up in secret to Christ, as friends, favourites, children, spouses, or else lay down these names.

[1] Plutarch, *Life of Alexander.*

18: Special Marks of God's Favour

EIGHTEENTHLY, consider *that God has set a special mark of favour, honour, and observation, upon those who have prayed in secret*. As you may see in Moses (*Exod.* 34:28); and in Abraham (*Gen.* 21:33); and in Isaac (*Gen.* 24:63); and in Jacob (*Gen.* 32:24–29); and in David (*Psa.* 55:16, 17); and in Daniel (*Dan.* 6:10); and in Paul (*Acts* 9:11); and in Cornelius (*Acts* 10:2, 4); and in Peter (*Acts* 10:9–12); and in Manasseh (2 *Chron.* 33:18, 19). God has put all these worthies that have exercised themselves in secret prayer upon record, to their everlasting fame and honour.

The Persians seldom write their king's name but in characters of gold. God has written, as I may say, their names in characters of gold who have made conscience of exercising themselves in secret prayer. The precious names of those that have addicted themselves to closet-duties are as statues of gold which the polluted breath of men can in no way stain; they are like so many shining suns that no clouds can darken; they are like so many sparkling diamonds that shine brightest in the darkest night.

A Christian can never get into a hole, a corner, a closet, to pour out his soul before the Lord, but the Lord makes an honourable observation of him, and sets a secret mark of favour upon him (*Ezek.* 9:4–6). And how should this provoke all Christians to be much with God alone!

The Romans were very ambitious of obtaining a great name, a great report, in this world; and why should not Christians be as divinely ambitious of obtaining a good name, a good report, in the other world? (*Heb.* 11:39). A *good* name is always better than a *great* name, and a name in heaven is infinitely better than a thousand names on earth; and the way to both these is to be much with God in secret.

19: Satan's Enmity to Secret Prayer

NINETEENTHLY, consider that *Satan is a very great enemy to secret prayer.* Secret prayer is a scourge, a hell to Satan. Every secret prayer adds to the devil's torment, and every secret sigh adds to his torment, and every secret groan adds to his torment, and every secret tear adds to his torment.

When a child of God is on his knees in his secret addresses to God, oh, the strange thoughts, the earthly thoughts, the wandering thoughts, the distracted thoughts, the hideous thoughts, the blasphemous thoughts, that Satan often injects into his soul! and all to wean him from secret prayer.[1] Sometimes he tells the soul, that it is vain to seek God in secret; and at other times he tells the soul it is too late to seek God in secret; for the door of mercy is shut, and there is no hope, no help for the soul. Sometimes he tells the soul that it is enough to seek God in

---

[32] There is no one thing that many hundred Christians have more sadly lamented and bewailed, as many faithful ministers can witness, than the sad interruptions that they have met with from Satan, when they have been with God alone in a room, in a corner. Oh! how often have they been scared, frightened, and amazed by noises and strange apparitions, at least in their imaginations, when they have been alone with God in a corner.

public; and at other times he tells the soul, that it is but a precise trick to seek the Lord in private. Sometimes he tells the soul, that it is not elected and therefore all his secret prayers shall be rejected; and at other times he tells the soul, that it is sealed up unto the day of wrath, and therefore a secret prayer can never reverse that seal; and all this to dishearten and discourage a poor Christian in his secret retirements. Sometimes Satan will bring before a poor Christian the greatness of his sins; and at other times he will bring before a Christian the greatness of his unworthiness. Sometimes he will bring before a Christian his lack of grace; and at other times he will bring before a Christian his lack of gifts to manage such a duty as it should be managed. Sometimes he will bring before a Christian his past difficulties in secret prayer; and at other times he will bring before a Christian his weak desire for secret prayer; and all to work the soul out of love with secret prayer, yes, to work the soul to loathe secret prayer; so deadly an enemy is Satan to secret prayer.

Oh, the strange fears, thoughts, and conceits, that Satan often raises in the spirits of Christians, when they are alone with God in a corner; and all to work them to cast off private prayer. It is none of Satan's least designs to interrupt a Christian in his private trade with God. Satan watches all a Christian's actions; so that he cannot turn into his closet, nor creep into any hole to converse privately with his God, but he follows him hard at heel, and will be still injecting one thing or another into the soul, or else bringing one thing or another against the soul. A Christian is as well able to count the stars of heaven, and to number the sands of the sea, as he is able to number up the several devices and sleights that Satan uses to obstruct the soul's private approaches to God. Now from that great opposition that Satan makes against private prayer, a Christian may safely conclude these five things:

1. First, *the excellency of private prayer.* Certainly if it were not an excellent thing for a man to be in secret with God, Satan would never make such head against it.

2. Secondly, *the necessity of this duty.* The more necessary any duty is to the internal and eternal welfare of a Christian, the more Satan will stir himself up to blunt a Christian's spirit in that duty.

3. Thirdly, *the utility or profit that attends a conscientious discharge of this duty.* Where we are like to gain most, there Satan loves to oppose most.

4. Fourthly, *the prevalency of private prayer.* If there were not a kind of omnipotency in it, if it were not able to do wonders in heaven, and wonders on earth, and wonders in the hearts and lives and ways of men, Satan would never have such an aching tooth against it as he has.

5. Fifthly, *that God is highly honoured by this duty,* or else Satan would never be so greatly enraged against it. This is certain. The more glory God has from any service we do, the more Satan will strive by all his wiles, and sleights to take us, either off from that service, or so to interrupt us in that service, that God may have no honour,

nor we no good, nor himself no hurt, by our private retirements.

20: The Lord's Secret Ones Should Engage in Secret Prayer

B UT IN THE twentieth and last place, consider that *you only are the Lord's secret ones, his hidden ones; and therefore if you do not apply yourselves to private prayer, and to your secret retirements, that you may enjoy God in a corner, none will.*

It is only God's hidden ones, his secret ones, that are spirited, principled, and prepared to wait on God in secret: *Exod.* 19:5, 'Then shall ye be a peculiar treasure unto me above all people.' The Hebrew word *segullah* signifies God's special jewels, God's proper ones, or God's secret ones, that he keeps in store for himself, and for his own special service and use. Princes lock up with their own hands in secret their most precious and costly jewels; and so does God his: *Psa.* 135:4, 'For the LORD hath chosen Jacob unto himself, and Israel for his peculiar treasure', or for his secret gem; *Psa.* 83:3, 'They have taken crafty counsel against thy people, and consulted against thy hidden ones', or 'thy secret ones'; so called partly because God hides them in the secret of his tabernacle (*Psa.* 31:26), and partly because God sets as high a value upon them as men do upon their hidden treasure, their secret treasure; yes, he makes more reckoning of them than he does of all the world besides. And so the world shall know when God shall arise to revenge the wrongs and injuries that have been done to his secret ones. Neither are there any on earth that knows so much of the secrets of his love, of the secrets of his counsels, of the secrets of his purposes, of the secrets of his heart, as his secret ones do. Neither are there any in all the world that are under those secret influences, those secret assistances, those secret incomes, those secret anointings of the Spirit, as his secret ones are under. And therefore, no wonder if God calls them again, and again, and again, his secret ones.

Now, what can be more attractive or more desirable than to see their natures and their practices to answer to their names? They are the Lord's secret ones, his hidden ones; and therefore how highly does it concern them to be much with God in secret, and to hide themselves with God in a corner!

Shall Nabal's nature and practice answer to his name? *1 Sam.* 25:25, 'Let not my Lord, I pray thee, regard this man of Belial, even Nabal: for as his name is, so is he: Nabal is his name, and folly is with him.' Nabal signifies a *fool*, a sot, a churl; it notes one that is void of wisdom and goodness; it signifies one whose mind, reason, judgment, and understanding is withered and decayed. Now, if so you look into the story, you shall find that as face answers to face, Nabal's nature and practice echoes and answers to his name. And why then, should not our natures and practices answer to our names also? We are called the Lord's secret ones, his hidden ones; and how highly therefore does it concern us to be much with God in secret!

Why should there be any jarring or discord between our names and our practices? It is observable that the practice and behaviour of other saints have been answerable to their names.

Isaac signifies 'laughter', and Isaac was a gracious son, a dutiful son, a son that kept clear of those abominations with which many of the patriarchs had defiled themselves, a son that proved a matter of laughter to his father and mother all their days.

So Josiah signifies 'the fire of the LORD'; and his practice did answer to his name. Witness the pulling down of Jeroboam's altar, and his burning of the vessels that were made for Baal, and pulling down the idolatrous priests whom the kings of Judah had set up, and his burning the grove at the brook Kidron, and his stamping it to powder, and his breaking down the houses of the Sodomites, and his defiling of the high places where the priests had burnt incense, and his breaking in pieces the images, and cutting down the groves, and filling their places with the bones of men, etc. (*1 Kings* 2; *2 Kings* 23:4–21).

So Joshua signifies 'a saviour'; and his practice was answerable to his name. Though he could not save his people from their sins, yet he often saved them from their sufferings. Great and many were the deliverances, the salvations, that were instrumentally brought about by Joshua, as all know that have read the book of Joshua.

So John signifies 'gracious', and his practice was answerable to his name. He was so gracious in his teachings and in his walkings that he gained favour in the very eyes of his enemies.

By all these instances, and by many more that might be given, you see that other saints' practices have answered to their names; and, therefore, let every one of us look that our practices do also answer to our names, that as we are called the Lord's secret ones, so we may be much with God in secret, that so there may be a blessed harmony between our names and our practice, and we may never repent another day that we have been called God's secret ones, his 'hidden ones', but yet never made conscience of maintaining secret communion with God in our closets.

And thus you see that there are no less than twenty arguments to persuade you to closet prayer, and to maintain private communion with God in a corner.

PART 3

THE USE AND APPLICATION
OF THE DOCTRINE

I s it so, that closet prayer or private prayer is such an
indispensable duty that Christ himself has laid it upon
all that are not willing to lie under the woeful brand of
being hypocrites? Then this truth looks very sourly and
sadly upon these five sorts of persons.

1. *First, it condemns all those that put off secret prayer
till they are moved to it by the Spirit;* for by this sad delu-
sion many have been kept from secret prayer many weeks,
many months; oh, that I might not say, many years!

Though it be a very fit season to pray when the Spirit
moves us to pray, yet it is not the only season to pray (*Isa.*
62:1; *Psa.* 123:1, 2; *Gal.* 4:6). He that makes religion his
business, will pray as daily for daily grace as he prays
daily for daily bread: *Luke* 18:1, 'And he spake a parable
unto them to this end, that men ought always to pray, and
not to faint'; *1 Thess.* 5:17, Pray without ceasing'; *Eph.*
6:18, 'Praying always[1] with all prayer and supplication in

[1] Ev παντι χαιρω, in every season, as occasion and opportunity offers
itself, we must pray.

the Spirit, and watching thereunto with all perseverance, and supplication for all saints'; *Rom.* 12:12, 'Continuing instant in prayer.' The Greek is a metaphor taken from hunting dogs, that never give up the game till they have got their prey. A Christian must not only pray, but hold on in prayer, till he has got the heavenly prize. We are lacking always; and therefore we have need to be praying always. The world is always alluring; and therefore we need to be always a-praying; Satan is always a-tempting; and therefore we need to be always a-praying; and we are always a-sinning; and therefore we need to be always a-praying; and we are in dangers always; and therefore we need to be praying always; and we are dying always (*1 Cor.* 15:31); and therefore we need to be praying always.

Man's whole life is but a lingering death; man no sooner begins to live, but he begins to die. When one was asked why he prayed six times a day, he only gave this answer, 'I must die, I must die, I must die.' Dying Christians need to be praying Christians, and they that are always a-dying need to be always a-praying. Certainly prayerless families are graceless families, and prayerless persons are graceless persons (*Jer.* 10:25). It were better ten thousand times that we had never been born into the world, than that we should go still-born out of the world. But,

2. *Secondly,* This truth condemns those *that pray not at all, neither in their families nor in their closets.* Among all God's children, there is not one possessed with a dumb devil. Prayerless persons are forsaken by God, blinded by Satan, hardened in sin, and every breath they draw liable to all temporal, spiritual, and eternal judgments. Prayer is

that part of natural worship due to God, which none will deny but stark atheists (*Psa.* 14:1).[1]

It is observable that amongst the worst of men, Turks, and the worst of Turks, the Moors, it is a just exception against any witness, by their law, that he has not prayed six times in every natural day, it being usual with them to pray six times a day.

1. Before the daybreak they pray for day.
2. When it is day, they give thanks for day.
3. At noon, they thank God for half the day past.
4. After that, they pray for a good sunset.
5. And after that, they thank God for the day past.

And then, sixthly and lastly, they pray for a good night after their day.

Certainly these very Moors will one day rise in judgment against those who cast off prayer, who live in a total neglect of prayer, who suffer so many suns and moons to rise and set upon their heads without any solemn calling upon God.

I have read of a man who, being sick and afraid of death, fell to his prayers; and, to move God to hear him, told him 'that he was no common beggar, and that he had never troubled him with his prayers before; and if he would but hear him at that time, he would never trouble him again'. This world is full of such profane, blasphemous, atheistic wretches. But,

---

[1] That wicked men ought to pray, and the grand objection against their prayers is answered at large in my treatise called 'The Crown and Glory of Christianity'. [See *The Works of Thomas Brooks*, 1861–7, repr. Edinburgh: Banner of Truth, 1980, vol. 4.]

3. *Thirdly,* This truth condemns those *who are all for public prayer, but never regard private prayer; who are all for going up to the temple, but never care for going into their closets.*

This is most palpable hypocrisy, for a man to be very zealous for public prayer, but very cold and careless as to private prayer. He that pretends to be conscientious in the one, and is not conscientious in the other, is an ingrained hypocrite (*Matt.* 23:5; 6:1, 2, 5); and the devil knows well enough how to trade in such hypocrites who are all for the prayers of the church, but perfect Gallios as to private prayer (*Acts* 18:17). Such as perform all their private devotion in the church, but not in the closet, despise the authority of Christ, who says, 'When thou prayest, enter into thy closet': he does not say, 'When thou prayest, go to the church', but, 'When thou prayest, go into thy closet.' But,

4. *Fourthly,* this truth condemns those *who in their closets pray with a loud clamorous voice.*

A Christian should shut both the door of his closet and the door of his lips so close that none should hear outside what he says inside. 'Enter into thy closet', says Christ, 'and when thou hast *shut thy door,* pray.' But why does a man need to shut his closet door, if he prays with a clamorous voice, if he makes such a noise as all in the street or all in the house may hear him?

The hen, when she lays her eggs, gets into a hole, a corner; but then she makes such a noise with her cackling, that she tells all in the house where she is, and what she is doing. Such Christians that imitate the hen in their closets, rather pray to be seen, heard, and observed by men, than out of any noble design to glorify God, or to pour out their souls before him who sees in secret. Sometimes children, when they are vexed, or afraid of the rod, will run behind the door, or get into a dark hole, and there they will lie crying, and sighing, and sobbing, that all the house may know where they are. Oh, it is a childish thing so to cry, and sigh, and sob in our closets, as to tell all in the house where we are, and about what we are doing. Well! Christians, for an effectual redress of this evil, frequently and seriously consider of these five things.

First, that God sees in secret.

Secondly, that God has a quick ear, and is taken the more with the voice of the heart, than he is with the clamour of the mouth. God can easily hear the most secret breathings of your soul. God is more curious in observing the messages delivered by the heart, than he is those that are only delivered by the mouth. He that prays aloud in private, seems to tell others, that God does not understand the secret desires, and thoughts, and workings of his people's hearts.

Thirdly, it is not fitting, it is not convenient nor expedient, that any should be acquainted with our secret prayers, except God and our own souls. Now it is as much our duty to look to what is expedient, as it is to look to what is lawful, *2 Cor.* 8:10; *1 Cor.* 6:12, 'All things are lawful unto me, but all things are not expedient.' So, *1 Cor.* 10:23, 'All things are lawful for me, but all things are not expedient: all things are lawful for me, but all things edify not.'

Now it is so far from being expedient, that it is very high folly for men to lay open their secret infirmities unto others, that will rather deride them, than lift up a prayer for them.

Fourthly, loud prayers may be a hindrance and disturbance to others that may be occupied near us, in some religious or civil exercises.

Fifthly and lastly, Hannah *prayed and yet spoke never a word.* Her heart was full, but her voice was not heard (*1 Sam.* 1:11). Moses prays and cries, and yet lets fall never a word: *Exod.* 14:15, 'And the LORD said unto Moses, Wherefore criest thou unto me?' Moses did not cry with any audible voice, but with inward sighs, and secret breathings, and wrestlings of soul; and these inward and secret cries, which made no noise, carried the day with God; for Moses is heard and answered, and his people are delivered. Oh, the prevalency of those prayers that make no noise in the ears of others!

5. *Fifthly* and lastly, this truth condemns those *that do all they can to hinder and discourage others from this duty of duties, private prayer;* and that either by deriding or vilifying the duty, or else by denying it to be a duty, or else by their daily neglect of this duty, or else by denying them that are under them time and opportunity for the discharge of this duty.

In *Matt.* 23:13, you have a woe pronounced against those that will neither go to heaven themselves, nor suffer others to go that are willing to enter into an everlasting rest. And so I say, Woe to those parents, and woe to those husbands, and woe to those masters and mistresses, that will neither pray in their closets themselves, nor suffer their children, nor their wives, nor their servants, to pour out their souls before the Lord in a corner. O sirs! How will you answer this to your consciences when you shall lie upon a dying bed! And how will you answer it to the Judge of all the world, when you shall stand before a judgment seat?

Certainly all their sin, and all their neglects, and all their spiritual losses, that might have been prevented by their secret prayers, by their closet communion with God, will one day be charged to your accounts. And oh, that you were all so wise as to lay these things to heart, that you may never hinder any that are under your care or charge, from private prayer any more! But,

Secondly, this may serve *to exhort us to keep close to our closets, to be frequent and constant in private prayer, to be often with God in a corner.* The twenty considerations already laid down may serve as so many motives to provoke your hearts to this noble and necessary duty.

PART 4

SIX OBJECTIONS STATED AND ANSWERED

FIRST OBJECTION. But many will be ready to object and say, *We have much business upon our hands, and we cannot spare time for private payer; we have so much to do in our shops, and in our warehouses, and in public with others, that we cannot spare time to wait upon the Lord in our closets.*

Now to this objection I shall give these eight answers, so that this objection may never have a resurrection more in any of your hearts.

1. First, *what are all those businesses that are upon your hands, to those businesses and weighty affairs that lay upon the hands of Abraham, Isaac, Jacob, Moses, David, Daniel, Elijah, Nehemiah, Peter, Cornelius?*[1]

And yet you find all these worthies exercising themselves in private prayers. And the king is commanded every day to read some part of God's Word, notwithstanding all his great and weighty employments (*Deut.* 17:18–20). Now certainly, sirs, your great businesses are little more

---

[1] See the first argument, pp. 7–13.

than zeros compared with theirs. And if there were any on earth that might have pleaded an exemption from private prayer, upon the account of business, of much business, of great business, these might have done it; but they were more honest and more noble than to neglect so choice a duty, upon the account of much business. These brave hearts made all their public employments stoop to private prayer; they would never suffer their public employments to tread private prayer under foot. But,

2. *Secondly,* I answer, *No men's outward affairs did ever more prosper than theirs did, who devoted themselves to private prayer, notwithstanding their many and great worldly employments.*

Witness the prosperity and outward flourishing estates of Moses, Abraham, Isaac, Jacob, Nehemiah, David, Daniel, and Cornelius. These were much with God in their closets, and God blessed their blessings to them (*Gen.* 22:17). How their cups overflowed! What signal favours did God heap upon them and theirs! No families have been so prospered, protected, and graced, as theirs who have maintained secret communion with God in a corner (*1 Chron.* 11:9). Private prayer best expedites our temporal affairs. He that prays well in his closet, shall be sure to speed well in his shop, or at his plough, or whatever else he turns his hand to (*1 Tim.* 4:8). It is true, Abimelech was rich as well as Abraham, and so was Laban rich as well as Jacob, and Saul was a king as well as David, and Julian was an emperor as well as Constantine; but it was only Abraham, Jacob, David, and Constantine, who had their blessings blessed unto them; all the rest had their blessings cursed unto them (*Prov.* 3:33; *Mal.* 2:2). They had many good things, but they had not 'the good will of him that dwelt in the bush' with what they had; and therefore all their mercies were but bitter-sweets unto them. Though all the sons of Jacob returned laden from Egypt with corn and money in their sacks, yet only Benjamin had the silver cup in the mouth of his sack. So though the men of the world have their corn and their money, etc., yet it is only God's Benjamins that have the silver cup, the grace cup, the cup of blessing, as the apostle calls it, for their portion (*1 Cor.* 10:16). O sirs! as ever you would prosper and flourish in the world; as ever you would have your water turned into wine, your temporal mercies into spiritual benefits, be much with God in your closets. But,

3. *Thirdly,* I answer, *it is ten to one but that the objector every day fools away, or fritters away, or idles away, or sins away, one hour in a day,* and why then should he complain of a lack of time?

There are none that toil and moil and busy themselves most in their worldly employments but do spend an hour or more in a day to little or no purpose, either in gazing about, or in dallying, or toying, or courting, or in telling of stories, or in busying themselves in other men's matters, or in idle visits, or in smoking a pipe, etc.[1] And why then should not these men redeem an hour's time in a day for private prayer, out of that time which they usually spend so vainly and idly? Can you, notwithstanding all

---

[1] Myrmecides, a famous artist [a sculptor], spent more time in making a bee than an unskilful workman would do to build a house.

your great worldly employments, find an hour in the day to catch flies in, as Domitian the emperor did? and to play the fool in? and cannot you find an hour in the day to wait on God in your closets?

There were three special faults of which Cato professed himself to have seriously repented: one was travelling by water when he might have gone by land; another was trusting a secret in a woman's bosom; but the main one was spending an hour unprofitably. This heathen will one day rise up in judgment against them who, notwithstanding their great employments, spend many hours in a week unprofitably, and yet cry out with the Duke of Alva 'that they have so much to do on earth, that they have no time to look up to heaven'. It was a base and sordid spirit in King Sardanapalus, who spent much of his time amongst women in spinning and carding, which should have been spent in ruling and governing his kingdom. So it is a base, sordid spirit in any to spend any of their time in toying and trifling, and then to cry out that they have so much business to do in the world, that they have no time for closet prayer, they have no time to serve God, nor to save their own precious and immortal souls. But,

4. *Fourthly,* I answer, no man *dares plead this objection before the Lord Jesus in the great day of account* (*Eccles.* 11:9; *Rom.* 14:10; *2 Cor.*5:10). And why then should any man be so childish and foolish, so ignorant and impudent to plead that before men which is not pleadable before the judgment-seat of Christ? O sirs! as you love your souls, and as you would be happy for ever, never put off your own consciences nor others' with any pleas, arguments,

or objections now, that you dare not own and stand by when you shall lie upon a dying bed, and when you shall appear before the whole court of heaven. In the great day of account, when the secrets of all hearts shall be revealed, and God shall call men to a reckoning before angels, men, and devils, for the neglect of private prayer, all guilty persons will be found speechless: there will not be a man or woman found, that shall dare to stand up and say, 'Lord, I would have waited upon you in my closet, but that I had so much business to do in the world that I had no time to enjoy secret communion with you in a corner.' It is the greatest wisdom in the world, to plead nothing by way of excuse in this our day, that we dare not plead in the great day. But,

5. *Fifthly,* I answer, *that it is our duty to redeem time from all our secular businesses for private prayer.*[1]

All sorts of Christians, whether bond or free, rich or poor, high or low, superiors or inferiors, are expressly charged by God to redeem time for prayer, for private prayer, as well as for other holy exercises: *Col.* 4:2–3, 'Continue in prayer, and watch in the same with thanksgiving; withal praying also for us, that God would open unto us a door of utterance, to speak the mystery of Christ, for which I am also in bonds.'

But here some may object and say, We have so much business to do in the world that we have no time for prayer. The apostle answers this objection in verse 5, 'Walk in wisdom towards them that are without, redeem-

---

[1] It is said of blessed Hooper [John Hooper, c.1495–1555], that he was spare of diet, spare of words, and sparest of time.

ing the time.' So *Eph.* 5:16, 'Redeeming the time, because the days are evil'; εξαγοραζομενοι τον χαιρον, or buying out, or gaining the time. The words are a metaphor taken from merchants, who prefer the least profit that may be gained before their pleasures or delights, closely following their business whilst the markets are at best. A merchant when he comes to a mart or fair, takes the first season and opportunity of buying his commodities; he takes no risk in putting it off to the evening, or to the next morning, in the hope of getting a better bargain, but he makes the most of the present time, and buys before the market is over.

Others understand the words thus: 'Purchase at any rate, all occasions and opportunities of doing good, that by doing so you may, in some way, redeem that precious jewel of time which you have formerly lost.' Like travellers that have loitered by the way, or stayed long at their inn, when they find night coming upon them, they mend their pace, and go as many miles in an hour as they did before in many. Though time let slip is physically irrecoverable, yet in a moral consideration, it is accounted as regained, when men double their care, diligence, and endeavours to redeem it. The best Christian is he who is the greatest monopoliser of time for private prayer; who redeems time from his worldly occasions and his lawful comforts and recreations, to be with God in his closet. David having tasted of the sweetness, goodness, and graciousness of God, cannot keep his bed, but will borrow some time from his sleep, that he might take some turns in paradise, and pour out his soul in prayer and

praises when no eye was open to see him, nor no ear open
to hear him, but all were asleep round about him, *Psa.*
63:6; *Psa.* 119:62, 'At midnight will I arise to give thanks
unto thee.' Verse 147, 'I have prevented the dawning of
the morning, and cried.' David was up and at private
prayer before daybreak. David was no sluggish Christian,
no slothful Christian, no lazy Christian: he used to be in
his closet when others were sleeping in their beds. So
verse 148, 'Mine eyes prevent the night-watches, that I
might meditate in thy word.' So *Psa.* 130:6, 'My soul
waiteth for the LORD, more than they that watch for the
morning; I say, more than they that watch for the morning.' Look, as the weary sentinel in a dark, cold, wet
night, waits and peeps, and peeps and waits for the appearance of the morning; so David did wait and peep, and
peep and wait for the first and fittest season to pour out
his soul before God in a corner. David would never suffer
his worldly business to jostle out holy exercises; he would
often borrow time from the world for private prayer,
but he would never borrow time from private prayer to
bestow it upon the world.

John Bradford, the martyr, counted that hour lost in
which he did not do some good, either with his pen,
tongue, or purse.

Ignatius, when he heard a clock strike, used to say,
'Now I have one more hour to answer for.'

So the primitive Christians would redeem some time
from their sleep, that they might be with God in their
closets, as Clemens observes. And I have read of the
emperor Theodosius that after the variety of worldly

employments relating to his civil affairs in the day time were over, he was wont to consecrate the greatest part of the night to the studying of the Scriptures and private prayer; to which purpose he had a lamp so cleverly made, that it supplied itself with oil, that so he might not be interrupted in his private retirements.

That time ought to be redeemed is a lesson that has been taught by the very heathens themselves. It was the saying of Pittacus, one of the seven wise men, 'Know time, lose not a minute.' And so Theophrastus used to say, 'Time is of precious cost.' And so Seneca: 'Time is the only thing', says he, 'that we can innocently be covetous of; and yet there is nothing of which many are more lavishly and profusely prodigal.' And Chrestus, a sophist of Byzantium in the time of Hadrian the emperor, was much given to wine; yet, he always counted time so precious, that when he had misspent his time all the day, he would redeem it at night.

When Titus Vespasian, who revenged Christ's blood on Jerusalem, returned victor to Rome, remembering one night as he sat at supper with his friends, that he had done no good that day, he uttered this memorable and praiseworthy apophthegm, *Amici, diem perdidi*, 'My friends, I have lost a day.'

Chilo, one of the seven sages, being asked what was the hardest thing in the world to be done, answered, 'To use and employ a man's time well.' Cato held that an account must be given, not only of our labour, but also of our leisure. And Aelian gives this testimony of the Lacedaemonians, 'that they were hugely covetous of their time, spending it all about necessary things, and suffering no citizen either to be idle or play.' And, another says, 'We trifle with that which is most precious, and throw away that which is our greatest interest to redeem.'

Certainly, these heathens will rise in judgment, not only against Domitian the Roman emperor, who spent much of his time in killing flies; nor only against Archimedes, who spent his time in drawing lines on the ground when Syracuse was taken; nor against Artaxerxes, who spent his time in making handles for knives; nor only against Sulaiman the great Turk, who spent his time in making notches of horn for bows; nor only against Eropas, a Macedonian king, who spent his time in making lanterns; nor only against Hyrcanus the king of Parthia who spent his time in catching moles; but also against many professors who, instead of redeeming precious time, do trifle and fool away much of their precious time at the glass, the comb, the lute, the viol, the pipe, or vain sports, and foolish pastimes, or by idle jestings, immoderate sleeping, and superfluous feasting, etc.

O sirs! Good hours, and blessed opportunities for closet prayer are merchandise of the highest value and price; and therefore, whosoever has a mind to be rich in grace, and to be high in glory, should buy up that merchandise, they should continually redeem precious time.

O sirs! we should redeem time for private prayer out of our eating time, our drinking time, our sleeping time, our buying time, our selling time, our sinning time, our sporting time, rather than neglect our closet communion with God, etc. But,

6. *Sixthly,* I answer, *Closet prayer is either a duty or it is no duty.* Now that it is a duty, I have so strongly proved, I suppose, that no man nor devil can fairly or honestly deny it to be a duty. And therefore, why do men cry out of their great business? Alas! duty must be done whatever business is left undone; duty must be done, or the man who neglects it will be undone for ever. It is a vain thing to complain of business, when a required duty is to be performed; and, indeed, if the bare objecting of business, of much business, were enough to excuse men from duty, I am afraid that there are but few duties of the gospel, but men would try to evade under a pretence of business, of much business. He who pretends business to evade private prayer, will be as ready to pretend business to evade family prayer; and he that pretends business to evade family prayer, will be as ready to pretend business to evade public prayer.

Well, sirs! remember what became of those that excused themselves out of heaven, by their carnal apologies, and secular businesses: *Luke* 14:16–24. 'I have bought a piece of ground, and I must needs go and see it; I pray thee, have me excused,' says one. 'I have bought', says another, 'five yoke of oxen, and I go to prove them; I pray thee, have me excused.' And, 'I have married a wife', says another, 'and therefore I cannot come.' The true reason why they would not come to the supper that the King of kings had invited them to was, not because they had bought farms and oxen, but because their farms and oxen had bought them. The things of the world and their carnal relations had taken up so much room in their hearts and affections, that they had no stomach for heaven's delicacies; and therefore it is observable what Christ adds at the end of the parable, 'He that hateth not his father, and mother, and wife, and children, and brethren, and sisters, yea, and his own life also', much more his farm and oxen, 'he cannot be my disciple,' verse 26. By these words, it is evident, that it was not simply the farm nor the oxen, nor the wife, but a foolish, inordinate, carnal love and esteem of these things, above better and greater blessings, that made them refuse the gracious invitation of Christ. They refused the grace and mercy of God offered in the gospel, under a pretence of worldly business; and God peremptorily concludes, that not one of them should taste of his supper.

And indeed what can be more just and righteous, than that they should never so much as taste of spiritual and eternal blessings, who prefer their earthly business before heaven's dainties, prefer a country commodious for the feeding of their cattle, before an interest in the land of promise. Private prayer is a work of absolute necessity, both to the bringing of the heart into a good frame, and to the keeping of the heart in a good frame. It is of absolute necessity, both for the discovery of sin, and for the preventing of sin, and for the purging away of sin. It is of absolute necessity, both for the discovery of grace, and for a full exercise of grace, and for an eminent increase of grace. It is of absolute necessity to arm us, both against inward and outward temptations, afflictions, and sufferings. It is of absolute necessity to fit us for all other duties and services. For a man to glorify God, to save his

THE SECRET KEY TO HEAVEN

own soul, and to further his own everlasting happiness, is a work of the greatest necessity. Now private prayer is such a work; and therefore why should any man plead business, great business, when a work of such absolute necessity is before him? If a man's child or wife were dangerously sick, or wounded, or near to death, he would never plead, 'I have business, I have a great deal of business to do, and therefore I cannot stay with my child, my wife; and I have no time to go or send for the physician, etc. Oh no! but he would rather argue thus: 'It is absolutely necessary that I should look after the preservation of the life of my child, my wife, and this I will attend whatever becomes of my business.' O sirs! your souls are of greater concern to you than the lives of all the wives and children in the world; and therefore these must be attended to, these must be saved, whatever business is neglected. But,

7. Seventhly, I answer, *That God did never appoint or design any man's ordinary, particular calling to throw private prayer out of doors.*[1]

That it is a great sin for any professing Christian to neglect his particular calling under any religious pretence is evident enough by these Scriptures – *Exod.* 20:9, 'Six days shalt thou labour, and do all thy work'; *1 Cor.* 7:20, 'Let every man abide in the same calling wherein he was called'; *2 Thess.* 3:10–12, 'For even when we were with you, this we commanded you, that if any would not work, neither should he eat. For we hear that there are

[1] Paradise was man's workhouse as well as his storehouse, *Gen.* 2:15. Man should not have lived idly though he had not fallen from his innocency.

[98]

some which walk among you disorderly, working not at all, but are busy-bodies. Now them that are such we command and exhort by our Lord Jesus Christ, that with quietness they work, and eat their own bread'; *1 Thess.* 4:11–12, 'And that ye study to be quiet, and to do your own business, and to work with your own hands, as we commanded you; that ye may walk honestly toward them that are without, and that ye may have lack of nothing'; *Eph.* 4:28, 'But rather let him labour, working with his own hands the thing which is good, that he may have to give to him that needeth'; *1 Tim.* 5:8, 'But if any provide not for his own, and specially for those of his own house, he hath denied the faith, and is worse than an infidel.' Yes, our Lord Jesus Christ was a plain, downright carpenter, and was worked hard in that particular calling till he entered upon the public ministry, as all the old writers do agree (*Mark* 6:3; *Matt.* 13:55, 56). And we read also that all the patriarchs had their particular callings. Abel was a keeper of sheep (*Gen.* 4:2); Noah was a husbandman (*Gen.* 5:29); the sons of Jacob were shepherds and keepers of cattle (*Gen.* 46:34), etc.; and all the apostles, before they were called to the work of the ministry, had their particular callings. By the law of Mohammed, the great Turk himself is bound to exercise some manual trade or occupation.

Solon made a law,[1] that the son should not be bound to relieve his father when old, unless he had set himself in his youth to some occupation. And at Athens, every man gave a yearly account to the magistrate by what trade or

[1] Plutarch, *Life of Solon.*

course of life he maintained himself, which, if he could not do, he was banished. And it is by all writers condemned as a very great vanity in Dionysius that he must be the best poet, and Caligula, that he must be the best orator; and in Nero, that he must be the best fiddler; and so became the three worst princes, by minding more other men's business than their own particular calling.

But for a man to evade or neglect private prayer under pretence of his particular calling, is agreeable to no Scripture, but is contrary to very many Scriptures, as is evident by the many arguments formerly cited. Certainly no man's calling is a calling away from God or godliness. It never entered into the heart of God that our particular callings should ever drive out of doors our general calling of Christianity. Look, as our general calling must not eat up our particular calling, so our particular calling must not eat up our general calling. Certainly our particular calling must give place to our general calling. Did not the woman of Samaria leave her water-pot, and run into the city, and say, 'Come, see a man that told me all things that ever I did: is not this the Christ' (*John* 4:28, 29)? Did not the shepherds leave their flocks in the field, and go to Bethlehem, and declare the good tidings of great joy that they had heard of the angel, viz. 'That there was born that day, in the city of David, a Saviour, which was Christ the Lord' (*Luke* 2:8–21)? And did not Christ commend Mary for that holy neglect of her particular calling, when she sat at his feet, and heard his word (*Luke* 10:38 ff.)? And what do all these instances show, but that our particular callings must give the right hand to the general calling of

Christianity? Certainly the works of our general calling are far more great and glorious, more eminent and excellent, more high and noble, than the works of our particular callings are; and therefore it is much more tolerable for our general calling to borrow time of our particular calling than it is for our particular calling to borrow time of our general calling. Certainly those men are very ignorant or very profane, that either think themselves so closely tied up to follow their particular callings six days in the week, as that they must not intermeddle with any religious services, or that think their particular callings to be a gulf or a grave designed by God to swallow up private prayer in. God, who is the Lord of time, has reserved some part of our time to himself every day. Though the Jews were commanded to labour six days of the week, yet they were commanded also to offer up morning and evening sacrifice daily (*Deut.* 6:6–8; *Exod.* 19:38, 39; *Num.* 28:3).

The Jews divided the day into three parts:

The first, to prayer;

The second, for the reading of the law;

And the third, for the works of their lawful callings.

As bad as the Jews were, yet they every day set a part of the day apart for religious exercises. Certainly they are worse than Jews that spend all their time about their particular callings, and shut closet prayer quite out of doors. Certainly that man's soul is in a very ill case, who is so entangled with the encumbrances of the world, that he can spare no time for private prayer. If God be the Lord of your mercies, the Lord of your time, and the Lord of your soul, how can you, with any equity or honour, put off his service under a pretence of much business? That man is lost, that man is cursed, who can find time for anything, but none to meet with God in his closet. That man is doubtless upon the brink of ruin, whose worldly business eats up all thoughts of God, of Christ, of heaven, of eternity, of his soul, and of his soul concerns. But,

8. *Eighthly, and lastly,* I answer, *the more worldly business lies upon your hand, the more need you have to keep close to your closet.*

Much business lays a man open to many sins, and to many snares, and to many temptations. Now, the more sins, snares, and temptations a man's business lays him open to, the more need that man has to be much in private prayer, that his soul may be kept pure from sin, and that his foot may not be taken in the devil's trap, and that he may stand fast in the hour of temptation. Private prayer is so far from being a hindrance to a man's business, that it is the way of ways to bring down a blessing from heaven upon a man's business (*Psa.* 1:2, 3; 127:1, 2; 128:1, 2); as the first-fruits that God's people gave to him brought down a blessing from heaven upon all the rest (*Deut.* 26:10, 11). Whet is no let;[1] prayer and provender never hinders a journey.

Private prayer can be likened to Jacob, who brought down a blessing from heaven upon all that Laban had (*Gen.* 30:27, 30). Private prayer gives a man a sanctified use, both of all his earthly comforts, and of all his earthly business; and this David and Daniel found by experience:

[1] That is, it is no hindrance to labour to sharpen the scythe.

and therefore it was not their great public employments that could take them off from their private duties. Time spent in heavenly employments, is no time lost from worldly business (*Deut.* 28:1–8).

Private prayer makes all we take in hand successful. Closet prayer has made many rich, but it never made any man poor or beggarly in this world. No man on earth knows what may be the emergencies, or the occurrences of a day: *Prov.* 27:1, 'Boast not thyself of to-morrow, for thou knowest not what a day may bring forth.' Every day is, as it were, a heavily-pregnant day; every day is as it were with child of something, but what it will bring forth, whether a cross or a comfort, no man can tell; as when a woman is with child, no man can tell what kind of birth it will be.

No man knows what mercies a day may bring forth, no man knows what miseries a day may bring forth; no man knows what good a day may bring forth, no man knows what evil a day may bring forth; no man knows what afflictions a day may bring forth, no man knows what temptations a day may bring forth; no man knows what liberty a day may bring forth, no man knows what bonds a day may bring forth; no man knows what good success a day may bring forth, no man knows what bad success a day may bring forth; and therefore, a man had need be every day in his closet with God, that he may be prepared and fitted to entertain and improve all the occurrences, successes, and emergencies that may attend him in the course of his life. And let thus much suffice for answer to this first objection. But,

OBJECTION 2. *Secondly, others may object and say, Sir, we grant that private prayer is an indispensable duty that lies upon the people of God; but we are servants, and we have no time that we can call our own, and our master's business is such as will not allow us any time for private prayer, and therefore we hope we may be excused.*

Solution (1.) *First, The text is indefinite, and not limited to any sort or rank of persons, whether high or low, rich or poor, bond or free, servant or master.* 'But thou, when thou prayest, enter into thy closet; and when thou hast shut the door, pray to thy Father which is in secret.' Here are three 'thous', thou, thou, thou, which are to be understood indefinitely: servant as well as master, bondman as well as freeman, poor man as well as rich man, maid as well as mistress, child as well as father, wife as well as husband.

Private prayer is an indispensable duty that lies upon all sorts and ranks of persons. A man may as well say that that pronoun *tu*, 'thou', that runs through the Ten Commandments – *Exod.* 20:3–18, 'Thou shalt have no other gods before me. Thou shalt not make unto thee any graven image. Thou shalt not bow down thyself to them, nor serve them. Thou shalt not take the name of the Lord thy God in vain. Six days shalt thou labour. Thou shalt not kill. Thou shalt not commit adultery. Thou shalt not steal. Thou shalt not bear false witness against thy neighbour. Thou shalt not covet thy neighbour's house, thou shalt not covet thy neighbour's wife, nor his man-servant, nor his maid servant, nor his ox, nor his ass, nor anything that is thy neighbour's', etc. – relates to the rich, and not to the poor, to masters and not to servants, to the free and not to them that are in bonds, etc., as he may say, that the three 'thous' in the text relate to the rich and not to the poor, to masters and not to servants, to those that are free but not to those that are bound; but certainly there is no man in his right mind that will say so, that will affirm such a thing. Doubtless this pronoun 'thou' reaches every man, of what rank or quality soever he be in this world. But,

2. *Secondly*, I answer, *that the first, the third, the fourth, the fifth, the sixth, the seventh, and the eighth answers that are given to the first objection, are very applicable here;* and oh, that all masters and servants were so wise, so serious, and so ingenuous, as to lay all those answers warm on their own hearts! It might be a means to prevent much sin, and to encourage masters and mistresses to give their pious servants a little more time to lift up their hearts to Christ in a corner. But,

3. *Thirdly, if you are a servant that has liberty to choose a new master, you are better to change your position than live under a master's roof who is such an enemy to God, to Christ, to, religion, to himself, and to the eternal welfare of your poor soul, as that he will not give you half an hour's time in a day to spend in your chamber, your closet, though the glory of God, the good of his own family, and the everlasting happiness of your own soul, is concerned in it (Psa. 84:10; 120:5).*

It is better for you to shift your master, than to neglect your duty: 1 *Cor.* 7:21, 'Art thou called, being a servant? care not for it; but if thou mayest be made free, use it rather.' We lost our liberty by sin, and we desire nothing more than liberty by nature.

The Rabbis say of liberty, 'If the heavens were parchment, the sea ink, and every pile of grass a pen, the praises of it could not be comprised nor expressed.' Laban's house was full of idols. Great houses are often so. Jacob's tent was little, but the true worship of God was in it. It is infinitely better to live in Jacob's tent, than in Laban's house. It is best being with such masters where we may have least of sin, and most of God; where we may have the most helps, the best examples, and the choicest encouragements to be holy and happy.

The religious servant should be as careful in the choice of his master, as the religious master is careful in the choice of his servant. Gracious servants are great blessings to the families where they live; and that master may well be called the unhappy master, who will rather part with a gracious servant, than spare him a little time in a day to pour out his soul before the Lord in a corner. But,

4. *Fourthly*, I answer, *If you are a gracious servant, then you are spirited and principled by God, to this very purpose, that you may cry, Abba, Father, when you are alone, when you are in a corner, and no eye sees you, but his who sees in secret* (*Rom.* 8:15; *Gal.* 4:6; *1 Cor.* 6:19; *2 Tim.* 1:14). If you are a gracious servant, then you have received not the spirit of the world, but the Spirit which is of God (*1 Cor.* 2:12). Now, he who has this tree of life, has also the fruit that grows upon this tree: *Gal.* 5:22, 23, 'But the fruit of the Spirit is love, joy, peace, long-suffering, gentleness, goodness, faith, meekness, temperance,

etc. Now, grace is called, not the *works* of the Spirit, but the *fruits* of the Spirit.

i. Because all grace is derived from the Spirit as the fruit is derived from the root. And,

ii. To note the pleasantness and delightfulness of grace, for what is more pleasant and delightful than sweet and wholesome fruits? (*Song of Sol.* 4:16; 6:2).

iii. To note the profit and advantage that redounds to them that have the Spirit; for as many grow rich by the fruits of their gardens and orchards, so many grow rich in grace, in holiness, in comfort, in spiritual experiences, by the fruits of the Spirit. Now why has God given you his Spirit, and why has he laid into your soul a stock of supernatural graces, but that you may be every way qualified, disposed, and fitted for private prayer, and to maintain secret communion with God in a corner?

Certainly, God never gave any poor servant a talent of gifts, or a talent of grace, but in order that he might drive a secret trade heavenward.

5. *Fifthly*, I answer, *though king Darius had made a decree that none should ask any petition of any god or man, for thirty days, upon the penalty of being cast into the den of lions, yet Daniel, who was both a subject and a servant to king Darius, and one upon whose hands the most important and greatest affairs of the kingdom lay, kept up his private devotion.*

In the first and second verses of the sixth chapter of Daniel, you will find that Daniel had abundance of great and weighty employments upon his hands; he was set over the whole affairs of the whole empire of Persia, and he with two other presidents, of whom he was chief, were to receive the accounts of the whole kingdom from all those hundred and twenty princes, which in the Persian monarchy were employed in all public businesses. And yet, notwithstanding such a multiplicity of business as lay upon his hands, and notwithstanding his servile condition, yet he was very careful to redeem time for private prayer; yes, it is very observable that the heart of Daniel, in the midst of all his mighty businesses, was so much set upon private prayer, upon his secret retirements for religious exercises, that he runs the risk of losing all his honours, profits, pleasures, yes, and life itself, rather than he would be deprived of convenient time and opportunities to wait upon God in his chamber.

Certainly Daniel will one day rise in judgment against all those subjects and servants who think to evade private prayer by their pleas of much business, and of their being servants, etc. But,

6. *Sixthly,* I answer, *if you who are gracious servants, notwithstanding your masters' businesses, cannot redeem a little time to wrestle with God in a corner, what singular thing do you?* What do you do more than others? Do you hear? So do others. Do you read? So do others. Do you follow your masters to public prayers? So do others. Do you join with your masters in family prayers? So do others. Oh! but now gracious servants should go beyond all other servants in the world, they should do singular things for God: *Matt.* 5:47, 'What do you more than others?' Τι περισσον ποιειτε? What extraordinary thing do you? What more ordinary than to find servants follow

their masters to public prayers and to family prayers? Oh! but now to find poor servants to redeem a little time from their masters' business to pour out their souls before the Lord in a corner, this is not ordinary, yes, this is extraordinary, and this wonderfully well become gracious servants. Oh! that all men's servants, who are servants to the most high God, would seriously consider,

i. *How singularly they are privileged by God above all other servants in the world.* They are called, adopted, reconciled, pardoned, justified before the throne of God, which other servants are not, etc. (*1 Cor.* 3:22, 23). And why then should not such servants be singular in their services, who are so singular in their privileges?

ii. *Secondly, gracious servants are made partakers of a more excellent nature than other servants are.* 2 *Pet.* 1:4, 'Whereby are given unto us exceeding great and precious promises; that by these you might be made partakers of the divine nature.' The apostle in this expression does not aim at any essential change and conversion of our substance into the nature of God and Christ, but only at the elevation and dignifying of our nature by Christ. Though that real, that near, that dear, that choice, that mysterious, that peculiar, that singular union that Christians have with Christ, raises them up to a higher similitude and likeness of God and Christ than ever they had attained to in their primitive perfection; yet it does not introduce any real transmutation, either of our bodies or souls, into the divine nature. It is certain that our union and conjunction with Christ neither mingles persons nor unites substances, but it does enjoin our affections, and brings our wills into a league of friendship with Christ. To be made partaker of the divine nature notes two things, say some.[1]

First, A fellowship with God in his holiness;

Secondly, A fellowship with God in his blessedness, viz., in the beatifical vision and brightness of glory. To be made partakers of the divine nature, say others, is to be made partakers of those holy graces, those divine qualities, which sometimes are called, 'the image of God, the likeness of God, the life of God,' etc. (*Eph.* 4:24; *Col.* 3:10), whereby we resemble God, not only as a picture does a man in outward lineaments, but as a child does his father in countenance and conditions. Now, take the words which way you will, how highly does it concern those servants, that are made partakers of the divine nature, to do singular things for God, to do such things for God, that other servants, that are not partakers of the divine nature, have no mind, no heart, no spirit to do! yea, that they refuse and scorn to do!

iii. *Thirdly, gracious servants are worthily descended;* they have the most illustrious extraction and honourable original (*1 John* 5:19; *John* 3:8; *James* 2:5).

iv. *Fourthly, gracious servants are worthily attended, they are nobly guarded;* (*Psa.* 34:15; *Heb.* 1:14; *Deut.* 33:26, 27; *Zech.* 2:5).

v. *Fifthly, gracious servants are worthily dignified;* they are dignified with the highest and most honourable titles (*1 Pet.* 2:9; *Rev.* 1:5, 6; 5:10).

---

[1] None but Familists [a mystical 16th-century sect] will say that we are made partakers of the substance of the Godhead, for that is incommunicable to any creature. The essence of God cannot be imparted to any created beings.

vi. *Sixthly, Take many things in one: gracious servants have more excellent graces, experiences, comforts, communions, promises, assurances, discoveries, hopes, helps, principles, diet, clothes, portion, than all other servants in the world have;* and therefore God may well expect better and greater things from them than from all other servants in the world. God may very well expect that they should do singular things for his glory, who has done such singular things for their good. Certainly God expects that gracious servants should be blessing him, when other servants are blaspheming him; that they should be magnifying him, when other servants are debasing him, that they should be redeeming precious time, when other servants are trifling, fooling, playing, or sinning away precious time; that they should be weeping in a corner, when other servants are playing sports and making themselves merry among their jovial companions; that they should be mourning in secret, when other servants are sinning in secret; and that they should be at their private devotion, when other servants are sleeping, and snoring.

Solomon, that was the wisest prince that ever sat upon a throne, and who was guided by an infallible Spirit, has delivered it for a standing maxim over two thousand years ago that 'the righteous is more excellent than his neighbour' (*Prov.*12:26). When Solomon dropped this aphorism from his royal pen, there was not a man in the world that was legally righteous; Adam and all his posterity being fallen from all their honour, glory, dignity, and excellency, into a most woeful gulf of sin and misery; and therefore Solomon must be understood to speak of him who is evangelically righteous, be he master or servant; (*Psa.* 14:1–3; *Rom.* 3:9–12; *Lam.* 5:16). He that is evangelically righteous, be he master or servant, rich or poor, bond or free, high or low, is more excellent than his neighbour. And oh, that all masters would seriously consider this, that they may carry it no more so proudly, so loftily, so scornfully, so forwardly, so strangely, so sourly, so bitterly, so rigorously, towards their pious servants, as not to afford them a little time to pour out their souls before the Lord in a corner!

I have read of Ingo, an ancient king of the Draves and Veneds, who, making a stately feast, appointed all his pagan nobles to sit in the hall below; and at the same time commanded certain poor Christians to be brought up into his presence-chamber, to sit with him at his table, that they might eat of his kingly provisions; at which many wondering, he told them, that he accounted Christians, though never so poor, a greater ornament at his table, and more worthy of his company, than the greatest nobles that were not converted to the Christian faith; for says he, when these pagan nobles shall be thrust down to hell, these poor Christians shall be my consorts and fellow-princes in heaven. Certainly, this noble prince will one day rise in judgment against all sour, churlish Labans, who behave so harshly and so severely towards their gracious servants, as that they will not allow them a little time to wait upon God in a hole (*Eph.* 6:9). Why should gracious masters not give their gracious servants a little time for closet prayer now, considering that they are sharers with them in all the fundamental good that comes by Christ in this world; and considering, that they shall be partakers with them in all the glory of another world? The poorest servant in a family has a soul more precious than heaven and earth; and the greatest work that lies upon his hand in this world is to look to the eternal safety and security of that: for if that be safe, all is safe; if that be well, all is well; but if that be lost, all is lost.[1] Every gracious servant, though he be never so poor and mean, yet he has the image of God, the image of the King of kings stamped upon him; and woe to him that shall wrong, or despise, or trample upon that image! Certainly, God himself is wronged by the injury that is done to his image. The contempt and despite that is done to the image or coin of a king, is done to the king himself; and accordingly he will revenge it.

If it was a capital crime in the days of Tiberius, to carry the image of Augustus upon a ring or coin into any sordid place, as Suetonius says it was, what crime must it be in those masters who despise, revile, reproach, scorn, abuse, and tread under foot, such servants as have the image of the great God stamped upon their souls, and all because they look God-ward, Christ-ward, heaven-ward, holiness-ward, duty-ward? Masters should never taunt their servants in the teeth with their inferiority, penury, poverty, misery, mean parentage, or servile condition; but remember that these things are more the Creator's pleasure than the servant's fault, and that that God who has made the

---

[1] Every man has two things to look to more than all the world beside, a body and a soul; for the one, every one is either a fool or a physician; for the other, either a devil or a divine, says one.

THE SECRET KEY TO HEAVEN

master rich and the servant poor, can as quickly make the
master poor and the servant rich (*Prov.* 22:2; 17:5). God
often puts down the mighty from their seats, and exalts
those of low degree (*Luke* 1:52). Certainly, no master nor
mistress should dare to insult or triumph over such servants as have souls as noble as their own; but they should
seriously and frequently consider Solomon's aphorism,
'The righteous, though a servant', though the meanest
among all the servants, 'is more excellent than his neighbour', and accordingly give them a little time and liberty
to converse with God in secret. And oh, that all gracious
servants would discover themselves to be more excellent
than their neighbours, by making more conscience of
private prayer than their neighbours do, and by being
more in their closets than their neighbours are, and by
delighting themselves in their secret retirements more
than their neighbours will, and by redeeming some time
for God, for their souls, and for eternity, more than their
neighbours do. But,

7. *Seventhly*, I answer, *that God alone is the Lord of
time.*[1] Time is more the Lord's than it is your master's;
and therefore it is no neglecting of your master's business,
to take a little time daily for private prayer. Times do belong to providence as well as issues; and as God is the
God of our mercies, so he is the Lord of our times: 'My
times are in thy hands', saith David (*Psa.* 31:15). Not
only the times of his sorrows, but also the times of his
comforts; not only the times of his miseries, but also the

---

[1] *Hab.* 2:3; *Dan.* 11:27, 29, 35; *Job* 7:1; *Psa.* 102:13; *Eccles.* 3:1;
Dan. 2:21; *Isa.* 60:22; *Job* 14:14.

times of his mercies; not only the times of his dangers, but also the times of his duties, were in the hands of God.

It is observable the Psalmist does not say 'time', but 'times', in the plural, to show that every point and period of time depends upon the hand of God.

One,[1] complaining of those who say, Come, let us talk together, to pass away the time, with grief of spirit cries out, *O donec praetereat hora, etc.,* 'Oh, until the hour be gone, oh, until time be past, which the mercy of your Maker has bestowed upon you to perform repentance, to procure pardon, to gain grace, and to obtain glory.' That servant who borrows a little time every day to seek the face of God in a corner, borrows it rather of God than of his master; and therefore why should his master swell, or rage, or complain, considering that God never made him Lord of time? But,

8. *Eighthly,* I answer, *that servants should rather redeem time from their sleep, their recreations, their daily meals, than neglect their daily closet-duty.* And certainly those servants that, out of conscience towards God, and out of a due regard to the internal and eternal welfare of their own souls, shall every day redeem an hour's time from their sleep, or sports, or feedings, to spend with God in secret, they shall find by experience that the Lord will make a few hours' sleep sweeter and better than many hours' sleep to them; and their outward sports shall be made up with inward delights; and for their common bread, God will feed them with that bread that came

[1] Bernard. [2] The evangelist applies these words to Christ, *Matt.* 12:15–18. Christ is called God's servant in regard of his human nature, and in regard of his office of mediatorship.

down from heaven. Sirs, was not Christ his Father's servant?[2] *Isa.* 42:1, 'Behold my servant, whom I uphold, mine
elect' (or choice one), 'in whom my soul delighteth' (or is
well pleased)? 'I have put my Spirit upon him; he shall
bring forth judgment to the Gentiles.' And did he not redeem time from his natural rest, rather than he would
omit private prayer? *Mark* 1:35, 'And in the morning, rising up a great while before day, he went out, and departed
into a solitary place, and there prayed.' Christ spent the
day in preaching, in healing the sick, in working miracles;
and rather than these noble works should shut out private
prayer, he rises a great while before day, that he might
have some time to wrestle with his Father in secret. So
Luke 6:12, 'And it came to pass in those days, that he
went out into a mountain to pray, and continued all night
in prayer to God.' O sirs! did Christ spend whole nights
in private prayer for the salvation of your souls; and will
you think it much to redeem an hour's time from your
natural rest to seek and to serve him in a corner, and to
make sure the things of your everlasting peace?

The redeeming of time for private prayer is the redeeming of a precious treasure, which, if once lost, can never
fully be recovered again. If riches should make themselves
wings, and fly away, they may return again, as they did to
Job; or if credit, and honour, and worldly greatness and
renown, should fly away, they may return again, as they
did to Nebuchadnezzar; if success, and famous victories
and conquests, should make themselves wings, and fly
away, they may return again, as they did to many of the
Roman conquerors and others; but if time, whom the

poets paint with wings, to show the volubility and swiftness of it, fly from us, it will never more return unto us.

A great lady of this land [Queen Elizabeth], on her dying bed cried out, 'Call time again, call time again; a world of wealth for an inch of time!' but time past was never, nor could ever be, recalled.

The Egyptians drew the picture of time with three heads. The first was of a greedy wolf gaping for time past, because it has ravenously devoured even the memory of so many things past recalling; the second of a crowned lion roaring for time present, because it has the principality of all action, for which it calls aloud; and the third was of a deceitful dog, fawning for time to come, because it feeds fond men with many flattering hopes, to their eternal undoing. Oh, that all this might prevail with servants to redeem time for private prayer! And if my counsel might prevail, I should rather advise servants to redeem some time for private prayer from their sleep or lawful recreations, or set meals, etc., than to spend in private prayer that time which their masters call their time, especially if their masters are unconverted, and in 'the gall of bitterness and bond of iniquity'; and that for these five reasons:

i. *First, because this may be a means to prevent much sin on the master's side.* Masters who are in their unregenerate state are very likely to storm, and take on, and let fly against God, and Christ, and religion, and profession, etc., when they see their servants spend that time in private prayer, or in any other religious exercise, which, according to their understanding, is their time, and ought to be wholly spent in following their businesses. Now gracious servants should have that honourable respect, and that tender affection, and that Christian compassion to their masters' souls, as to do to the utmost all that lies in them to prevent their masters from contracting guilt upon their souls, or from making work for repentance, for hell, or for the physician of souls (*Jude* 22, 23).

The Persians, the Turks, and many Indians are so compassionate that they erect hospitals not only for lame and diseased men, but also for birds, beasts, and dogs that are either aged, starved, or hurt. Oh then, what tender compassions should gracious servants exercise towards their masters' souls, which are jewels worth more than heaven and earth! But,

ii. *Secondly, because this may be a means to convince the judgments and consciences of their masters, that there is some worth, some excellency, some sweetness. etc., to be found in private prayer, and in other closet-duties;* for when masters shall observe their servants to redeem time for closet duties, from their very sleep, recreations, dinners, suppers, they will be ready to conclude, that certainly there is more worth, more goodness, more sweetness, more excellency, more glory, more gain in closet duties, than ever they have understood, felt, or experienced, etc., and that their very poor servants are better and more righteous than themselves. Sozomen reports, that the devout life of a poor captive Christian woman made a king and all his family embrace the faith of Jesus Christ. Good works convince more than miracles themselves.

I have read of one Pachomius, a soldier under Constantine the emperor, how that his army being almost starved for want of necessary provision, he came to a city of Christians, and they of their own charity relieved them speedily and freely; he, wondering at their free and noble charity, inquired what kind of people they were whom he saw so bountiful? It was answered that they were Christians, whose profession it is to hurt no man, and do good to every man. Hereupon Pachomius, convinced of the excellency of this religion, threw away his arms, and became a Christian, a saint.

As husbands sometimes are won by the conversation of their wives without the word (*1 Pet.* 3:1, 2); so masters may sometimes be won by the gracious attitude and conversation of their servants, without the word. The servant's redeeming of time for private duties, upon the hardest and severest terms, may be so blessed to the master, that it may issue in his conviction, conversion, and salvation. There is a *may-be* for it; and a very may-be should be a sufficient encouragement for every gracious servant to do all he can to save the soul of his master from going down into the infernal pit. But,

iii. *Thirdly, because the servant's redeeming of time from his sleep, recreations, meals, for private prayer, will most clearly and abundantly evidence the singular love, the great delight, and the high esteem that he has of private prayer.* We say those children love their books well, and delight much in learning, who will be at their books when others are gone to their beds, and who will be at their books before others can get out of their beds. Certainly they love private prayer well, and they delight much in closet communion with God, who will still be praying when others are sleeping, and who will be dressing their souls before God in a corner, before their mistress is dressing herself at the mirror, or their fellow-servants dressing themselves in the workplace. But,

iv. *Fourthly, because the servant's redeeming of time for private prayer, from his sleep, set meals, recreations, etc., may be of most use to other fellow-servants, both to awaken them, and to convince them that the things of religion are of the greatest and highest importance, and that there is no trade, or pleasure, or profit, in comparison to that private trade that is carried on between God and a man's own soul;* and also to keep them from trifling, or fooling away of that time, which is truly and properly their masters' time, and by the royal law of heaven ought to be spent solely and wholly in their service and business. For what ingenuous servant is there in the world but will argue thus? I see that such and such of my fellow-servants will redeem time for private prayer, and for other closet-services, from their very sleep, meals, recreations, etc.; rather than they will borrow, or make bold with that time which my master says is his, etc.; and why then should I be so foolish, so brutish, so mad, to trifle, or idle, or play, or toy away that time which should be spent in my master's service, and for my master's advantage? But,

v. *Fifthly,* and lastly, *because the servant's redeeming of time for private prayer from his sleep, his meals, his recreations, etc., cannot but be infinitely pleasing to God; and that which will afford, him most comfort when he comes to die.* The more any poor heart acts contrary to flesh and blood, the more he pleases God; the more any poor heart denies himself, the more he pleases God; the more any poor heart acts against the stream of sinful examples, the more he pleases God; the more difficulties and discouragements a poor heart meets with in the discharge of his duty, the more love he shows to God; and the more love a poor heart shows to God, the, more he pleases God: *Jer.* 2:2, 3, 'Go and cry in the ears of Jerusalem, saying, Thus saith the LORD, I remember thee, the kindness of thy youth, the love of thine espousals, when thou wentest after me in the wilderness, in a land that was not sown. Israel was holiness unto the LORD, and the first-fruits of his increase: all that devour him shall offend; evil shall come upon them, saith the LORD.' God was very highly pleased and greatly delighted with the singular love and choice affections of his people towards him, when they followed after him, and kept close to him, in that tedious and uncouth passage through the waste, howling wilderness.

How all these things agree with that poor pious servant that redeems time for private prayer upon the hardest terms imaginable, I shall leave the ingenuous reader to judge. And certainly, upon a dying bed, no tongue can express, nor heart conceive but he who feels it, the unspeakable comfort that closet-duties will afford to him who has been exercised in them, upon those hard terms that are under present consideration. But,

9. *Ninthly,* I answer, *If you are a gracious servant, then the near and dear relations that are between God and*

you, and the choice privileges that you are interested in, call aloud for private prayer (*John* 8:32, 33, 36).

As you are your Master's servant, so you are the Lord's free-man: *1 Cor.* 7:22, 23, 'For he that is called in the Lord, being, a servant, is the Lord's freeman; likewise, also he that is called being free, is Christ's servant. Ye are bought with a price; be not ye servants of men', either when they command you things forbidden by Christ, or forbid you things commanded by Christ; or when they would exercise a dominion over your faith, or a lordship over your consciences. Suffer not yourselves in spiritual things to be brought into such bondage by any men or masters in the world, not to use that freedom and liberty that Christ has purchased for you with his dearest blood (*Gal.* 5:1; *Col.* 2:20; *Gal.* 2:4).

No servants are to serve their masters in opposition to Christ; nor are servants to serve their masters as spiritual masters; and no servants are to serve their masters as supreme masters, but as subordinate masters (*Eph.* 6:5–7). And as every gracious servant is the Lord's free-man, so every gracious servant is the Lord's friend (*Isa.* 41:8; *James* 2:23; *John* 15:13–15). And as every gracious servant is the Lord's friend, so every gracious servant is the Lord's son (*Gal.* 4:5, 6); *Rom.* 8:16). And as every gracious servant is the Lord's son, so every gracious servant is the Lord's spouse (*Hos.* 2:19, 20; *2 Cor.* 11:2).

And now I appeal to the consciences of all that have tasted that the Lord is gracious, whether the near and dear relations that are between the Lord and pious servants do not call aloud upon them to take all opportunities and advantages they possibly can to pour out their souls before the Lord in secret, and to acquaint him in a corner with all their secret needs, and weaknesses, and wishes, etc. And as gracious servants are thus nearly and dearly related to God, so gracious servants are very highly privileged by God. Gracious servants are as much freed from the reign of sin, the dominion of sin, and the damning power of sin, as gracious masters are (*Rom.* 6:14). Gracious servants are as much freed from hell, from the curse of the law, and from the wrath of God, as their gracious masters are (*Rom.* 8:1). Gracious servants are as much adopted, as much reconciled, as much pardoned, as much justified, and as much redeemed, as their gracious masters are (*Gal.* 3:13). Gracious servants are as much heirs, heirs of God, and joint heirs with Christ, as their gracious masters are.[1] Gracious servants are as much a chosen generation, a royal priesthood, an holy nation, a peculiar people, called out of darkness into his marvellous light, as their gracious masters are. And therefore they being all alike participants in all these great and glorious privileges which belong to saints as saints, they are, without all doubt, alike obliged and engaged to all those duties which lie upon saints as saints, among which private prayer is one; and therefore they are to buckle to this duty against all carnal reasons and objections whatsoever. But,

10. *Tenthly*, and lastly, I answer, *that the promised reward in the text lies as fair and as open to the servant as to the Master, to the bond as to the free, to the peasant as to the prince.*

[1] *1 Thess.* 1:10; *Col.* 3:11; *Gal.* 5:6; *Rom.* 8:17; *Gal.* 6:14; *1 Pet.* 2:9.

Whoever prays to his heavenly Father in secret, be he high or low, rich or poor, honourable or common, servant or master, he shall receive an open reward. The reward in the text is not to be confined or limited to this or that sort or rank of men, but it is to be extended to all ranks and sorts of men that make conscience of private prayer, of closet duties. So *Eph.* 6:5–8, 'Servants, be obedient to them that are your masters, according to the flesh, with fear and trembling, in singleness of your heart, as unto Christ. Not with eyeservice, as menpleasers, but as the servants of Christ, doing the will of God from the heart: with good will doing service, as to the Lord, and not to men: knowing that whatsoever good thing any man doth, the same shall he receive of the Lord, whether he be bond or free.' *Col.* 3:22–21, 'Servants obey, in all things, your masters, according to the flesh, not with eyeservice, as menpleasers, but in singleness of heart, fearing God. And whatsoever ye do, do it heartily, as to the Lord, and not unto men; knowing that of the Lord ye shall receive the reward of the inheritance; for ye serve the Lord Jesus Christ.'[1]

Such servants as serve their masters faithfully, cordially, and in singleness of spirit, shall receive the reward of grace and the reward of the inheritance. The meanest servant that is faithful in the service of his master, shall for a recompense receive the eternal inheritance (*Rom.* 8:15–17). The recompense of reward in the Scripture last cited is not of merit, but of mere grace, because the inheritance

---

[1] The Persian kings did usually reward the faithful services of their servants. Surely the King of kings will not fall short of the kings of Persia?

belongs only to children upon the account of their birth or adoption. Faithful servants shall of servants be made sons, and so enjoy the heavenly inheritance. Christ is so noble a master that he will not suffer any service that has been performed to men out of conscience to his command to pass unrewarded. Oh, how much more will he recompense pious servants for those spiritual services that they perform for his sake, for his glory! God is so liberal a paymaster, that no man shall so much as shut the door, or kindle a fire upon his altar, or give a cup of cold water – one of the least, readiest, and meanest refreshments – but he shall be rewarded (*Mal.* 1:10; *Matt.* 10:42).

It is an excellent observation of Calvin, upon God's rewarding of the Rechabites' obedience (*Jer.* 35:19), 'God', he says, 'often recompenses the shadows and seeming appearances of virtue, to show that complacency he takes in the ample rewards that he has reserved for true and sincere piety.' Nebuchadnezzar, though a tyrant, yet being engaged in God's service against Tyre, he shall have Egypt as his pay for his pains at Tyre (*Ezek.* 29:18–20). It is an ancient slur and slander that has been cast upon God, as if he were an austere master, an illiberal Lord, and as if there were nothing to be got in his service but knocks, blows, wounds, crosses, losses, etc., whereas he is a rewarder, not only of them that diligently seek him, but even of the very worst of men that do any service for him (*Heb.* 11:6).

I have read of Herod Agrippa, the same that was smitten by the angel and eaten up of worms, because he gave not glory to God (*Acts* 12:23), that, being, bound in chains, and sent to prison by Tiberius for wishing Gaius in the empire, one Thaumastus, a servant of Gaius, carrying a pitcher of water, met him, and Agrippa being very thirsty, desired him to give him some of his water to drink, which he willingly did: whereupon Agrippa said, 'This service you have done in giving me drink, shall do you good another day.' And he was as big and as good as his word; for afterwards, when Gaius was emperor, and Agrippa made king of Judea, he first got his liberty, then made him chief officer of his household, and after his decease took order that he should continue in the same office with his son. Now how much more then will the King of kings reward all those poor pious servants of his, that do not only give to him in his members cups of cold water, but do also redeem time from their very rest, meals, and recreations, that they may have some time to seek the face of God in a corner. Certainly, there shall not be a sigh, a groan, a prayer, a tear let fall by a poor servant in a corner, that shall not be at last regarded and rewarded by the great God.

Lyra says, that Mordecai waited six years, before his good service was rewarded by king Ahasuerus. It may be God may reward you sooner for all your closet services; but if he do not reward you sooner, he will certainly reward you better, he will reward you with higher honours, with greater dignities, with more glorious robes, and with a more royal crown, even an incorruptible crown, a crown of righteousness, a crown of life, a crown of glory (*1 Cor.* 9:29; *2 Tim.* 4:8; *Rev.* 2:10; *James* 1:12; *1 Pet.* 5:4). And therefore hold on and hold out in your secret

Objections Stated and Answered

retirements. Though some may deride you, and others revile you, and your carnal masters discourage you, yet God is faithful and will certainly reward you; yea, he will openly reward you for all the secret pourings out of your souls in his bosom.

OBJECTION 3. Some may further object and say, *Oh, but we cannot pray alone; we lack those gifts and endowments which others have; we are shut up and know not how to pour out our souls before God in a corner; we would willingly pray, but we lack the ability to pour out our souls before the Lord in secret, etc.*

Solution 1. God's dearest children may sometimes be shut up; they may with Zechariah, for a time, be struck dumb, and not able to speak, Luke 1:20; *Psa.* 77:4, 'I am so troubled that I cannot speak'; *Psa.* 38:9, 'Lord, all my desire is before thee: and my groaning is not hid from thee.' God's dearest children have sometimes been so shut up, that they have been able to say nothing, nor to do nothing but groan. A child of God may sometimes meet with such a blow from God, from conscience, from Scripture, from Satan, from the world, that may for a time so astonish him, that he may not be able to speak to others, nor speak to his own heart.

As the Holy Spirit is not always a teaching Spirit, nor always a leading Spirit, nor always a sealing Spirit, nor always a witnessing Spirit, nor always an assuring Spirit to any of the saints; so he is not always a supplicating Spirit in any of the saints. When he is grieved, vexed, quenched, provoked, he may suspend his gracious influences, and deny the soul his assistance; and what can a Christian then say or do? But,

2. *Secondly*, I answer, *You cannot pray; but can you not sigh, nor groan either?*

There may be the Spirit of adoption in sighs and groans, as well as in vocal prayer (*Rom.* 8:26). The force, the virtue, the efficacy, the excellency of prayer does not consist in the number and flourish of words, but in the supernatural motions of the Spirit, in sighs, and groans, and pangs, and strong affections of heart, that are unspeakable and unutterable. Certainly, the very soul of prayer lies in the pouring out of a man's soul before the Lord, though it be but in sighs, groans, and tears (*1 Sam.* 1:13–19). One sigh and groan from a broken heart, is better pleasing to God, than all human eloquence. But,

3 *Thirdly*, I answer, *Beg God to teach you to pray.*

Oh, beg the Holy Spirit, who is a Spirit of prayer. God has promised his Holy Spirit to those who ask for him, *Luke* 11:13, 'If ye then, being evil, know how to give good gifts unto your children: how much more shall your heavenly Father give the Holy Spirit to them that ask him!' *Ezek.* 36:26, 27, 'A new heart also will I give you, and a new spirit will I put within you: and I will take away the stony heart out of your flesh, and I will give you a heart of flesh, and I will put my Spirit within you, and cause you to walk in my statutes; and ye shall keep my judgments, and do them.' *Ezek.* 11:19, 'And I will give them one heart, and I will put a new spirit within them; and I will take the stony heart out of their flesh, and will give them a heart of flesh.' *Zech.* 12:10, 'I will pour upon the house of David and upon the inhabitants of Jerusalem, the spirit of grace and of supplications.'

Now gracious promises are God's bonds, and he loves to see his people put them in suit. God expects that we should be his remembrancers, and that we should pray over his promises (*Isa.* 62:6, 7; *Isa.* 42:25, 26). When he had promised great things to his people concerning justification, sanctification, and preservation, he subjoins, 'Yet, I will for this be inquired of by the house of Israel to do it,' (*Ezek.* 36:37). God looks that we should spread his gracious promises before him, as Hezekiah did Sennacherib's letter (*Isa.* 37:14). God is never better pleased than when his people importune him in his own words, and urge him with arguments taken from his own promises. Though God be a very affectionate father, and a very liberal father, yet he is not a prodigal father, for he will never throw away his mercies on such as will not stoutly and humbly plead out his promises with him. God loves to take state upon him, and will be sought unto, both for his giving in of mercies, and for his making good of precious promises.

You say you cannot pray; why! can you not go into a corner, and spread the promises last cited before the Lord, and tell him how much it concerns his honour and glory, as well as your own internal and eternal good, to make good those gracious promises that he has made concerning his giving of his Spirit to those who ask him, and his putting his Spirit within them, and his pouring out a Spirit of grace and supplication upon them? We read of Tamar (*Gen.* 38:18, 25), that, when Judah her father-in-law lay with her, she took as a pledge his signet, bracelets, and staff; and afterwards, when she was in great distress, and ready to be burnt as an harlot, she then brought out her staff, and signet, and bracelets, and said, 'By the man whose these are, am I with child', and by doing so she saved her life. The promises are as so many rich mines, they are as so many choice flowers of paradise, they are the food, life, and strength of the soul. They are as a staff to support the soul, and they are as a signet and bracelets to adorn the soul, and to enrich the soul; and therefore poor sinners should bring them forth, and lay them before the Lord, and urge God with them, there being no way on earth to save a man's soul, and to prevent a burning in hell like this. Concerning precious promises, let me give you these eight hints.

i. *First, that they are truly propounded and stated by God* (Mark 10:30).

ii. *Secondly, that they shall certainly be performed* (2 Cor. 1:20), they being all made in and through Christ. They are made first to Christ, and then to all that have union and communion with him. Sirtorius, says Plutarch, paid what he promised with fair words but God does not so do. Men many times say and unsay; they often eat their words as soon as they have spoken them; but God will never eat the words that are gone out of his mouth: *Isa.* 46:10, 11, 'My counsel shall stand, and I will do all my pleasure: yea, I have spoken it, I will also bring it to pass: I have purposed it, I will also do it.'

iii. *Thirdly, that they all issue from free grace, from special love, from divine goodness* (Hos. 14:4).

iv. *Fourthly, That they are all as unchangeable as he is that made them* (*Jer.* 31:3).

v. *Fifthly, that they are all bottomed and founded upon the truth, faithfulness, and all-sufficiency of God* (*Mal.* 3:6).

vi. *Sixthly, that they are pledges and pawns of great things that God will do for his people in time* (*Heb.* 13:5).

vii. *Seventhly, that they are most sure and certain evidences of divine favour, and a declaration of the heart and good-will of God to his poor people* (*Heb.* 6:12; *Num.* 23:19).

viii. *Eighthly, that they are the price of Christ's blood.*

Now how should all these things encourage poor souls to be still pressing God with his promises. But,

4. *Fourthly, You* say *you cannot pray, etc. Oh, that you would leave off objecting, and fall upon praying.*

If you cannot pray as you would, nor as you should, pray as well as you can. Joseph's brethren stood so long dallying, and delaying, and trifling out the time, that, having a journey to go to buy corn, they might have bought and returned twice before they went and bought once. When Elijah called Elisha, he beats about the bush, and he must go bid his father and mother farewell before he could follow the prophet (*1 Kings* 19:20). O friends! take heed of dallying, delaying, trifling, and beating about the bush, when you should be getting down to the work of prayer. What though with Hannah you can't but weep out a prayer, or with Moses stammer out a prayer, or with Hezekiah chatter out a prayer, yet do as well as you can, and you shall find acceptance with God: 2 *Cor.* 8:12, 'For if there be first a willing mind, it is accepted according to that a man hath, and not according to that he hath not.'

The publican's prayer did not have much rhetoric or eloquence in it, 'God be merciful to me a sinner,' (*Luke* 18:13), and yet God accepted it. He prayed much, though he spoke little, and God did not turn a deaf ear upon him. That God who once accepted a handful of meal for a sacrifice, and a handful of goat's hair for an oblation, and the poor widow's two mites, as if they had been two millions, will certainly accept of what you are able to do, though you fall short, yea, much short of what you ought to do (*Lev.* 2:1, 2; and 6:15; *Luke* 21:3). 'Lord', says Luther, 'you command me to pray. I cannot pray as I would, yet I will obey; for though my prayer be not acceptable, yet your own commandment is acceptable to you.'

If weak Christians would but put forth in prayer that little strength they have, God would quickly renew their spiritual strength; he would certainly carry them on from strength to strength; he would still, by secret assistances and secret influences, help them on in their heavenly trade (*Isa.* 49:20–22; *Psa.* 84:7). As a loving indulgent father will take his little child in his arms, and carry him on in his way homeward, when his strength begins to fail him, and he can walk no further, and the way proves dirty, slippery, or uneven, so God does by his: *Hos.* 11:3, 'I taught Ephraim also to go' (as a nurse does the infant), 'taking them by their arms.' When God's poor children come to a foul way, or a rough place, he takes them up in his own arms, and helps them over the quagmire of crosses, and the difficulties of duties, and over all that straitness, and narrowness, and weakness of spirit that attends them in their closet performances.

It is observable that, when the king of Israel was to shoot the arrow, he did put his hand upon the bow, and Elisha did put his hand upon the king's hand (2 *Kings* 8:16). So when we go into our closets, we are to put up our hands, and then the Spirit of God likewise will put his hand upon our hand, he will put his strength to our strength, or rather to our weakness: *Rom.* 8:26, 'Likewise the Spirit also helpeth our infirmities', lifts with us, or helps together. The Greek word συναντιλαμβανεται properly signifies such a help as when another man of strength and ability steps in to sustain the burden that lies upon our shoulders, be it a log, or a piece of timber, setting his shoulders under it, to lift up, and bear part of it with us, or to help us as the nurse helps her little child, upholding it by the sleeve.

When a poor Christian sets himself to closet prayer, or to mourn, or to believe, or to obey, etc., then the Spirit comes in with new help, and new influences, and new assistances, and so carries him on in all these noble services. That child that does but stammer at first, in time will speak plainly and fluently. Oh, how many Christians are there that now can pray with much freedom, liberty, and fluency, who at first could only sigh out a prayer, or stammer out a prayer, or weep out a prayer! You say you cannot pray, but did you but stir up yourself to obey that command (*Matt.* 6:6), as well as you can, you do not know but that a power may go forth with the command, that may enable you to act suitable to the command. In

Matt. 9:1–9, Christ bid the palsied man rise and walk: 'Take up thy bed, and go unto thine house.' The palsied man might have objected, 'Alas! I am carried by four, I am not able to stir a limb, much less to rise, but least of all to take up my bed and walk', etc. Oh, but he rouses himself up as well as he could, and a power went forth with the command, that enabled him to do what was commanded. So, *Matt.* 12:10–14, there was a poor man who had a withered hand, and Christ commands him to stretch forth his hand; he might have replied, 'My hand is withered, and if I might have as many worlds as there be men in the world, to stretch it forth, I could not stretch it forth; yea, if my very life, if my very salvation lay upon stretching forth my withered arm, I could not stretch it forth.' Oh! but he throws away all such pleas, and complies with Christ's command as well as he could, and a power went forth and healed his hand.

O sirs! if you would but pray in your closets as well as you can, you do not know but that such a power and virtue might flow from Christ into your hearts, as might carry you on in your closet-duties, beyond expectation, even to admiring wonder; others have found it so, and why not you, why not you? Well! remember, that God is no curious nor critical observer of the incongruous expressions that falls from his poor children when they are in their closet-duties; he is such a Father as is very well pleased with the broken expressions and divine stammerings of his people when they are in a corner. It is not a flood of words, nor studied notions, nor seraphical expressions, nor elegant phrases in prayer, that takes the ear, or that delights the heart of God, or that opens the gates of glory, or that brings down the best of blessings upon the soul; but uprightness, holiness, heavenliness, spiritualness, and brokenness of heart: these are the things that make a conquest upon God, and that turns most to the soul's account. But,

5. *Fifthly,* You say you cannot pray, *but if you are a child of God, you have the Spirit of God, and the Spirit of God is a Spirit of prayer and supplication.*

That all the children of God have the Spirit of God is most evident in the blessed Scriptures. Take these for a taste: *Zech.* 12:10, 'I will pour upon the house of David, and upon the inhabitants of Jerusalem, the spirit of grace and of supplications'; *Psa.* 51:11, 'Take not thy Holy Spirit from me'; *Rom.* 8:15, 'Ye have received the Spirit of adoption, whereby we cry, Abba, Father'; *1 Cor.* 2:12, 'We have received, not the spirit of the world, but the Spirit which is of God; that we might know the things that are freely given to us of God'; *1 Thess.* 4:8, 'Who hath given unto us his Holy Spirit'; *1 John* 3:4, 'Hereby we know that he abideth in us, by the Spirit which he hath given us'; *1 Thess.* 4:13, 'Hereby we know that we dwell in him, and he in us, because he hath given us of his Spirit.'

That all the children of God have the Spirit of God, may be further made evident by an induction of these seven particulars.

i. First, *they are all sanctified by the Spirit:* *1 Cor.* 6:11, 'Ye are sanctified by the Spirit of our God.' I do not say, that they are all equally sanctified by the Spirit, but I say they are all really sanctified by the Spirit. Though all the servants of Christ have their talents, yet all have not their ten talents, nor have all their five talents, nor have all their two talents; some have only their one talent (*Matt.* 25:15). Though Benjamin's portion of food was five times as much as his brethren's portions, yet every one of his brethren had their portion (*Gen.* 43:32–34), so though some Christians have five times more measures of the Spirit, and more measures of light, of love, of holiness, of heavenly-mindedness, etc., than others have, yet every Christian has some measures of the Spirit, and some measures of grace and holiness, etc.

Though some are babes in Christ, and others are children in Christ, though some are young men in Christ, and others old men in Christ, yet every one of them is born of the Spirit of Christ (*1 Pet.* 2:2; *1 John* 2:12–14; *John* 3:8). Though none of the people of God in this life have the Spirit in perfection, yet every one of them have so much of the Spirit as will bring him to salvation. Every Christian has so much of the Spirit as will bring Christ and his soul together; and therefore without all doubt, every Christian has so much of the Spirit, as will at last bring heaven and his soul together.

ii. *Secondly, they are all led by the Spirit: Rom.* 8:14, 'As many as are led by the Spirit of God, they are the sons of God.' Every child of God has a twofold guide: the Word without, and the Spirit within (*Isa.* 30:20, 21). How the Spirit leads by the rule of the Word, and how he leads to God, and leads to Christ, and leads to truth, and leads to righteousness, and leads to holiness, and leads to happiness, I shall not now undertake to show (*Prov.* 6:22; *Eph.* 5:9).

iii. *Thirdly, they are all upheld and strengthened by the Spirit:* Psa. 51:12, 'Uphold me with thy free Spirit'; or under-prop me or sustain me, as the Hebrew has it, with your free, voluntary Spirit; or, as the Greek turns it, with your noble, princely Spirit. So *Eph.* 3:16, 'To be strengthened with might by his Spirit in the inner man.' By the inner man, some understand the regenerate part of man; others, by the inner man, do understand the soul with all its noble faculties and motions.

Take the words which way you will, it is certain that all the spiritual might and strength that a Christian has, he has it from the Holy Spirit. Though the Spirit strengthens every Christian in the inner man, yet I do not say that the Spirit strengthens every Christian alike in the inward man. Some have stronger corruptions to subdue than others, and more violent temptations to withstand than others, and greater difficulties to wrestle with than others, and choicer mercies to improve than others, and higher and harder duties of religion to manage than others, and accordingly they are more strengthened in the inner man than others.

iv. *Fourthly, they are all partakers of the first-fruits of the Spirit: Rom.* 8:23, 'Ourselves . . . have the first-fruits of the Spirit', which are but as a handful of corn in respect of the whole crop. All the grace and all the holiness which we have from the regenerating Spirit at first conversion is but a drop to that sea, a mite to those talents, which we shall receive in the life to come (2 *Cor.* 1:22).

v. *Fifthly, they are all taught by the Spirit, John* 14:26, 'The Holy Ghost, whom the Father will send in my name, he shall teach you all things'; (*Isa.* 59:21).

This promise primarily belongs to the apostles; Secondarily, to all believers. Though these words were spoken at first to the apostles only, yet they were not spoken of the apostles only: Isa. 54:13, 'And all thy children shall be taught of the Lord; and great shall be the peace of thy children.' In these words there are three things promised to the apostles: *First,* Immediate illumination by the Spirit of God. *Secondly,* A full knowledge of all those truths belonging to their apostolical office, and that were necessary for them at that juncture of time. *Thirdly,* Absolute infallibility as to matter of doctrine. There are also three things promised to all believers: *First,* Mediate illumination, teaching truths by the Spirit of truth, in the use of the means of grace. *Secondly,* Knowledge of all truth necessary to salvation. *Thirdly,* Infallibility too, so far forth as they adhere and keep close to the Spirit's teaching in the Word.

Philo says that the primitive Christians were called tillers, because, as husbandmen till their fields and manure their grounds, so did they teach their families and nurture their children and servants with good instructions. Oh, what choice teachings of the Spirit were these primitive Christians under, who made it so much their business, their work, to teach those that were under their charge (*1 Thess.* 4:9; *2 Cor.* 3:8). So *1 John* 2:27, 'But the anointing which ye have received of him abideth in you; and ye need not that any man teach you: but as the same anointing teacheth you of all things, and is truth.' Not that we know all things simply, or that we need not a ministry to teach and instruct us; but he speaks comparatively: you shall not be so helped by any instructions without the Spirit, as with the Spirit. The Spirit shall declare the truth as it is in Jesus more clearly, more freely, more particularly, more certainly, more universally, more effectually, than any other is able to do.[1] The Spirit, this holy unction, shall teach the saints all things; not all things knowable, for that is impossible for finite creatures to attain unto. Who knows the motions of the heavens, the influences of the stars, the nature of the creatures, or how the bones grow in the womb of her that is with child? Who knows the reason why the river Nile should overflow in the summer, when waters are at the lowest; or why the loadstone should draw iron to it, or incline to the pole star?

Pliny tells us of one that spent fifty-eight years in learning about the nature of the bee, and yet had not fully attained to it.[2] How is it possible, then, for the wisest naturalist to enter into the deep things of God?

Paul, who learned his theology among the angels, and who had the Holy Ghost for his immediate teacher, tells us plainly that 'he knew but in part' (*1 Cor.* 13:9–11); and oh then, how little a part of that part do we know! But the Spirit teaches the saints all things; that is, *First*, He teaches them all things needful for the salvation of their souls, all things necessary to bring them to heaven (*John* 17:3). *Secondly*, All things needful to life and godliness (2

---

[1] *1 Cor.* 6:9–11; *1 Tim.* 4:1; *John* 16:25; *Isa.* 48:17; *Eccles.* 11:5.
[2] Aristomachus of Soli.

THE SECRET KEY TO HEAVEN

Pet. 1:3). *Thirdly,* All things needful to their places, callings, sexes, ages, and conditions. *Fourthly,* All things needful for you to know to preserve you in the truth, and to preserve you from being deluded and seduced by those false teachers of whom he speaks (*1 John* 2:10, 19, 22, 23, 26). And certainly this is the main thing that John hints at in that expression. The 'all things', spoken of in verse 27, according to the ordinary Scripture style, must necessarily be interpreted only of all those things which are there spoken of. But,

vi. Sixthly, *they are all comforted by the Spirit:*[1] *Acts* 9:31, 'They walked in the fear of the Lord, and in the comfort of the Holy Ghost'; *Rom.* 14:17, 'For the kingdom of God is not meat and drink, but righteousness, and peace, and joy in the Holy Ghost'; *1 Thess.* 1:6, 'And ye became followers of us, and of the Lord, having received the word in much affliction, with joy of the Holy Ghost.' Not that all Christians have always actual comfort, actual joy. Oh no! For as the air is sometimes clear and sometimes cloudy, and as the sea is sometimes ebbing and sometimes flowing; so the comforts and joys of the people of God are sometimes ebbing and sometimes flowing, sometimes clear and sometimes cloudy.

Thomas Hudson [c.1528–58] the martyr being deserted at the stake, went from under his chain; and having prayed earnestly, was comforted immediately, and suffered valiantly. So Robert Glover, the martyr [d. 1555] was deserted in prison, but as he was going to the stake he looked back, and cried out to his friend, 'He is come, he

[1] *John* 14:16, 26; 15:26; 16:7.

is come', meaning the Comforter, and so he laid down his life with joy.

Rachel wept, and would not be comforted; she gave so much way to weeping, that she would not give the least way to comfort; and so it is many times with the choicest saints, 'My soul refused to be comforted' (*Psa.* 72:2). It is not my purpose at present to insist on the several ways whereby the people of God refuse comfort, and fall short of those strong consolations which God is willing that they should receive. The sun may operate where it does not shine, and a man may be in a state of salvation, and yet lack consolation; a man may fear the Lord, and obey the voice of his servant, and yet walk in darkness and see no light (*Isa.* 50:10). There is no Christian but may sometimes have trouble in his conscience, and grief in his heart, and tears in his eyes, and fears and questionings in his soul, whether God be his Father, and whether Christ be his Redeemer, and whether mercy belongs to him, yes, whether any promise in the book of God belongs to him?

Joy and comfort are those delicacies, those sweetmeats of heaven, that God does not every day feast his people with (*Psa.* 30:6, 7); every day is not a wedding day, nor every day is not a harvest day, nor every day is not a summer's day. The fatted calf is not killed every day, nor the robe and the ring is not every day put on; every day is not a festival day nor a dancing day (*Luke* 15:22, 23; *Eccles.* 3:4; *Rom.* 12:15).

As there is a time to sing, so there is a time to sigh; as there is a time to laugh, so there is a time to weep; and as there is a time to dance, so there is a time to mourn. All tears will never be wholly wiped from our eyes till all sin be quite taken out of our hearts.

But notwithstanding all this, yet gracious souls have always sure and choice grounds of consolation; they have the promises, they have the 'first-fruits of the Spirit', they have union with Christ, and they have right to eternal life, though they have not always sensible comforts. The children of God have always cause to exercise faith and hope on God in their darkest condition, though they have not always actual joy and consolation (*Job* 13:15; *Psa.* 42:5). The Comforter always abides with the saints, though he does not always actually comfort the saints (*John* 1:16). The Spirit many times carries on his sanctifying work in the soul when he does not carry on his comforting work in the soul; the Spirit many times acts in a way of humiliation when he does not act in a way of consolation; the Spirit many times fills the soul with godly sorrow when he does not fill the soul with holy joy. The actings of the Spirit, as to his comforting work, are all of his own sovereign will and pleasure; and therefore he may abide in the soul when he does not actually comfort the soul. But,

vii. *Seventhly, The people of God, first or last, are sealed by the Spirit: Eph.* 1:13, 'In whom, after ye believed, ye were sealed with that Holy Spirit of promise.'[1] The nature of sealing consists in the imparting of the image, or character of the seal to the thing sealed. To seal a thing is to stamp the character of the seal on it. Now, the Spirit of

---

[1] Zanchius [1516–90] says that this is a metaphor taken from merchants, who having bought goods, seal them as their own, and so transport them to other places (*Eph.* 4:24).

God really and effectually communicates the image of God to us, which image consists in righteousness and true holiness. Then are we truly sealed by the Spirit of God when the Holy Ghost stamps the image of grace and holiness so obviously, so evidently upon the soul, as that the soul sees it, feels it, and can run and read it; then the soul is sealed by the Holy Spirit. So *Eph.* 4:30, 'And grieve not the Holy Spirit of God, whereby ye are sealed unto the day of redemption.'

The person of the Holy Ghost is here set forth in the Greek with a very great energy, such as our tongue is not able fully to express. Here are three words, that have three articles, every word his several article by itself, το πνευμα, το αγιον, του Θεου: *the* Spirit, not *a* Spirit; and not holy, but *the* holy; nor of God, but of *that* God: 2 *Cor.* 1:22, 'Who hath also sealed us, and given the earnest of the Spirit in our hearts.'

In these Scriptures you see that the Spirit is a seal. Now, a seal among men is, first, for *secrecy*; secondly, for *distinction*; thirdly, for *authority*; fourthly, for *certainty*. A writing sealed is authentic, and to give assurance. In the three texts last cited, if you compare them together, you may observe these six things:

First, The person sealing, and that is, the *Father.*

Secondly, In whom: in *Christ.*

Thirdly, With what seal: the *Spirit of promise.* Where all the Persons in the Trinity are making us sure of our inheritance.

Fourthly, When: *after ye believed.*

Fifthly, The end, which is twofold:

[143]

i. *Subordinate,* and that is the certainty of our salvation;

ii. *Ultimate,* and that is, the praise of his glory.

Sixthly, The time, how long this seal and earnest shall assure us, and that is, 'till we have the complete possession of that of which it is an earnest'. To prevent mistakes and disputes about the sealings of the Spirit on the one hand, and to support, comfort, and encourage the poor people of God on the other hand, let me briefly hint at the Spirit's special sealing times.

i. *First, conversion times are often the Spirit's sealing times* (*Luke* 15:22–23). Upon the prodigal's return, the fatted calf is killed, and the best robe is put upon his back, and the ring is put upon his hand, and shoes on his feet. Some by the robe understand the royalty of Adam, others, the righteousness of Christ. And by the ring, some understand the pledges of God's love, rings being given as pledges of love; and by the ring others understand the seal of God's Holy Spirit, men using the seal with their rings. Among the Romans the ring was an ensign of virtue, honour, and nobility, whereby they that wore them were distinguished from the common people.

I think the main thing intended by the robe and the ring is, to show us, that God sometimes upon the sinner's conversion and returning to him, is graciously pleased to give him some choice manifestations of his gracious pleasure and good-will, and to seal up to him his everlasting love and favour. And hence it comes to pass that some that are but babes in Christ (*1 Pet.* 2:2, 3; *1 John* 2:12–14), are so diligent and active in religious duties, and so conscientious and dexterous in the exercise of their graces. At first conversion, God helps some of his people to read their own names written in legible letters in the book of life (*Acts* 9:3–6). No sooner are some converted, but the Spirit stamps his seal upon them.

ii. *Secondly, believing times are sealing times* (*Eph.* 1:13). When they were in the very exercise of their faith, when they were acting their faith – for so much the original imports – the Spirit came and sealed them up to the day of redemption (*Rom.* 15:13; *1 Pet.* 1:8). He that honours Christ by frequent actings of faith on him, him will Christ honour, by setting his seal and mark upon him.

iii. *Thirdly, humbling times, mourning times, are sealing times.* When a holy man was asked, which were the most joyful days, the most comfortable days, that ever he enjoyed, he answered that his mourning days were his most joyful days; and therefore he cried out, 'Oh, give me my mourning days, give me my mourning days; for they were my most joyful days.' Those were days in which God sealed up his everlasting love to his soul (*Job* 22:29; *Isa.* 29:19). When the prodigal had greatly humbled himself before his father, then the best robe and ring were put upon him (*Luke* 15:17–24). There are none that long for the sealings of the Spirit like humble souls; none set so high a price upon the sealings of the Spirit, as humble souls; none make so choice an improvement of the sealings of the Spirit, as humble souls. And therefore when men's hearts are humble and low, the Spirit comes and sets the privy-seal of heaven upon them.

iv. *Fourthly, sin-killing, sin-mortifying, sin-subduing times, are the Spirit's sealing times; Rev.* 2:17, 'To him that overcomes I will give to eat of the hidden manna, and will give him a white stone, and in the stone a new name written, that no man knows saving he that receiveth it.'

God will give to the victorious Christian a secret love-token, whereby his soul may rest assured of the unspeakable love of God, and of its freedom from condemnation. White stones were of very great use among the Romans and the Athenians, and served to acquit the accused in courts of justice. When malefactors were accused, arraigned, and condemned in their courts, they gave them a black stone in token of condemnation; but when they were acquitted, they gave them white stones, in token of absolution; and to this practice the Holy Ghost seems to allude.

He that is victorious over his lusts shall have a new name, 'better than the names of sons and daughters' (*Isa.* 56:5); and he shall have the pardon of his sins written in fair letters upon the white stone, so that he may run and read his absolution. The victorious Christian shall have assurance of the full discharge of all his sins, he shall have a clear evidence of his justification, and a blessed assurance of his eternal election; all which are hidden and mysterious things to all but those that have experienced and tasted what these sweet-meats of heaven mean (*1 John* 1:7).

Among the Romans there were solemn feasts held in honour of those that were victorious in their sacred games. Now those that were to be admitted to those feasts used to have their names written on white shells, and white stones, and by these tickets they were admitted.

Now some think the Holy Ghost alludes to this practice, and so would hint to us a personal mark by which victorious Christians may be known, and admitted as bidden guests to the heavenly banquet of the hidden manna, according to *Rev.* 19:9. O sirs! when predominant lusts are brought under, when cherished sins lie slain in the soul, then the Spirit comes and seals up love, and life, and glory to the soul.

v. *Fifthly, suffering times are sealing times* (*Acts* 7:55, 56, 59, 60; *Rev.* 1:9, 10; 2 *Cor.* 4:15–17). The primitive Christians found them so, and the suffering saints in the Marian days found them so. When the furnace is seven times hotter than ordinary, the Spirit of the Lord comes and seals up a man's pardon in his heart, and his peace with God, and his title to heaven.

When the world frowns most, then God smiles most; when the world puts their iron chains upon the saints' legs, then God puts his golden chains about the saints' necks; when the world puts a bitter cup into one hand, then the Lord puts a cup of consolation into the other hand; when the world cries out, 'Crucify them, crucify them', then commonly they hear that sweet voice from heaven, 'These are my beloved ones, in whom I am well pleased.'

Blessed John Bradford looked upon his sufferings as an evidence to him that he was in the right way to heaven. And says Ignatius, 'It is better for me to be a martyr than to be a monarch.'

vi. *Sixthly, self-denying times are the Spirit's sealing times* (*Matt.* 19:27–29).

First, there is sinful self, which takes in a man's lusts.

Secondly, there is natural self, which takes in a man's arts, parts, gifts, and reason.

Thirdly, there is religious self, which takes in all a man's religious duties and services, whether ordinary or extraordinary.

Fourthly, there is moral self, which includes a freedom from gross, heinous, enormous wickednesses, and a fair, sweet, harmless behaviour towards men.

Fifthly, there is relative self, which takes in our nearest and dearest relations in the flesh; as wife, children, father, mother, brothers, sisters, etc. (*Psa.* 45:7–11). Now when a man comes thus universally to deny himself for Christ's sake, and the gospel's sake, and religion's sake, then the Spirit of the Lord comes and seals him up unto the day of redemption. This is a truth confirmed by the experiences of many martyrs now in heaven, and by the testimony of many Christians still alive.

vii. *Seventhly, sacrament times are sealing times.* In that 'feast of fat things', God by his Spirit seals up his love to his people, and his covenant to his people, and pardon of sin to his people, and heaven and happiness to his people. There are many precious souls that have found Christ in this ordinance, and when they could not find him in other ordinances, though they have sought him sorrowingly. In this ordinance many a distressed soul has been strengthened, comforted and sealed. I might give you many instances. Take one for all. There was a gracious woman, who, after God had filled her soul with comfort and sealed up his everlasting love to her, fell under former fears and trouble of spirit, and being at the Lord's supper, a little before the bread was administered to her, Satan seemed to appear to her, and told her that she should not presume to eat; but at that very nick of time, the Lord was pleased to bring into her mind that passage in the Song of Solomon, 'Eat, O my friend' (*Song of Sol.* 5:1). But notwithstanding this, Satan still continued terrifying her, and when she had eaten, he told her that she should not drink; but then the Lord brought that second clause of the verse to her remembrance, 'Drink, yea drink abundantly' (or, 'be drunk', as the Hebrew has it) 'my beloved' (or, 'my loves', as the Hebrew has it – all faithful souls are Christ's loves), and so she drank also, and presently was filled with such unspeakable joys, that she hardly knew how she got home; which soul-ravishing joys continued for a fortnight after, and filled her mouth with songs of praise, so that she could neither sleep nor eat, more than she forced herself to do out of conscience of duty. At the fortnight's end, when God was pleased to abate her measure of joy, she came to a settled peace of conscience and assurance of the love of God; so that for twenty years after she had not so much as a cloud upon her spirit, or the least questioning of her interest in Christ. But,

viii. *Eighthly, when God calls his people to some great and noble work, when he puts them upon some high services, some difficult duties, some holy and eminent employments, then his Spirit comes and sets his seal upon them: Jer.* 1:5, 'Before I formed thee in the belly I knew thee: and before thou camest forth out of the womb I sanctified thee, and I ordained thee to be a prophet unto the nations.' The Lord sending the prophet Jeremiah to denounce most dreadful judgments against a rebellious people, an impudent brazen-faced nation, he assures him of his eternal election, and of his choice presence, and singular assistance in that work that he set him about, *Jer.* 1:8, 17–19. Thus the Lord dealt with Peter, James, and John (*Matt.* 17:1–6), and thus he dealt with Paul (*Acts* 9:1–23).

ix. *Ninthly, when they are taken up into more than ordinary communion with God, then is the Spirit's sealing time.* When was it that the spouse cried out, 'My beloved is mine, and I am his!', but when Christ brought her to his banqueting house, and his banner over her was love (*Song of Sol.* 2:16; 3–6, compared)?

x. *Tenthly* and lastly, *when Christians give themselves up to private prayer, when Christians are more than ordinarily exercised in secret prayer, in closet duties, then the Spirit comes and seals up the covenant and the love of the Father to them.* When Daniel had been wrestling and weeping, and weeping and wrestling all day long with God in his closet, then the angel tells him, 'that he was a man greatly beloved of God', or 'a man of great desires', as the original has it (*Dan.* 9:20–23). There was a gracious woman who, after much frequenting of sermons, and walking in the ways of the Lord, fell into great desertions; but in secret prayer, God came in with abundance of light and comfort, sealing up to her soul that part of his covenant, viz., 'I will take the stony heart out of their flesh, and will give them an heart of flesh; that they may walk in my statutes, and keep mine ordinances, and do them: and they shall be my people, and I will be their God' (*Ezek.* 11:19, 20). And thus I have given you a brief account of the Spirit's special sealing times. Now mark, this seal God sets upon all his wares, upon all his adopted children; for sooner or later there are none of his but are sealed with this seal. God sets his seal of regeneration, he stamps his image of holiness upon all his people, to difference and distinguish them from all profane, unholy, and hypocritical persons in the world (*John* 3:3; *2 Thess.* 2:13; *Heb.* 12:14). Doubtless the sanctifying work of the Holy Ghost, imprinting the draughts and lineaments of God's image of righteousness and holiness upon man, as a seal or signet leaves an impression and stamp of its likeness upon the thing sealed, is the seal of the Spirit spoken of in Scripture: *2 Tim.* 2:19, 'The foundation of God standeth sure, having this seal, The Lord knoweth them that are his. And let every one that nameth the name of Christ depart from iniquity.'

But to prevent mistakes, you must remember, that though the Spirit of the Lord, first or last, will set his seal upon every real saint, yet the impression of that seal is not alike visible in all; for some bear this impression as babes, others as men grown up to some maturity. All God's adopted children bear this impression truly, but none of them bear it perfectly in this life. Sometimes this seal of regeneration, this seal of holiness, is so plain and obvious that a man may run and read it in himself and others; and at other times it is so obscure and dark, that he can hardly discern it, either in himself or others. This seal is so lively stamped on some of God's people, that it discovers itself very visibly, eminently, gloriously; but on others it is not alike visible. And thus I have made it evident by these seven particulars, that all the children of God have the Spirit of God.

Now mark, the Spirit of God that is in all the saints is a Spirit of prayer and supplication: *Rom.* 8:15, 'Ye have received the Spirit of adoption, whereby we cry, Abba, Father.' While the child is in the womb it cannot cry, but as soon as it is born it cries. Whilst Paul did lie in the womb of his natural estate, he could not pray; but no sooner was he born of the Spirit, but the next news is, 'Behold he prayeth!' (*Acts* 9:11). Prayer is nothing but the turning of a man's inside outward before the Lord. The very soul of prayer lies in the pouring out of a man's soul into the bosom of God. Prayer is nothing but the breathing of that out before the Lord that was first breathed into us by the Spirit of the Lord. Prayer is nothing but a choice, a free, a sweet, and familiar intercourse of the soul with God. Certainly, it is a great work of the Spirit to help the saints to pray: *Gal.* 4:6, 'Because you are sons, God hath sent forth the Spirit of his Son into your hearts, crying, Abba, Father.' God has no still-born children. The doubling, 'Abba, Father,' notes fiducial, filial, and vehement affection. The first is a Hebrew or Syriac word, the second a Greek, which signifies the union of the Hebrews and Grecians, or the Jews and Gentiles, in one church, 'Abba, Father.'

'Father' is added because in Christ the corner-stone both peoples are joined, alike becoming sons, from wherever they come: circumcision from one place, whereupon

Abba; uncircumcision from another, whereupon *Father* is named: the concord of the walls being the glory of the corner-stone.

The word *Abba*, say others, signifies *father* in the Syriac tongue, which the apostle here retains, because it is a word full of affection, which young children retain almost in all languages, when they begin to speak. And he adds the word *father*, not only to expound the same, but also the better to express the eager movings and the earnest and vehement desires and singular affections of believers, in their crying unto God; even as Christ himself redoubled the word Father (*Mark* 14:36), to the same purpose, when he was in his greatest distress. This little word Father, says Luther, lisped forth in prayer by a child of God, exceeds the eloquence of Demosthenes, Cicero, and all other famed orators in the world. It is certain that the Spirit of God helps the saints in all their communions with God, viz., in their meditations of God, in their reading and hearing of the Word of God, in the communions one with another, and in all their solemn addresses to God. And as to this the apostle gives us a most special instance in *Rom.* 8:26, 'Likewise the Spirit also helpeth our infirmities: for we know not what we should pray for as we ought; but the Spirit itself maketh intercessions for us with groanings which cannot be uttered.'

When we are to pray, there is in us sometimes an infirmity of ignorance, so that we know not what to pray for, either in regard of the matter or the manner. And there is in us at other times an infirmity of pride and conceitedness, so that we cannot pray with that humility and lowliness of spirit as we should, spiritual pride having fly-blown our prayers. Sometimes there is in us an infirmity of deadness, dullness, drowsiness, etc., so that we cannot pray with that warmth, heat, life, spirit, and fervency, as we should, or as we would; and at other times there is in us an infirmity of unbelief and slavish fears, so that we cannot pray with that faith and holy boldness, as becomes children that draw near to a throne of grace, to a throne of mercy, etc.

But now the Spirit helps these infirmities by way of instruction, prompting and teaching us what to pray for, and how we should spell our lesson; and by telling us as it were within, what we should say, and how we should sigh and groan; and by rousing and quickening, and stirring of us up to prayer, and by his singular influence and choice assistance opening and enlarging our hearts in prayer; and by tuning the strings of our affections he prepares us and fits us for the work of supplication, and therefore every one that derides the spirit of prayer in the saints, saying, These are the men and the women that pray by the Spirit! blaspheme against the Holy Spirit; it being a main work of the Spirit to teach the saints to pray and to help them in prayer.

Now, all the saints having the Spirit, and the Spirit being a Spirit of prayer and supplication, there is no reason in the world why a saint should say, I would pray in secret, but I cannot pray, I cannot pour out my soul nor my complaint before the Lord in a corner.

6. *Sixthly and lastly,* you say you cannot pray, you have not the gifts and parts which others have. *But you can*

manage your callings, your worldly business as well as others; and why then can you not pray as well as others?

Ah, friends! did you but love private prayer as well as you love the world, and delight in private prayer as much as you delight in the world, and were your hearts as much set upon closet prayer as they are set upon the world, you would never say you could not pray. You would as quickly pray as others. It is not so much from lack of ability to pray in secret, that you don't pray in secret, as it is from lack of a will, a heart to pray in secret. Jacob's love to Rachel, and Shechem's love to Dinah, carried them through the greatest difficulties (*Gen.* 29 and 34). Were men's affections but strongly set upon private prayer, they would quickly find abilities to pray.

He that sets his affections upon a virgin, though he be not learned nor eloquent, will find words enough to let her know how his heart is taken with her. The application is easy. One in Seneca complained of a thorn in his foot, when his lungs were rotten. So many complain of lack of ability to pray in their closets, when their hearts are rotten. Sirs! Do but get better hearts, and then you will never say you can't pray. It is one of the saddest sights in all the world to see men strongly parted and gifted for all worldly businesses cry out that they can't pray, that they have no ability to pour out their souls before the Lord in secret. You have sufficient parts and gifts to tell men of your sins, your needs, your dangers, your difficulties, your mercies, your deliverances, your duties, your crosses, your losses, your enjoyments, your friends, your foes; and are you not ashamed to complain of your lack of parts and gifts to tell those very things to God in a corner which you can tell to men even upon the housetops?

OBJECTION 4. Some may further object and say, *God is very well acquainted with all our desires, necessities, straits, trials; and there is no moving of him to bestow any favours upon us which he does not intend to bestow upon us, whether we pray in our closets or no; and therefore to what purpose do you press secret prayer so hard upon us?*

To this objection I shall give these answers.

1. *First, that this objection lies as strong against family prayer and public prayer as it does against private prayer.*

God knows all your wants and necessities, all your straits and trials, etc., and therefore why do you need to pray in your family, why do you need to attend public prayers in the communion of saints? There is no wringing of any mercy out of the hands of heaven which God does not intend to bestow. This objection faces all kind of prayer, and fights against all kinds of prayer. But,

2. *Secondly*, I answer, *that private prayer is a piece of divine worship and adoration, it is a part of that homage which we owe to God upon the account of a divine command, as I have already proved.*

Now, all objections must bow before the face of divine commands; as Joseph's brethren bowed before him (*Gen.* 42:6); or as king Ahasuerus' servants bowed before Haman (*Est.* 3:2). Indeed, every objection that is formed up against a divine command, should fall before it, as Dagon fell before the ark, or as Goliath fell before David. He that casts off private prayer under any pretence whatever, casts off the dominion of God, the authority of God, and this may be as much as a man's life and soul is worth.

3. *Thirdly*, I answer, *though prayer be not the ground, the cause of obtaining favours and mercies from God, yet it is the means, it is the silver channel, it is the golden pipe, through which the Lord is pleased to convey to his people all temporal, spiritual, and eternal favours*[1] (Ezek. 36:26–37). God promises to give them the cream, the choicest, the sweetest of all spiritual, eternal, and temporal blessings; but mark, verse 37, 'I will yet for this be inquired of by the house of Israel, to do it for them.' Though God be very prompt and ready to bestow upon his people the best and the greatest of blessings, yet he will by prayer be sought for the actual enjoyment of them. He that has no heart to pray for a mercy he needs, has no ground to believe that God will ever give him the mercy he needs. There is no receiving without asking, no finding without seeking, no opening without knocking. The threefold promise annexed to the threefold precept in *Matt.* 7:7 should encourage all Christians to be instant, fervent, and constant in prayer. The proud beggar gets nothing of men, and the dumb sinner gets nothing of God. As there is no mercy too great for God to give, so there is no mercy too little for us to crave. Certainly that man has little worth in him that thinks any mercy not worth a seeking. But,

4. *Fourthly* and lastly, I answer, *Every Christian should labour to enjoy his mercies in mercy, he should labour to have his blessings blessed unto him; he should labour to*

[1] Isa. 55:6; James 1:5; Isa. 62:7; Psa. 22:24.

have 'the good will of him that dwelt in the bush', with all he has (Gen. 22:17). Now this is an everlasting truth, a maxim to live and die with, that whatever mercy does not come in upon the wing of prayer is not given in mercy. Oh, how sweet is that mercy that comes flying in upon the wing of prayer! How sweet was that water to Samson which streamed to him in the channel of private prayer (Judg. 15:19); he called the name of it En-hakkore, the well of him that prayed. Samson prayed as for life, and that water that was handed to him was as sweet as life. Every mercy that is gathered by the hand of prayer is as sweet as the rose of Sharon (Song of Sol. 2:1). But that mercy that comes not in at the door of prayer, comes not in at the right door; and that mercy that comes not in at the right door will do a man no good: such mercies will make themselves wings and fly from us (Prov. 23:5).

Every Christian should narrowly look that all his mercies are sanctified mercies. Now, every mercy is sanctified by the Word and prayer (1 Tim. 4:4–5). Prayer prepares and fits us for mercy, and mercy for us. It is prayer that gives us a right and holy use of all our mercies. Such mercies are but great miseries that come not in upon the wing of prayer. Prayerless men's mercies are all given in wrath; their blessings are cursed unto them (Prov. 3:33; Mal. 2:2). Look, as every sacrifice was to be seasoned with salt, so every mercy is to be sanctified by prayer. Look, as gold sometimes is laid not only upon cloth and silks, but also upon silver itself, so prayer is that golden duty that must be laid not only upon all our natural and civil actions, as eating, drinking, buying, selling, etc., but also upon all our silver duties, upon all our most religious and spiritual performances, as hearing, reading, meditating, conference, church-fellowship, breaking of bread, etc.

Certainly prayer is very necessary to make every providence, and every ordinance, and every mercy to be a blessing to us. Every mercy that comes in upon the wing of private prayer is a double mercy; it is a great-bellied mercy; it is a mercy that has many mercies in its womb. Happy is that Christian that can lay his hand upon every mercy that he enjoys, and say of them all as once Hannah said of her Samuel: *1 Sam.* 1:27, 'For this child I prayed, and the LORD hath given me my petition which I asked of him.' But,

OBJECTION 5. Some may further object and say, *I would drive a private trade with God, I would exercise myself in secret prayer, but I lack a convenient place to retire into; I lack a private corner in which to unburden my soul to my Father, etc.*

To this objection I shall give these three short answers

1. First, *I suppose this objection concerns but a few Christians in our days.* The God who has given a Christ to believers commonly gives them a convenient corner in which to enjoy private communion with himself (*Rom.* 8:32). Most Christians, I am afraid, do rather need a heart for private prayer, than a convenient place for private prayer. What men set their hearts upon, they will find time and place to effect it, whether it be good or whether it be evil, whether it concerns temporals or spirituals, whether it concerns this world or another world, this life

or a better life. If most men would but get better hearts, they would quickly find or make convenient places for private prayer. He who has an inflamed love to God will certainly find out a corner to enjoy secret communion with God. True lovers will find out corners to enjoy one another in. How many men are there that can easily find out private places for their dogs to lie in, and their swine to sleep in, and their horses to stand in, and their oxen to feed in, etc., who can't find out a private place to seek the face of God in! But did these men but love their God, or their souls, or private prayer, or eternity, as well or better than their beasts, they would not be such brutes but that they would quickly find out a hole, a corner, to wait upon the Lord in. But,

2. *Secondly,* I answer, *if a Christian be on the top of a house with Peter, he may pray there; or if he be walking in the field with Isaac, he may pray there; or if be on the mountain with Christ, he may pray there; or if he be behind the door with Paul, he may pray there; or if he be waiting at table with Nehemiah, he may secretly pray there; or if he be in a wood, he may pray there, as the primitive Christians in times of persecution did; or if he be behind a tree, he may pray there; or if he be by the seaside, he may pray there, as the apostles did.*

It was a choice saying of Augustine, 'Every saint is God's temple, and he that carries his temple around with him, may go to prayer when he pleases.' Some saints have never had so much of heaven brought down into their hearts, as when, they have been with God in a corner. Oh, the secret manifestations of divine love, the secret kisses, the secret embraces, the secret influences, the secret communion with God, that many a precious Christian has had in the most solitary places: it may be behind the door, or behind the wall, or behind the hedge, or behind the arbour, or behind the tree, or behind the rock, or behind the bush, etc. But,

3. *Thirdly,* and lastly, *did you never in your unregenerate estate make use of all your wits, and parts, and utmost endeavours, to find out convenient seasons, and secret corners, and solitary places to sin in, and to dishonour your God in, and to undo your own and others souls in?*

Yes! I remember with shame and blushing, that it was so with me when I was dead in trespasses and sins, and walked according to the course of this world (*Eph.* 2:1–3). Oh, how much then does it concern you in your renewed, sanctified, and raised estate, to make use of all your wits, and faculties, and utmost endeavours, to find out the fittest seasons, and the most secret corners, and solitary places you can, to honour your God in, and to seek the welfare of your own and others' souls in! Oh, that men were but as serious, studious, and industrious, to find out convenient seasons, secret places to please and serve and glorify the Lord in, as they have been serious, studious, and industrious to find out convenient seasons, and secret places to displease and grieve the Spirit of the Lord in. But,

OBJECTION 6. *Sixthly,* and lastly, others may further object and say, *We would be often in private with God, we would give ourselves up to closet prayer, but no sooner*

[161]

*do we shut our closet doors, than a multitude of infirm-
ities, weaknesses, and vanities face us, and rise up against
us.* Our hearts being full of distempers and follies, and
our bodies, say some, are under great indispositions; and
our souls, say others, are under present indispositions;
and how then can we seek the face of God in a corner?
how can we wrestle with God in our closets ? etc.

Now, to this objection I shall give these six answers.

1. *If these kinds of reasonings or arguments were sufficient to shut* private prayer out of doors, where lives that
man or woman, that husband or wife, that father or
child, that master or servant, that *would ever be found in
the practice of that duty?*[1]

Where is there a person under heaven whose heart is
not full of infirmities, weaknesses, follies, and vanities;
and whose body and soul is not too often indisposed to
closet duties? *1 Kings* 8:46, 'If they sin against thee, for
there is no man that sinneth not, etc.';[2] *Eccles.* 7:20, 'For
there is not a just man upon the earth that doeth good
and sinneth not'; *Prov.* 20:9, 'Who can say, I have made
my heart clean, I am pure from my sin?' *Job* 14:4, 'Who
can bring a clean thing out of an unclean? not one.' *Job*
9:30, 31, 'If I wash myself with snow-water, and make my
hands never so clean; yet shall thou plunge me in the
ditch, and mine own clothes shall abhor me.' *Job* 9:20, 'If
I justify myself, my own mouth shall condemn me: if I say,
I am perfect, it shall also prove me perverse.' *Psa.* 143:2,

---

[1] *Psa.* 40:12; *Psa.* 51:5; *Rom.* 7:15, 24; *Psa.* 130:3; *1 Cor.* 4:4;
2 Chron. 6:36; *Phil.* 3:12.

[2] Grace in this life is like gold in the ore, full of mixture.

'And enter not into judgment with thy servant: for in thy sight shall no man living, be justified.' *James* 3:2, 'For in many things we offend all.' *1 John* 1:8, 'If we say we have no sin, we deceive ourselves, and the truth is not in us.' Such that affirm that men may be fully perfect in this life, or without sin in this life, they do affirm that which is expressly contrary to the Scriptures last cited, and to the universal experience of all saints, who daily feel and lament over that body of sin and death that they bear about with them; yes, they do affirm that which is quite contrary to the very state or constitution of all the saints in this life. In every saint, 'the flesh lusteth against the Spirit, and the Spirit lusteth against the flesh, and these are contrary one to the other, so that they cannot do the things that they would' (*Gal.* 5:17). In every good man there are two men, the old man and the new; the one must be daily put on, and the other daily put off (*Eph.* 4:22–24). All saints have a law in their members rebelling against the law of their minds; so that the good that they would do, they do not; and the evil that they would not do, that they do (*Rom.* 7:23, 25). They have two contrary principles in them, from whence proceeds two manner of actions, motions, and inclinations, continually opposite one to another; hence it is that there is a continual combat within them, like the struggling of the twins in Rebekah's womb. An absolute perfection is peculiar to the triumphant state of God's elect in heaven: heaven is the only privileged place, where no unclean thing can enter in (*Rev.* 23:21); that is the only place where neither sin nor Satan shall ever get a footing.

THE SECRET KEY TO HEAVEN

Such as dream of an absolute perfection in this life confound and jumble heaven and earth together; the state of the church militant with the state of the church triumphant, which are certainly distinct both in time and place, and in order, measure, and concomitants (*Heb.* 12:22, 23). This dangerous opinion of absolute perfection in this life, shakes the very foundation of religion, and overthrows the gospel of grace; it renders the satisfaction of Christ, and all his great transactions, null and void; it tells the world that there is no need of faith, of repentance, of ordinances, of watchfulness. They that say they have no sin, say they have no need of the blood of Christ to cleanse them from sin (*1 John* 1:7). Such as say they have no sin, say they have no need of faith to rest upon Christ for imputed righteousness to justify their persons. Such as say they have no sin, say they have no need of Christ as king to subdue their lusts; nor as priest, to expiate offences; nor as prophet, to teach and instruct them; nor as a Saviour, to save them from their sins, or from wrath to come (*Matt.* 1:21; *1 Thess.* 1:10). They that have a perfect righteousness of their own, need not be indebted to Christ for his pure, perfect, spotless, matchless righteousness. Such as are without sin have no cause to repent of sin, nor yet to watch against sin. Such as are perfect cannot say, We are unprofitable servants.

But are they indeed just? Then they must live by faith (*Heb.* 2:1). Are they men, and not angels? Then they must repent, Acts 17:30, 'For now he commands men everywhere to repent.' Surely the best of men are but men at the best. Oh, how bad those men must be, who make God himself a liar (1 *John* 1:10). But if these men are absolutely perfect, how is it that they are afflicted and diseased as other men? How is it that they eat, and drink, and sleep, and buy, and sell, and die as other men? Are these things consistent with an absolute perfection? Surely not. An absolute perfection is not a step short of heaven; it is heaven on this side of heaven; and they that would obtain it must step to heaven before they have it. But,

2. *Secondly, I answer that this objection lies as strong against family prayer, and against all other kinds of prayer, as it does against closet prayer.*

He that shall upon any grounds make this objection a great bugbear to scare his soul from closet prayer, he may upon the same ground make it a great bugbear to scare his soul not only from all other kind of prayer, but from all other duties of religion also, whether private or public. The spirit of this objection fights against all religion at once; and therefore you should say to it, as Christ said to Peter, 'Get thee behind me, Satan.' But,

3. *Thirdly, I answer, It is not the infirmities and weaknesses of a Christian which are seen, lamented, bewailed, and resisted, that can obstruct or hinder the efficacy and success of his prayers.*[1]

Let me clear up this in a few instances. Jonah, you know, was a man full of sinful passions, and other weaknesses, etc., and yet his prayer was very prevalent with God (*Jon.* 2:1, 2, 7, 10, compared). So Elijah's prayers were exceeding prevalent with God; he could open and

---

[1] A spiritual infirmity is the sickness or indisposition of the soul, that arises from weakness of grace.

shut heaven at his pleasure; and yet subject to like passions as we are (*James* 3:17). Elijah was a man of extraordinary sanctity and holiness, a man that lived in heaven whilst he dwelt on earth; Enoch-like, he walked with God, and yet subject to like passions as we are (*1 Kings* 19:8; *Rom.* 11:2, 3). God did in an eminent way communicate to him his counsel and secrets; he lay in the bosom of the Father; and yet was a man subject to like passions as we are. He was a very powerful and prevalent prophet; his very name imports as much. In *1 Kings* 17:1, it is *Eli-jahu,* that is, 'the LORD is my strong God'; and yet subject to like passions as we are. He was a man much in fasting and prayer; he was an inferior mediator between God and his people; and yet subject to like passions as we are. Now because some from hence might object and say, No wonder if such a man as he was, could by his prayers open and shut heaven at his pleasure; but I am a poor, weak, low, sinful, and unworthy creature; I am full of infirmities, weaknesses, and passions; and shall my prayers ever find access to God, and acceptance with God, or gracious answers and returns from God?

Now to obviate this objection, and to remove this discouragement out of the thoughts and hearts of poor sinners, the Holy Ghost adds this clause, that he was not a god, nor an angel, but a man, and such a man as was not exempted from common infirmities; for he had his passions, frailties, and weaknesses as well as other saints; intimating to us, that infirmities in the meanest saints should no more prejudice the acceptance and success of their prayers with God, than they did in Elijah himself.

The word *passion* sometimes signifies, *first*, a motion of the sensual appetite, arising from the imagination of good or ill, with some commotion of the body; secondly, sometimes passions signify sinful infirmities, sinful perturbations of the mind; and thirdly, sometimes passion is taken more strictly for the especial affection of sinful anger and wrath, which Chrysostom calls *brevis daemon,* 'a short devil'. It makes a man speak he knows not what, as you may see in Jonah; and to do he knows not what, as you may see in Saul. Now in these two last senses Elijah was a man subject to like passions as we are, and yet a man so potent with God, that by private prayer he could do even what he pleased in the court of heaven.

In *1 Sam.* 21 you may read of David's round lies, and of his other failings, infirmities, and unseemly behaviour before Achish, king of Gath, for which, he was turned out of the kings presence, under the notion of a madman; and yet at that very time he prays, and prevails with God for favour, mercy, and deliverance: *Psa.* 34:4, 'I sought the LORD, and he heard me, and delivered me out of all my fear.' But when was this? Read the title of the Psalm, and you shall find it: 'A Psalm of David, when he changed his behaviour before Abimelech; who drove him away, and he departed.'

In *Num.* 20:10–12, Moses' infirmities are pointed out. (1.) You have there his immoderate anger. (2.) His speaking to the people when he should have spoken to the rock, verse 8. (3.) His smiting of it, when he should only have spoken to it with the rod in his hand; and smiting it twice, as in a pang of passion and impatience. (4.) His distrusting of the Lord's Word, verse 12. (5.) His reviling of the people, when he should have convinced them, 'Hear, ye rebels.' (6.) He seems to be so offended at his commission that he can hardly forbear murmuring: 'Must we bring water out of the rock?' Mark that word, 'Must *we*?'. Oh, how is the meekest man in all the world transported into passion, and anger, and unbelief, and hurried into sad indecencies (*Num.* 12:3)! And yet there was not a man on earth whose prayers were so powerful and prevalent with God as Moses' were (*Psa.* 106:23; *Exod.* 32:9–15; 33:11–17; 14:13–16).

King Asa was a man full of infirmities and weaknesses; he relies on the king of Syria, and not on the Lord (2 *Chron.* 16:7–13); he is very impatient, and under a great rage upon the seer's reproof. He imprisons the seer; he oppressed some of the people; or, as the Hebrew has it, 'he crushed', or he trampled upon some of the people at the same time; and being greatly diseased in his feet, he sought the physicians and not the Lord; and yet this man's prayer was wonderfully prevalent with the Lord.

The saints' infirmities can never make void those gracious promises by which God stands engaged to hearken to the prayers of his people (*Psa.* 50:15; *Isa.* 30:19; 65: 24). God's hearing of our prayers does not depend upon sanctification, but upon Christ's intercession; not upon what we are in ourselves, but upon what we are in the Lord Jesus; both our persons and our prayers are acceptable in the beloved (*Eph.* 1:6; *1 Pet.* 2:5). When God hears our prayers, it is neither for our own sakes nor yet for our prayers' sake, but it is for his own sake, and his Son's sake, and his glory's sake, and his promise's sake. Certainly God will never cast off his people for their infirmities.

First, It is the glory of a man to pass by infirmities (*Prov.* 19:11); Oh, how much more then, must it be the glory of God to pass by the infirmities of his people!

Secondly, Saints are children; and what father will cast off his children for their infirmities and weaknesses? (*Psa.* 103:13, 14; *1 Cor.* 12:27).

Thirdly, Saints are members of Christ's body; and what man will cut off a member because of a scab or wart that is upon it? 'What man will cut off his nose', said Luther, 'because there is some filth in it?'

Fourthly, Saints are Christ's purchase; they are his possession, his inheritance.[1] Now what man is there that will cast away, or cast off his purchase, his possession, his inheritance, because of thorns, bushes, or briars that grow upon it?

Fifthly, Saints are in a marriage-covenant with God (*Hos.* 2:19–20). Now what husband is there who will cast off his wife for her failings and infirmities? So long as a man is in covenant with God, his infirmities can't cut him off from God's mercy and grace. Now it is certain a man may have very many infirmities upon him, and yet not break his covenant with God, for no sin breaks a man's covenant with God but such as unties the marriage knot. As in other marriages, every offence or infirmity does not disannul the marriage union; it is only the breach of the marriage vow, viz. adultery, that unties the marriage knot;

[1] *Eph.* 1:22–23; *1 Cor.* 6:20; 7:23; *1 Pet.* 18–20.

THE SECRET KEY TO HEAVEN

so here it is only those sins which breaks the covenant
which unties the marriage knot between God and the
soul: (1.) When men freely subject themselves to any lust
as a new master; or (2.) When men take another husband;
and this men do, when they enter into a league with sin or
the world, when they make a new covenant with hell and
death (*Isa.* 28:15, 18). Now from these mischiefs God
secures his chosen ones. In a word, if God should cast off
his people for their infirmities, then none of the sons or
daughters of Adam could be saved: 'For there is not a just
man upon the earth that doeth good and sinneth not'
(*Eccles.* 7:20). Now if God will not cast off his people for
their infirmities, then certainly he will not cast off the
prayers of his people because of those invincible infirmities that hang upon them; and therefore our infirmities
should not discourage us, or take us off from closet
prayer, or from any other duties of religion. But,

4. *Fourthly,* I answer, *the more infirmities and weaknesses hang upon us, the more cause we have to keep
close and constant to our closet-duties.*[1]

If grace be weak, the omission of private prayer will
make it weaker. Look, as he that will not eat will certainly
grow weaker and weaker, so he that will not pray in his
closet will certainly grow weaker and weaker. If corruptions be strong, the neglect of private prayer will make
them stronger. The more the remedy is neglected, the
more the disease is strengthened. Whatsoever the distempers of a man's heart be, they will never be abated, but
augmented, by the omission of private prayer. The more

---

[1] The omission of a good diet breeds diseases.

bodily infirmities hang upon us, the more we have need of the physician; and so the more sinful infirmities hang upon our souls, the more need we have of private prayer. All sinful omissions will make work for repentance, for hell, or for the Physician of souls. Sinful omissions lead to sinful commissions, as you may see in the angels that fell from heaven to hell, and in Adam's Fall in paradise.

Origen going to comfort and encourage a martyr that was to be tormented was himself apprehended by the officers, and constrained either to offer to the idols, or to have his body abused by an executioner who was standing ready for that purpose; of which hard choice, to save his life, he bowed unto the idol; but afterwards, making a sad confession of his foul deed, he said, 'That he went forth that morning before he had been with God in his closet'; and so peremptorily concludes, 'that his neglect of prayer was the cause of his falling into that great sin'.

The neglect of one day, of one duty, of one hour, would undo us for ever, if we had not an Advocate with the Father (1 *John* 2:1, 2). Those years, those months, those weeks, those days, those hours that are not filled up with God, with Christ, with grace, with duty, will certainly be filled up with vanity and folly. All omissions of duty, will more and more unfit the soul for duty. A key thrown by gathers rust; a pump not used, will be hard to get going; and armour not used, will be hard to make bright, etc. Look, as sinful commissions will stab the soul, so sinful omissions will starve the soul. Such as live in the neglect of private prayer may well cry out, *Isa.* 24:16; *Job* 16:8, 'Our leanness, our leanness!' And therefore away with all these pleas and reasonings about infirmities, and weaknesses, and indispositions, and address yourselves to closet prayer. But,

5. *Fifthly,* I answer, *it may be your distemper and indisposition of body is not so great but that you can buy, and sell, and get gain.*[1]

Notwithstanding your aching head, and your shooting back, and your pained sides, and your feeble knees, yet you can, with Martha, burden yourself down with your worldly affairs. In *Song of Sol.* 5:3, Christ calls upon his spouse to open the door, and let him in. But, sin and shifting coming into the world together, see how poorly and unworthily she labours to shift Christ off: 'I have put off my coat; how shall I put it on? I have washed my feet; how shall I defile them?' Rather than she will make no excuse for herself, she will make a silly excuse, a worthless excuse. She was past a child; and what a great business had it been for her to have risen to have let in such a guest, that brings everything with him that heart can wish or need require (*Rev.* 3:17–18). She was not grown so decrepit with old age, but that she was able to make herself ready; at least, she might easily have slipped on her morning-coat and stepped to the door without any danger of taking cold, or of being wet to the skin, and so have let him in, who never comes empty handed (*Rev.* 22:12); yes, who was now come full of the dew of divine blessings to enrich her; for so some take those words, 'Mine head is filled with dew, and my locks with the

---

[1] The body itself, if you set too high a price upon it, will make a cheap soul; and he is the most unhappy man whose outside is his best side.

drops of the night.' Oh, the frivolous pretences, and idle excuses that even gracious persons are apt sometimes to take up to over-colour their neglect of duty!

But some may say, It may be the spouse of Christ was asleep. Oh, no! for she says, verse 2, 'I sleep, but my heart waketh.' She slept with open eyes, as the lion does; she slept but half-sleep; though her outward man was drowsy, yet her inward man was wakeful; though the flesh took a nap, yet her spirit did not nod.

Oh! but it may be Christ made no noise, he gave no notice that he was at the door! O yes! he knocked, he knocked and bounced by the hammer of his Word, and the hand of his Spirit; he knocked by outward corrections and inward admonitions; he knocked by providences, and he knocked by mercies. His importunity and vehemency for admission was very great.

Oh! but it may be he did but only knock, he should have called as well as knocked; for none but madmen would open their doors in the night, except they knew the voice of him who knocks. Oh, yes! he did not only knock, but called also.

Oh! but it may be she did not know his voice, and therefore she would not open. No chaste wife will at unseasonable hours arise and open her doors unto a stranger, especially in her husband's absence. Oh, yes, she knew his voice: verse 2, 'It is the voice of my beloved that knocketh.' She was not so fast asleep, but that she knew the voice of her beloved from all other voices, and could understand every little word that he said.' The calls of Christ were so strong, so loud, and his knockings so mighty, that she could not but know and confess, that it was the voice of her beloved, though she was not so respectful and dutiful as to obey that voice.

Oh! but it may be Christ knocked and called, like a friend in his journey, only to inquire how it was with her, or to speak to her at the window. Oh, no! he speaks plainly, he speaks with authority, 'Open to me.'

Oh! but it may be she had no power to open the door. Oh, yes; for when he commands his people to open, he lends them a key to open the door that he may enter in (*Phil.* 1:6, 2:13; *1 Cor.* 15:10). Infused grace is a living principle that will enable the soul to open to Christ. If a man be not a free agent to work and act by the helps of grace received, to what purpose are counsels, commands, exhortations and directions, given to perform this, and that, and the other work? And certainly it is our greatest honour and happiness in this world to co-operate with God in those things which concern his own glory, and our own internal and eternal good.

Oh! but it may be Christ had given his spouse some distaste, or it may be he had let fall some hard words, or some unkind speeches, which made her a little froward and pettish. Oh, no! for he owns her as his beloved, and courts her highly, with the most winning and amicable terms of love: 'My sister, my love, my dove, my undefiled, or my perfect one.' He calls her so for her dovelike simplicity, purity, and integrity. All these endearing and honouring titles, are the rhetoric of divine love; and should have been as so many sacred engagements upon her to open to her beloved.

Oh! but it may be Christ was too quick for her, it may be he gave but a knock and a call, and was gone before she could rise and open the door. O no! Christ stayed till his head was filled with dew, and his locks with the drops of the night; which most passionate expression notes the tender goodness, patience, and gentleness of our Lord Jesus, who endures far greater and harder things for his spouse's sake, than ever Jacob did for his Rachel's sake. After Christ had suffered much for her sake, and waited her leisure a long while, she very unkindly, and very unmannerly and unworthily turns her back upon all his sweet and comfortable compellations, and blessed and bleeding embracements, and turns him away to look for his lodging in some other place; so that he might well have said, Is this thy kindness to your friend, your husband, your Lord, to suffer him to stand bareheaded, and that in foul weather, yea, in the night time, wooing, entreating, and beseeching admittance; and yet to turn him away as one in whom your soul could take no pleasure?

Now, if you will but seriously weigh all these circumstances in the balance of the sanctuary, you clearly read the fault and folly, the weakness and madness, the slightness and laziness of the spouse; and by her you may make a judgment of those sad and sinful distempers that may seize upon the best of saints, and see how ready the flesh is to frame excuses; and all to keep the soul off from duty, and the doors fast bolted against the Lord Jesus.

It is sad when men are well enough to sit, and chat, and trade in their shops, but are not well enough to pray in their closets. Certainly, that man's heart is not right with

God, at least at this time, who, under all his physical weaknesses, can maintain and keep up his public trade with men, but is not well enough to maintain his private trade with heaven. Our bodies are but dirt, handsomely tempered, and artificially formed; we derive our pedigree from the dirt, and are akin to clay. One calls the body 'the blot of nature'; another calls it the 'the soul's beast', 'a sack of dung', 'worms' meat'; another calls it 'a prison, a sepulchre'; and Paul calls it 'a body of vileness'. Now for a man to make so much fuss about the weaknesses of his body to excuse the neglects of his soul, is an evil made up of many evils. But really, sir, I am so ill, and my body is so out of sorts and indisposed, that I am not able to mind or meddle with the least things of the world! Well! if this be so, then know that God has on purpose knocked you off from the things of this world, that you may look the more effectually after the things of another world.

The design of God in all the weaknesses that affect your body, is to wind you more off from your worldly trade, and to work you to follow your heavenly trade more closely. Many a man had never found the way to his closet, if God by bodily illnesses had not turned him out of his shop, his trade, his business, his all, etc.

Well, Christians! remember this once for all, if your indisposition to closet prayer really arises from bodily illnesses, then you may be confident that the Lord will pity you much, and bear with you much, and kindly accept of a little. You know how affectionately parents and ingenuous masters behave towards their children and servants, when they are ill and indisposed; and you may be confident that God will never carry it worse towards you than they do towards them. Ponder often upon *Ezek.* 34:4, 16, 21, 22. But,

6. *Sixthly,* and lastly, I shall answer this objection by way of distinction, thus:

First, There is a contracted indisposition to private prayer, and there is an involuntary indisposition to private prayer. There is a contracted indisposition, and that is when a man, by his wilful sinning against light, knowledge, conviction, etc., contracts that guilt that lies as a load upon his conscience. Now guilt makes the soul shy of God; and the greater the guilt is, the more shy the soul is of drawing near to God in a corner. The child that is sensibly under guilt hides himself, as Adam did, in the day from his father's eye, and at night he slips to bed, to avoid either a chiding or a whipping from his father (*Gen.* 3:7, 8). Guilt makes a man fly from God, and fly from prayer. It is a hard thing to look God in the face, when guilt stares a man in the face (*Job* 11:14, 15). Guilt makes a man a terror to himself (*Jer.* 20:3–4); now when a man is a terror to himself, he is neither fit to live, nor fit to die, nor fit to pray.

When poison gets into the body, it works upon the spirits, and it weakens the spirits, and it endangers life, and unfits and indisposes a man to all natural actions. It is so here; when guilt lies heavy upon the conscience, it works upon the soul, it weakens the soul, it endangers the soul, and it wonderfully unfits and indisposes the soul to all holy actions. Guilt fights against our souls, our consciences, our comforts, our duties, yes, and our very graces also (1 *Pet.* 2:11). There is nothing that wounds and lames our graces like guilt; there is nothing that weakens and wastes our graces like guilt; there is nothing that hinders the activity of our graces like guilt; and there is nothing that clouds our evidences of grace like guilt. Look, what water is to the fire, that our sinnings are to our graces, evidences, and duties.

Guilt is like Prometheus' vulture, that ever lies gnawing. It is better with Evagrius to lie on a bed of straw with a good conscience, than to lie on a bed of down with a guilty conscience. What the probationer-disciple said to our Saviour, *Matt.* 8:19 – 'Master, I will follow thee whithersoever thou goest' – that a guilty conscience says to the sinner, 'Wherever you go I will follow you.' If you go to a fast, I will follow you, and fill your mind with black and dismal apprehensions of God; if you go to a feast, I will follow you, and show you the handwriting on the wall (*Dan.* 5:5); if you go abroad, I will follow you, and make you afraid of every leaf that wags; you shall look upon every bush as an armed man, and upon every man as a devil; if you stay at home, I will follow you from room to room, and fill you with horror and terror; if you lie down to rest, I will follow you with fearful dreams and tormenting apparitions; if you go into your closet, I will follow you, and make your very closet a hell to hold you.

It is reported of King Richard III that, after he had murdered his two nephews in the Tower, guilt lay so hard upon his conscience, that his sleeps were very unquiet; for he would often leap out of his bed in the dark, and catching his sword, which hung by his bed-side, in his hand, he would go distractedly about his bedroom seeking for the traitor.

So Charles IX of France, after he had made the streets of Paris run down with the blood of the Protestants, he could seldom take any sound sleep, nor could he endure to be awakened out of his sleep without music.[1]

Judge Morgan, that passed the sentence of condemnation upon Jane Grey, a virtuous lady, shortly after fell mad, and in his raving cried out continually, 'Take away the Lady Jane from me, take away the Lady Jane from me', and in that horror ended his wretched life.

James Abyes, going to execution for Christ's sake, as he went along he gave his money and his clothes to one and another, till he had given all away to his shirt, whereupon one of the sheriff's men scoffed and derided him, and told him that he was a madman and an heretic, and not to be believed; but as soon as the good man was executed, this wretch was struck mad, and threw away his clothes, and cried out, 'James Abyes was a good man, and gone to heaven, but I am a wicked man, and am damned', and thus he continued crying out till his death. Certainly he that derides or smites a man for walking according to the Word of the Lord, the Lord will, first or last, so smite and wound that man's conscience, that all the physicians in the world shall not be able to heal it.

Now if your indisposition to private prayer springs from contracting guilt upon your conscience, then your best way is speedily to renew your repentance, and greatly

[1] See *Works of Richard Sibbes*, vol. 1. p. 149.

to judge and humble your own soul, and so to act faith afresh upon the blood of Christ, both for pardoning mercy and for purging grace. When a man is stung with guilt, it is his highest wisdom in the world to look up to the brazen serpent, and not to spend his time or create torments to his own soul by perpetual poring over his guilt. When guilt upon the conscience works a man to water the earth with tears, and to make heaven ring with his groans, then it works kindly. When the sense of guilt drives a man to God, to duty, to the throne of grace, then the darkness will not be long with that man. He that thinks to shift off private prayer under the pretence of guilt, does but in that increase his own guilt. Neglect of duty will never get guilt off the conscience.

But then there is an *involuntary* indisposition to private prayer; as in a sick man, who would work and walk, but cannot, being hindered by his disease; or as it is with a man who has a great chain on his leg, he would very gladly walk or get away, but his chain hinders him. Now if your indisposition to private prayer be an involuntary indisposition, then God will in mercy, in course, both pardon it and remove it.

Secondly, there is a total indisposition to private prayer, and there is a partial indisposition to private prayer.

A total indisposition to private prayer is, when a man has no mind at all to private prayer, and no will at all to private prayer, and no love at all to private prayer, and no delight, or any heart at all to private prayer (*Jer.* 4:22; 44:17–19). Now where this frame of heart is, there all is nothing, very nothing, stark nothing. A partial indispos-

ition to private prayer is when a man has some will to private prayer, though not such a will as once he had; and
some mind to private prayer, though not such a mind as
once he had; and some affections to private prayer,
though not such warm and burning affections as once he
had. Now if your indisposition to private prayer be total,
then you must wait upon the Lord in all his appointments
for a changed nature, and for union with Christ; but if
your indisposition to private prayer be only partial, then
the Lord will certainly pardon it, and in the very use of
holy means in time remove it. But,

Thirdly, and lastly, *there is a transient, accidental, occasional, or fleeting indisposition to private prayer; and there
is a customary, a constant, or permanent indisposition to
private prayer.*

Now a transient, accidental, occasional, or fleeting indisposition to that which is good may be found upon the
best of saints, as you may see in Moses (*Exod.* 4:10–14);
and in Jeremiah (*Jer.* 1:5–8, 17–19; 20:9); and in Jonah
(*Jon.* 1); and in David (*Psa.* 39:2, 3). Now if this be the
indisposition that you are under, then you may be confident that it will certainly work off by degrees, as theirs
did that I have last cited (*Isa.* 65:2).

But then there is a customary, a constant or permanent
indisposition to private prayer, and to all other holy
duties of religion. Now if this be the indisposition that
you are under, then I may safely conclude that you are in
the very gall of bitterness and in the bond of iniquity
(*Acts* 8:21–23), and your work lies not in complaining of
your indisposition, but in repenting and believing, and in

labouring for a change of your heart and state; for till your heart, your state, be changed, you will remain for ever indisposed both to closet prayer and to all other duties of religion and godliness. To see a sinner sailing towards hell with wind and tide on his side alter his course, and tack about for heaven, to see the earthly man become heavenly, the carnal man become spiritual, the proud man become humble, the vain man become serious, to see a sinner move contrary to himself in the ways of Christ and holiness, is as strange as to see the earth fly upward, or the bowling ball run contrary to its own bias; and yet a divine power of God upon the soul can effect it; and this must be effected before the sinner will be graciously inclined and sincerely disposed to closet prayer.

And let thus much suffice by way of answer to this objection also.

PART 5

ELEVEN INSTRUCTIONS
CONCERNING PRIVATE PRAYER

Now, FOR THE BETTER MANAGEMENT of this great duty of closet prayer, I urge you take my advice and counsel in these eleven following particulars.

1. *First, be frequent in closet prayer, and not now and then only.* He will never have a yearning for closet prayer who is not frequent in closet prayer. Now, that this counsel may stick, consider,

i. *First, other eminent servants of the Lord have been frequent in this blessed work: Neh.* 1:6, 'Let thine ear now be attentive, and thine eyes open, that thou mayest hear the prayer of thy servant, which I pray before thee, day and night.' So Daniel kneeled upon his knees three times a day and prayed and gave thanks before his God as he always did (*Dan.* 6:10). So David, 'My voice shalt thou hear in the morning, and in the evening will I direct my prayer unto thee, and will look up' (*Psa.* 5:3). So *Psa.* 88:13, 'But unto thee have I cried, O Lord; and in the morning shall my prayer prevent thee.' So *Psa.* 119:147, 'I prevented the dawning of the morning, and cried unto the Lord.' So *Psa.* 55:17, 'Evening, and morning, and at noon, will I pray and cry aloud.' Yes, he was *vir orationis* [a man of prayer] for his frequency in it. *Psa.* 109:4, 'For my love they are my adversaries: but I give myself unto prayer'; or, as the Hebrew may be read, 'But I am a man of prayer.' Of Carolus Magnus [Charlemagne] it was said, *Carolus plus cum Deo quam hominibus loquitur,* that he spoke more with God than with men.

ii. *Secondly, consider the blessed Scripture not only enjoins this duty, but requires frequency in it also* (*Luke* 18:1; *1 Thess.* 5:17; *Col.* 4:2). In the former part of this discourse, I have given light into these Scriptures ; and therefore the bare citing of them must now suffice.

iii. *Thirdly, Christ was frequent in private prayer, as you may easily see by comparing these Scriptures together, Mark* 1:35; *Matt.* 14:23; *Luke* 22:39; *John* 18:2. In my second argument for private prayer you may see these Scriptures opened and amplified. But,

iv. *Fourthly, consider that you have the examples of the very worst of men in this case.* Papists are frequent in their private devotions. And the Muslims, whatever occasion they have, either by profit or pleasure, to divert them, will yet pray five times every day. Yes, the very heathens sacrificed to Hercules morning and evening upon the great altar at Rome. Now, shall blind nature do more than grace? But,

v. *Fifthly, consider you cannot have too frequent communion with God, you cannot have too frequent conversation with Jesus, you cannot have your hearts too frequently filled with joy unspeakable and full of glory, and with that peace that passes understanding, you cannot have heaven too frequently brought down into your hearts, and you cannot have your hearts too frequently carried up to heaven;* and therefore you cannot be too frequent in closet prayer. But,

vi. *Sixthly, consider that you are under frequent needs, and frequent sins, and frequent snares, and frequent temptations, and frequent allurements, and frequent trials, and frequent cares, and frequent fears, and frequent favours (1 Pet. 5:8; Job 1:7);* and therefore you had need be frequent with God in your closets. But,

vii. *Seventhly, consider you are the favourites of heaven, you are greatly beloved, you are highly honoured, you are exceedingly esteemed and valued in the court of the Most High;* and remember, that the petitions of many weak Christians, and of many benighted Christians, and of many tempted Christians, and of many clouded Christians, and of many staggering Christians, and of many doubting Christians, and of many bewildered Christians, and of many fainting Christians, etc., are put into your hands, for a quick and speedy despatch to the throne of grace; so that you had need be frequent in your closets, and improve your interest in heaven, or else many of these poor hearts may be wronged, betrayed, and prejudiced by your neglect.

Such as are favourites in princes' courts, if they are active, diligent, careful, and watchful for others, they may come as often as they please into their prince's presence, and with Queen Esther have for asking what they please, both for themselves and others (*Est.* 7). Oh, what a world of good may such do for others that are God's favourites, if they would be but frequent with God in their closets! O sirs! if you have not that love, that regard, that pity, that compassion to your own souls, as you should have, yet, let not others suffer by your neglect of private prayer! Oh, let not Zion suffer! Oh, let not any particular saint suffer by your being found seldom in your closets.

Certainly, it might have gone better with the churches of Christ, and with the concerns of Christ, and with many of the poor people of Christ, if most Christians had been more frequent with God in their closets. But,

viii. *Eighthly and lastly, consider that this liberty to approach near to God in your closets, cost Christ his dearest blood (Eph. 2:13; Heb. 10:20).* Now, he that is not frequent with God in his closet reveals that he sets no great value upon that liberty that Christ has purchased with his blood. The incomparable, the unparalleled price which Christ has paid down upon the nail, above sixteen hundred years ago, that we might have liberty and free access to his Father in our closets, argues very strongly, yes, irrefragably, the superlative excellency of that liberty (*1 Pet.* 1:19). Oh, therefore, let us improve to purpose this blessed purchase of our Lord Jesus by being frequent with God in our closets. It is disputed by some whether one drop of Christ's blood was sufficient for the pardon of our sins and redemption of our souls.[1] My intention is not to dispute, but to offer a few things to your consideration.

First, It must be granted, that by reason of the hypo-statical union, a drop of Christ's blood was of an

---

[1] One little drop of Christ's blood is worth more than heaven and earth – *Luther.*

inestimable worth and excellency; and the value of his passion is to be measured by the dignity of his Person. But,

Secondly, a proportion was to be observed between the punishment due to men, and that which was suffered for man; that his sufferings might be satisfactory, two things were necessary, *Poenae gravitas,* as well as *personae dignitas.*[1] That the least drop of Christ's blood was not sufficient for the redemption of our souls may thus appear:

First, If it were, then the circumcision of Christ was enough, for there was a drop, if not many drops of blood shed.

Secondly, Then his being crowned with a crown of thorns, was sufficient; for it is most probable that they drew blood from him.

Thirdly, Then all Christ's sufferings besides were superfluous and vain.

Fourthly, Then God was unjust and unrighteous to take more than was due to his justice. But for any man to affirm that God has taken beyond what was his just due, is high blasphemy.

Fifthly, Then Christ was weak and imprudent to pay more than he needed; for what need was there of his dearest heart blood, if a drop from his hand would have saved our souls? Let schoolmen imagine what they please, it is certain that not one dram of that bitter cup from which Christ drunk could be abated, in order to his Father's full

[1] [Gravity of penalty, as well as dignity of person.] What is the blood of a grape, or the blood of a son, an only son, to the blood of a Saviour?

THE SECRET KEY TO HEAVEN

satisfaction, and man's eternal redemption. Christ has given under his own hand that it was necessary that he should suffer many things (*Luke* 24:26). O sirs! shall Christ shed not only a few drops of blood, but his very heart blood, to purchase you a freedom and liberty to be as often in your closets with his Father as you please; and will you only now and then give God a visit in private? The Lord forbid.

2. My second advice and counsel is this, *Take the fittest seasons and opportunities that you possibly can for closet* prayer. Many take unfit seasons for private prayer, which more obstruct the importunity of the soul in prayer than all the suggestions and instigations of Satan. As,

First, When the body is drowsy and sleepy; this is a very unfit season for closet prayer (*Song of Sol.* 3:1). Take heed of laying cushions of sloth under your knees, or pillows of idleness under your elbows, or of mixing nods with your petitions, or of being drowsily devoted when you draw near to God in your closets.

Secondly, When a man's head and heart is filled with worldly cares and distractions; this is a very unfit season for closet prayer (*1 Cor.* 7:35; *Ezek.* 33:31). When Dinah feels the need to be out and about to see the latest fashions, Shechem, prince of that country, meets with her, and forces himself upon her and rapes her. So when our hearts, Dinah-like, feel the need to be roving and gadding abroad after the things of the world, then Satan, the prince of the air, usually seizes upon us, commits a rape upon our souls, and either leads us off from prayer, or else he so distracts us from prayer, that it were better not to have prayed at all, than to have offered the sacrifice of foolish and distracted prayer.

I have read a story, how that one offered to give his horse to his fellow, upon condition he would but say the Lord's prayer, and think upon nothing but God; the offer was accepted, and he began, '"Our Father which art in heaven, hallowed be thy name." But I must have the bridle too', he said. 'No, nor the horse neither', said the other, 'for you have lost both already.' The application is easy.

Certainly, the most free and lively season for closet prayer is the mornings, before a man's spirit be blunted or cooled, deadened, damped, or flattened by worldly businesses. A man should speak with God in his closet, before he speaks with his worldly affairs and occasions. A man should say to all his worldly business, as Abraham said unto his young men, when he went to offer up his only Isaac, 'Abide you here . . . and I will go yonder and worship, and come again to you.' He that will attend to closet prayer without distraction or disturbance, must not, first, slip out of the world into his closet, but he must first slip into his closet before he be encompassed about with a crowd of worldly employments.

It was a precept of Pythagoras, that when we enter into the temple to worship God, we must not so much as speak or think of any worldly business, lest we make God's service an idle, perfunctory, and lazy recreation. The same I must say of closet prayer. Jerome complains very much of his distractions, dullness, and indisposition to prayer, and chides himself thus, 'What! do you think that Jonah prayed like this when he was in the fish's belly; or Daniel when he was among the lions; or the thief when he was upon the cross?'

Thirdly, When men or women are under rash and passionate distempers (*1 Tim.* 2:8); for when passions are up, holy affections are down, and this is a very unfit season for closet prayer; for such prayers will never reach God's ear which do not first warm our own hearts. In the Muscovy churches, if the minister makes a mistake in reading, or stammers in pronouncing his words, or speaks any word that is not well heard, the hearers blame him very much, and are ready to take the book from him, as one who is unworthy to read from it. And certainly God is no less offended with the giddy, rash, passionate, precipitate, and inconsiderate prayers of those who, without a deliberate understanding, do send their petitions to heaven in post-haste. Solomon's advice is worthy of all commendation and acceptation: 'Be not rash with thy mouth, and let not thy heart be hasty, to utter any thing before God' (*Eccles.* 5:2); or as the Hebrew may be read, 'Let not your heart through haste be so troubled or disturbed, as to tumble over, and throw out words without wisdom or premeditation.' Good men are apt many times to be too hasty, rash, and unadvised in their prayers, complaints, and deprecations. Witness David, Job, Jeremiah, Jonah, and the disciples.[1] A Christian will wisely and seriously weigh up his prayers and praises before he pours out his soul before the Lord. He never repents of his requests, who first duly deliberates what to request; but

---

[1] *Psa.* 31:2–3; *Psa* 116:11; *Job.* 10:1–3; *Jer.* 18:15, 18; *Jon.* 4:2–4; *Matt.* 20:20–21.

he that blurts out whatever lies uppermost, and that brings into the presence of God his rash, raw, tumultuous, and indigested petitions, confessions, complaints, etc., he but provokes God, he but brawls with God, instead of praying to him or wrestling with him. Those who bring their grievances to court observe their fittest times and seasons for pleading; they commonly take that very nick of time, when they have the king in a good mood, and so seldom or never come off without good success.

Sometimes God strongly inclines the heart to closet prayer; sometimes he brings the heart beforehand into a praying frame; sometimes both body and soul are more enlivened, quickened, raised, and divinely inflamed than at other times; sometimes conscience is more stirring, working, and tender, etc. Oh, now, strike while the iron is hot! Oh, now, lay hold on all such blessed opportunities, by applying yourself to private prayer. O sirs! can you take your fittest times, seasons, and opportunities for ploughing, and sowing, and reaping, and buying and selling, and eating, and drinking, and marrying, etc. And can you not as well take your fittest times and seasons to seek the Lord in your closets? Must the best God be put off with the least and worst of your time? The Lord forbid. Neglect not the seasons of grace, do not let slip your opportunities for closet prayer; thousands have lost their seasons and their souls together.

3. My third advice and counsel is this, *Be extremely careful that you do not perform closet duties merely to still your consciences.*

You must perform them out of conscience, but you must not perform them only to quiet conscience. Some have such a light set up in their understandings that they cannot omit closet prayer, but conscience is upon their backs, conscience is still upbraiding and disquieting them, and therefore they are afraid to neglect closet prayer, lest conscience should question, arraign, and condemn them for their neglects.[1] Sometimes when men have greatly sinned against the Lord, conscience becomes impatient, and is still accusing, condemning, and terrifying them; and now in these agonies they run to their closets, and cry, and pray, and mourn, and confess, and bitterly bewail their transgressions, but all this is only to quiet their consciences; and sometimes they find upon their performance of closet-duties, that their consciences are a little allayed and quieted; and for this very end and purpose do they take up closet prayer as a charm to allay their consciences; and when the storm is over, and their consciences quieted, then they lay aside closet prayer – as the monk did the net when the fish was caught – and are ready to transgress again.

O sirs! take heed of this, for this is but plain hypocrisy, and will be bitterness in the end. He that performs closet prayer only to bribe his conscience that it may not be clamorous, or to stop the mouth of conscience that it may not accuse him for sin, will at length venture upon such a trade, such a course of sinning against conscience, as will certainly turn his troubled conscience into a seared

[1] An ill conscience, says Augustine, is like a scolding wife; a man, he says, who has an ill conscience, cares not to be at home, he cares not to look into his own soul, but loves to be abroad.

conscience (2 *Tim.* 4:2); and a seared conscience is like a sleepy lion, when he awakes he roars, and tears his prey in pieces; and so will a seared conscience, when it is awakened, roar and tear the secure sinner in pieces.

When Dionysius' conscience was awakened, he was so troubled with fear and horror of conscience that, not daring to trust his best friends with a razor, he used to singe his beard with burning coals, as Cicero reports. All the mercy that a seared, a benumbed conscience affords the sinner, when it most befriends him, when it deals most seemingly kind with him, is this, that it will not cut, that it may kill; it will not convince, that it may confound; it will not accuse, that it may condemn; it will spare the sinner a while, that it may torment him for ever; it will spare him here, that it may gnaw him hereafter; it will not strike till it be too late for the sinner to ward off the blow.

Oh, cruel mercy, to observe the sin, and let alone the sinner till the gates of mercy be shut upon him, and hell stands gaping to devour him: *Gen.* 4:7, 'Sin lieth at the door.' The Hebrew word, *robets* signifies *to lie down, or couch,* like some wild beast at the mouth of his cave, as if he were asleep, but indeed watching and waking, and ready to fly at all that come near it. O sirs! sin is rather *couchant* [lying down] than *dormant* [sleeping]; it sleeps dog's sleep, that it may take the sinner at the greater advantage, and fly the more furiously in his face. But,

4. My fourth advice and counsel is this, *Take heed of resting upon closet duties, take heed of trusting in closet duties.*

Noah's dove made use of her wings, but she did not trust in her wings, but in the ark; so you must make use of closet-duties, but you must not trust in your closet-duties, but in Jesus, of whom the ark was but a type. There are many that go a round of duties, as mill horses turning a mill, and rest upon them when they have done, using the means as mediators, and so fall short of Christ and heaven at once. Closet-duties, rested in, will as eternally undo a man as the greatest and foulest enormities; open wickedness slays her thousands, but a secret resting upon duties slays her ten thousands. Multitudes bleed inwardly of this disease, and die for ever. Open profaneness is the broad dirty way that leads to hell, but closet-duties rested in is a sure way, though a cleaner way, to hell. Profane persons and formal, professing Christians shall meet at last in one hell. Ah, Christians! do not make duties your money, lest you and your money perish together.

The phoenix gathers sweet odoriferous sticks in Arabia together, and then blows them with her wings and burns herself with them; so do many shining professing Christians burn themselves by resting in their duties and services. You know, in Noah's flood all that were not in the ark, though they climbed up the tallest trees, and the highest mountains and hills, yet were really drowned; so let men climb up to this duty and that, yet, if they don't get into Christ, they will be really damned. It is not your closet, but your Christ that must save you. If a man has no share in Christ, he may perish with 'Our Father' in his mouth. It is as natural to a man to rest in his duties as it is for him to rest in his bed.

This was Bernard's temptation, who, being a little assisted in duty, could stroke his own head with *bene fecisti Bernarde* [well done, Bernard], this was gallantly done, now cheer up yourself. Ah, how apt is man, when he has been a little assisted, heated, melted, enlarged, etc., in a way of duty, to go away and stroke himself, and bless himself, and hug himself, and warm himself with the sparks, with the fire of his own kindling (*Isa.* 50:11).

Adam was to win life and wear it; he was to be saved by his doings: 'Do this and live.' Hence it is that all his posterity are so prone to seek for salvation by doing: *Acts* 2:37; 16:30, 'What shall we do to be saved?' and 'Good Master, what shall I do that I may inherit eternal life?' (*Mark* 10:17, 20). Like father, like son. But if our own duties or doings were sufficient to save us, to what purpose did Christ leave his Father's bosom, and lay down his precious life? etc. Closet-duties rested in may pacify conscience for a time, but this will not always hold. 'When Ephraim saw his sickness, and Judah saw his wound, then went Ephraim to the Assyrian, and sent to king Jareb; yet could they not heal him, nor cure him of his wound' (*Hos.* 5:13). If we rest on closet-duties, or on anything else on this side of Christ, we shall find them as weak as the Assyrian, or as Jareb; we shall find to our cost that they cannot help us nor heal us; they cannot comfort us nor cure us of our wounds.

As creatures, so duties, were never true to any that have trusted in them. When the Israelites were in great distress the Lord bids them go and cry unto the gods which they had chosen, and let them deliver you, says God, in the time of your tribulation (*Judges* 10:14). O sirs! if, when you are under distress of conscience, or lying upon a dying bed, God should say to you, Go to your closet prayers and performances, that you have made and rested in, go to your closet tears that you have shed and rested in, and let them save you and deliver you; oh, what miserable saviours and comforters would they be for you! Look, what the ark of God was to the Philistines (*1 Sam.* 5), that closet-duties are to Satan; he trembles every time he sees a poor sinner go into his closet and come out of his closet, resting, and glorying in Jesus, and not in his duties; but when he sees a poor creature confide in his closet-duties, and rest upon his closet-duties, then he rejoices, then he claps his hands and sings, Aha! so would I have it.

Oh, rest not on anything on this side of Jesus Christ; say to your graces, say to your duties, say to your holiness, You are not my saviour, you are not my mediator; and therefore you are not to be trusted in, you are not to be rested in. It is my duty to perform closet-duties, but it is my sin to rely upon them, or to put confidence in them; do them I must, but glory in them I must not. He that rests in his closet-duties, makes a saviour of his closet-duties. Let all your closet-duties lead you to Jesus, and leave you more in communion with him, and in dependence upon him; and then thrice happy will you be (*Heb.* 7:25). Let all your closet prayers and tears, your closet fastings and meltings, be a star to guide you to Jesus, a Jacob's ladder by which you may ascend into the arms of eternal love; and then you are safe for ever.

Ah ! it is sad to think, how most men have forgotten their resting place, as the Lord complains: *Jer.* 50:6, 'My people have been like lost sheep, their shepherds have caused them to go astray, and have turned them away to the mountains; they have gone from mountain to hill and forgotten their resting-place.' Ah! how many poor souls are there, that wander from mountain to hill, from one duty to another, and here they will rest, and there they will rest, and all on this side their resting place! O sirs! it is God himself that is your resting-place; it is his free grace, it is his singular mercy, it is his infinite love that is your resting place; it is the arms of Christ, the favour of Christ, the satisfaction of Christ, and the pure, perfect, spotless, matchless, and glorious righteousness of Christ, that is your resting-place; and therefore say to all your closet duties and performances, Farewell; prayer, farewell; reading, farewell; fasting, farewell; tears, farewell; sighs and groans, farewell; meltings and humblings, I will never trust more to you, I will never rest more on you; but I will now return to my resting-place, I will now rest only in God and Christ, I will now rest wholly in God and Christ, I will now rest for ever in God and Christ.

It was the saying of a precious saint, that 'he was more afraid of his duties than of his sins; for the one made him often proud, the other made him always humble'. But,

5. My fifth advice and counsel is this, *Work hard to put your hearts into all your closet prayers and performances.*

Look that your tongues and your hearts keep time and tune. *Psa.* 17:1, 'Give ear unto my prayer, that goeth not out of feigned lips', or, as it is in the Hebrew, 'without lips of deceit'. Heart and tongue must go together; word and work, lip and life, prayer and practice, must echo one to another, or else your prayers and your soul will be lost together. The labour of the lips and the travail of the heart must go together.

The Egyptians of all fruits made choice of the peach to consecrate to their goddess, and for no other cause, but that its fruit is like to one's heart, and the leaf to one's tongue. These very heathens in the worship of their gods thought it necessary that men's hearts and tongues should go together. Ah, Christians! when in your closet duties your hearts and your tongues go together, then you make that sweet and delightful melody that is most taking and pleasing to the King of kings. The very soul of prayer lies in the pouring out of the soul before God (*1 Sam.* 1:15); *Psa.* 42:4, 'When I remember these things I pour out my soul in me.'

So the Israelites poured out their souls like water before the Lord. So the church: 'The desire of our soul is to thy name, and to the remembrance of thee. With my soul have I desired thee in the night, yea, with my spirit within me will I seek thee early' (*Isa.* 26:8,9).So *Lam.* 3:41, 'Let us lift up our heart with our hands unto God in the heavens.' So *Heb.* 10:22, 'Let us draw near with a true heart', etc. So *Rom.* 1:9, 'For God is my witness, whom I serve in the spirit.' *1 Cor.* 14:15, 'I will pray with the spirit, and sing with the spirit.' *Phil.* 3:3, 'We are the circumcision which worship God in the spirit.' Under the law the inward parts were only to be offered to God in sacrifice; the skin belonged to the priests. From which we may easily gather, that truth in the inward parts, is that which is most pleasing in a sacrifice. When the Athenians would know of the oracle the cause of their often unprosperous success in battle against the Lacedaemonians, seeing they offered the choicest things they could get, in sacrifice to the gods, which their enemies did not, the oracle gave them this answer, that 'the gods were better pleased with their inward supplication without ambition, than with all their outward pomp in costly sacrifices'. Ah, sirs! the reason why so many are so unsuccessful in their closet-duties and services is because there is no more of their hearts in them. No man can make sure work or happy work in prayer but he that makes heart-work of it. When a man's heart is in prayers, then great and sweet will be his returns from heaven. That is no prayer in which the heart of the person bears no part. When the soul is separated from the body the man is dead; and so when the heart is separated from the lips in prayer, the prayer is dead.

The Jews at this day write upon the walls of their synagogues these words, *Tophillah belo cavannah ceguph belo neshamah;* that is, a prayer without the heart, or without the intention of the affection, is like a body without a soul.

In the law of Moses the priest was commanded to wash the inwards and the feet of the sacrifices in water; and this was done, says Philo, 'not without a mystery, to teach us to keep our hearts and affections clean when we draw near to God'. In all your closet-duties God looks first and most to your hearts: 'My son, give me thy heart' (*Prov.*

26). It is not a piece, it is not a corner of the heart, that will satisfy the Maker of the heart; the heart is a treasure, a bed of spices, a royal throne in which he delights. God looks not at the elegancy of your prayers, to see how neat they are; nor yet at the geometry of your prayers, to see how long they are; nor yet at the arithmetic of your prayers, to see how many they are; nor yet at the music of your prayers, nor yet at the sweetness of your voice, nor yet at the logic of your prayers; but at the sincerity of your prayers, how hearty they are.

There is no prayer acknowledged, approved, accepted, recorded, or rewarded by God, but that in which the heart is sincerely and wholly engaged. The true mother would not have the child divided. As God loves a broken and a contrite heart, so he loathes a divided heart (*Psa.* 51:17; *James* 1:8). God neither loves halting nor halving; he will be loved truly and totally. The royal law is, 'Thou shalt love and serve the LORD thy God, with all thy heart, and with all thy soul.'

Among the heathens, when the beasts were cut up for sacrifice, the first thing the priest looked on was the heart, and if the heart was naught, the sacrifice was rejected. Verily, God rejects all those services and sacrifices, in which the heart is not, as you may see by comparing the Scriptures below together.[1] Prayer without the heart is but as sounding brass or a tinkling cymbal. Prayer is only lovely and weighty as the heart is in it, and not otherwise. It is not the lifting up of the voice, nor the wringing of the

---

[1] *Prov.* 21:27; *Isa.* 1:11–12; 29:13; *Matt.* 15:7–9; *Ezek.* 33:30–32; *Zech.* 7:4–6; 2 *Chron.* 25:1–2; *Psa.* 78:36–37.

hands, nor the beating of the breast, nor an affected tone, nor studied motions, nor seraphical expressions, but the stirrings of the heart, that God looks at in prayer. God hears no more than the heart speaks. If the heart be dumb, God will certainly be deaf. No prayer is acceptable to God but that which is the travail of the heart.

The same day Julius Caesar came to the imperial dignity, sitting in his golden chair he offered a beast in sacrifice to the gods; but when the beast was opened, it was without a heart, which the soothsayers looked upon as an ill omen. It is a sad omen, that you will rather provoke the Lord than prevail with him, who are habitually heartless in your closet duties. Of the heart, God seems to say to us, as Joseph did to his brethren, concerning Benjamin, 'Ye shall not see my face without it.' It was the saying of blessed John Bradford, that, 'he would never leave a duty, till he had brought his heart into the frame of the duty; he would not leave confession of sin, till his heart was broken for sin; he would not leave petitioning for grace, till his heart was quickened and enlivened in a hopeful expectation of more grace; he would not leave thanksgiving, till his heart was enlarged with the sense of the mercies he enjoyed, and quickened in the return of praise.'

6. My sixth advice and counsel is this, *Be fervent, be warm, be importunate with God in all your closet duties and performances.*

James 5:16, 'The effectual fervent prayer of a righteous man availeth much'; or, as the Greek has it, 'The working prayer [ενεργουμενη]'; that is, such working prayer as sets the whole man to work, as sets all the faculties of the soul, and all the graces in the soul, to work. The word signifies such a working as shows the liveliest activity that can be. Certainly, all those usual phrases of crying, wrestling, and striving with God, which are scattered up and down in Scripture, do strongly argue that holy importunity and sacred violence that the saints of old have expressed in their addresses to God.[1]

Fervency feathers the wings of prayer, and makes them fly the swifter to heaven. An arrow, if it be drawn up but a little way, flies not far; but if it be drawn up to the head, it will fly far, and pierce deeply: so fervent prayer flies as high as heaven, and will certainly bring down blessings from thence.[2] Cold prayers speak of a denial, but fervent prayers offer a sacred violence both to heaven and earth. Look, as in a painted fire there is no heat, so in a cold prayer there is no heat, no warmth, no omnipotency, no devotion, no blessing. Cold prayers are like arrows without heads, as swords without edges, as birds without wings: they pierce not, they cut not, they fly not up to heaven. Such prayers as have no heavenly fire in them, do always freeze before they reach as high as heaven. But fervent prayer is very prevalent with God: *Acts* 12:5, 'Peter, therefore, was kept in prison, but prayer was made without ceasing.' The Greek word εκτενης signifies instant

---

[1] *Psa.* 55:1; 61:1; 64:1; 88:1, 13; 119:164; *Jon.* 2:1–2; *Joel* 2:13; *Psa.* 119:145, 147; 119:20.

[2] *Qui timide rogat, docet negare* [he who asks timidly courts a refusal], says the philosopher.

prayer, earnest prayer, stretched out prayer; prayer stretched out upon the rack, as it were. These gracious souls did in prayer strain and stretch themselves, as men do that are running in a race; they prayed with all the strength of their souls, and with all the fervency of their spirits; and accordingly they carried the day with God, as you may see in the following verses.

So *Acts* 26:7, 'Unto which promise, our twelve tribes instantly serving God day and night', or rather as the Greek has it, εν εκτενεια, 'in a stretched out manner, serving God day and night'. These twelve tribes, or the godly Jews of the twelve tribes of Israel, stretched out their hearts, their affections, their graces, to the utmost in prayer. In all your private retirements, do as the twelve tribes did. *Rom.* 12:11, 'Fervent in spirit, serving the Lord.' The Greek word ζεοντες, signifies *seething hot.* God loves to see his people zealous and warm in his service. Without fervency of spirit, no service finds acceptance in heaven. God is a pure act, and he loves that his people should be lively and active in his service; verse 12, 'Continuing instant in prayer'; 'continuing with all your might in prayer'. It is a metaphor from hunting dogs, that will never give over the game till they have got it.

Rom. 15:30, 'That ye strive together with me, in your prayers to God for me'; συναγωνισασθαι, strive mightily, strive as champions strive, even to an agony, as the word imports. It is a military word, and notes such fervent wrestling or striving, as is for life and death. *Col.* 4:12, 'Always labouring fervently for you in prayer.' The Greek word that is here used, signifies to strive or wrestle, as those do that strive for mastery; it notes the vehemency and fervour of Epaphras' prayers for the Colossians. Look, as the wrestlers do bend, and writhe, and stretch, and strain every joint of their bodies, that they may be victorious, so Epaphras did bend, and writhe, and stretch, and strain every joint of his soul – if I may so speak – that he might be victorious with God on the Colossians' account. So, when Jacob was with God alone, ah how earnest and fervent was he in his wrestlings with God (*Gen.* 32:24–27; *Hos.* 12:4, 5). He wrestles and weeps, and weeps and wrestles; he tugs hard with God, he keeps his hold, and he will not let God go till, as a prince, he has prevailed with him.

Fervent prayer is the soul's contention, the soul struggling with God; it is a sweating work, it is the sweat and blood of the soul, it is a laying out to the uttermost all the strength and powers of the soul. He that would gain victory over God in private prayer, must strain every muscle of his heart; he must, in beseeching God, besiege him, and so get the better of him; he must be like importunate beggars that will not be put off with frowns, or silence, or sad answers. Those that would be masters of their requests, must, like the importunate widow, press God so far as to put him to an holy blush, as I may say with reverence: they must with an holy impudence, as Basil speaks, make God ashamed to look them in the face, if he should deny the importunity of their souls.

Had Abraham had a little more of this impudence, says one, when he made suit for Sodom, it might have done well. Abraham brought down the price to ten righteous, and there his modesty stayed him; had he gone lower, God only knows what might have been done, for 'God went not away', says the text, 'till he had left communing with Abraham', that is, till Abraham had no more to say to God. Abraham left over asking, before God left over granting; he left over praying, before God ceased abating; and so Sodom was lost.

Oh, the heavenly fire, the holy fervency that was in Daniel's closet prayer! 'O Lord, hear; O Lord, forgive; O Lord, hearken and do, defer not for thine own sake' (*Dan.* 9:19). Look, as there be two kinds of antidotes against poison, viz., hot and cold, so there are two kinds of antidotes against all the troubles of this life, viz., fervent prayers and holy patience: the one hot, the other cold; the one quickening, and the other quenching, and holy Daniel made use of them both. Fervency is to prayer as the fire was to the spices in the censer, or as wings to the bird, or as oil to the wheels; and this Daniel found by experience.

God looks not for any James with horny knees, through assiduity of prayer; nor for any Bartholomew with a century of prayers for the morning, and as many for the evening; but for fervency of spirit in prayer, which alone carries all with God. Feeble prayers, like weak pangs, go over, and never bring a mercy to the birth. Cold prayers are still-born children, in whom the Father of spirits can take no pleasure. Look, as a painted man is no man, and as painted fire is no fire; so a cold prayer is no prayer. Such prayers never win upon the heart of God that do not first warm our own hearts. As a body without a soul,

much wood without a fire, a bullet in a gun without powder; so are all prayers without fervency of spirit. Luther
terms prayer *bombarda Christianorum*, the gun or
cannon of Christians, or the Christian's gunshot.

The hottest springs send forth their waters by
ebullitions. Cold prayers make a smoke, a smother in the
eyes of God. Lazy prayers never procure noble answers;
lazy beggars may starve for all their begging (*Isa.* 1:15;
65:5).

Such as have a male in their flock, and offer to the Lord
a female; such as offer to the Lord the torn, and the lame,
and the sick; such as turn off God with their cold, lazy,
sleepy, and formal devotions, are condemned, cast, and
cursed by God (*Mal.* 1:13, 14). David compares his
prayers to incense, and no incense was offered without
fire (*Psa.* 141:2); it was fire that made its smoke ascend.
It is only fervent prayer that hits the mark, and that
pierces the walls of heaven, though, like those of Gaza
(*Isa.* 45:2), made of brass and iron. While the child only
whimpers and whines in the cradle, the mother lets it
alone; but when once it sets up its note, and cries out-
right, then she runs and takes it up. So it is with a
Christian: *Psa.* 34:6, 'This poor man cried.' There is his
fervency, he *cried*; but it was silently and secretly, in the
presence of King Achish, as Moses did at the Red Sea, and
as Nehemiah did in the presence of the king of Persia.
'And the LORD heard him, and delivered him out of all his
troubles'; here is his *prevalency*.

So Latimer plied the throne of grace with great fervency,
crying out, 'Once again, Lord, once again restore the

gospel to England', and God heard him. Hudson the martyr, deserted at the stake, went from under his chain, and having prayed fervently, he was comforted immediately, and suffered valiantly.[1]

I have read of one Giles of Brussels, a Dutch martyr, who was so fervent in his prayer, kneeling by himself in some secret place of the prison where he was, that he seemed to forget himself; and being called to his meat, he neither heard nor saw who stood by him, till he was lifted up by the arms, and then he would speak gently to them, as one awaked out of a trance.

So Gregory Nazianzen, speaking of his sister Gorgonia, says, that, in the vehemency of her prayer, she came to a religious impudency with God, so as to threaten heaven, and tell God that she would never depart from his altar till she had her petition granted.[2]

Let us make it our business to follow these noble examples, as ever we would so prince it in prayer as to prevail with God. An importunate soul in prayer is like the poor beggar, that prays and knocks, that prays and waits, that prays and works, that knocks and persists, that begs and perseveres, and will not stir from the door till he receives an alms.

Well, friends, remember this, God no more respects lukewarm prayers than he does lukewarm persons, and they are such that he has threatened to spue out of his mouth. Those prayers that are but lip-labour are lost labour; and therefore, in all your closet prayers, look to the fervency of your spirits.

[1] See p. 140. [2] *Paulin. Epist.*, lib. epist. 4.

7. My seventh advice and counsel is this, *Be constant, as well as fervent, in closet prayer.*

Look that you hold on and hold out, and that you persevere to the end in private prayer: *1 Thess.* 5:17, 'Pray without ceasing.' A man must always pray habitually, though not actually; he must have his heart in a praying, disposition in all estates and conditions. Though closet prayer may have an intermission, yet it must never have a cessation: *Luke* 18:1, 'And he spake a parable unto them, to this end, that men ought always to pray, and not to faint', or, as the Greek has it, εκκανειν, not to shrink back, as sluggards in work, or cowards in war. Closet prayer is a fire like that on the altar, that was never to go out, day nor night: *1 Thess.* 3:10, 'Night and day praying exceedingly.' Paul speaks like a man made up all of prayer, like a man that minded nothing so much as prayer. So *Eph.* 6:18, 'Praying always with all prayer and supplication in the Spirit, and watching thereunto with all perseverance.'

Calvin makes this difference between 'praying always' in the beginning of this verse, and 'praying with perseverance' in the end of this verse: 'By praying always', he says, 'he exhorts us to pray in prosperity as well as in adversity, and not to quit the duty of prayer in a prosperous estate, because we are not driven to it by outward pressing necessities and miseries; and by praying with perseverance, he admonishes us that we be not weary of the work, but continue instant and constant in its performance, though we have not presently what we pray for.' So that 'praying always' is opposed to a neglect of the duty in its proper times and reasons, and 'praying with perseverance' is opposed to a fainting in our spirits, in respect of this or that particular suit or request that we put up to God. When God turns a deaf ear to our prayers, we must not fret nor faint, we must not be dismayed nor discouraged, but we must hold up and hold on in the duty of prayer with invincible patience, courage, and constancy, as the church did, *Lam.* 3:8, 44, 55–57, compared. *Col.* 4:2, 'Continue in prayer, and watch in the same with thanksgiving.' We must be constant and instant in closet prayer; we must wait upon it, and lay all aside for it.

He that is only in his closet by fits and starts, will neither glorify God nor advantage his own soul. If we do not make a trade of closet prayer, we shall never have any yearnings for closet prayer. Look, as they that get money by their iron mills do keep a continual fire in them, so they that will get any soul-good by closet duties, they must keep close and constant to closet duties. The hypocrite is only constant in inconstancy; he is only in his closet by fits and starts. Now and then, when he is in a good mood, you shall find him step into his closet, but he never holds to it. *Job* 27:10, 'Will he always call upon God?' or, as the Hebrew has it, 'Will he in every time call upon God?' When they are under the smarting rod, or when they are upon the tormenting rack, or when they are under grievous wants, or when they are struck with panic-fears, etc., then you shall have them run to their closets, as Joab ran to the horns of the altar, when he was in danger of death; but they never persevere, they never hold out to the end; and therefore in the end they lose both their closet prayers and their souls together (*Isa.* 26:16; *Psa.* 78:34; *Zech.* 7:5).

It was a most profane and blasphemous speech of that atheistical wretch that told God 'that he was no common beggar, and that he never troubled him before with prayer, and if he would but hear him that time, he would never trouble him again'.

Closet prayer is a hard work; and a man must tug hard at it, and stick close to it as Jacob did, if ever he intends to make any internal or eternal advantages by it (*Gen.* 32). Daniel chose rather to run the hazard of his life, than to give up praying in his chamber (*Dan.* 6). It is not he that begins in the spirit and ends in the flesh (*Gal.* 3:3); it is not he that puts his hand to the plough and looks back (*Luke* 9:62); but he that perseveres to the end in prayer, that shall be saved and crowned (*Matt.* 24:13). It is he that perseveres in well doing, that shall eat of the hidden manna, and that shall have the white stone, 'and in the stone a new name written, which no man knows save him that receiveth it' (*Rev.* 2:17). Those precious, praying, mourning souls in Ezekiel 9:4, 6, that were marked to be preserved in Jerusalem, were distinguished, say some of the learned, by the character *tau,* which is the last of all the Hebrew letters, to teach them that they must hold out and hold on to the end in well doing. It is constancy in closet duty that crowns the Christian and commends the duty.

But would God have his people to cast off their callings, and to cast off all care of their relations, and shut themselves up in their closets, and there spend their whole time in secret prayer? Oh, no! Every duty must have its time and place; and as one friend must not shut out another, so one duty must not shut out another (*Eccles.* 3:1). The duties of my particular calling, as I am a man, must not shut out the duties of my general calling, as I am a Christian, nor must the duties of my general calling, as I am a Christian, shut out the duties of my particular calling, as I am a man. But that you may be fully satisfied in this case, you must remember that a man may be said to pray always,

i. First, *when his heart is always in a praying frame.* Look, as a man may be truly said to give always whose heart is always in a giving frame, and to suffer always whose heart is always in a suffering frame – 'For thy sake are we killed all the day long' (*Psa.* 44:22) – and to sin always whose heart is always in a sinning frame (2 *Pet.* 2:14; *Jer.* 9:3), so a man may be as truly said to pray always whose heart is always in a praying frame.

ii. Secondly, a man prays always when *he takes hold on every fit season and opportunity for the pouring out of his soul before the Lord in his closet.* To pray *always* is εν παντι χαιρω, to pray in every opportunity; but of this before.

It is observed by some of Proteus, that he used to give certain oracles, but it was hard to make him speak and deliver them, for he would turn himself into several shapes and forms; yet if they would hold out, and press him hard without fear, into whatsoever form or shape he appeared, they were sure to have satisfactory oracles.[1] So if we continue constant in our closet-wrestlings with God,

---

[1] Homer, *Odyssey,* Book 4.

if we hold on in private prayer though God should appear to us in the form or shape of a judge, an enemy, a stranger, we shall certainly speed at last: 'O woman, great is thy faith, be it unto thee even as thou wilt; and her daughter was made whole from that very hour' (*Matt.* 15:28).

The philosopher, being asked in his old age why he did not give over his practice and take his ease, answered, 'When a man is to run a race of forty furlongs, would you have him sit down at the thirty-ninth, and so lose the prize, the crown for which he ran?'[1] O sirs! if you do not hold out to the end in closet prayer, you will certainly lose the heavenly prize, the crown of life, the crown of righteousness, the crown of glory. To continue in giving glory to God in this way of duty, is as necessary and requisite as to begin to give glory to God in this way of duty; for though the beginning be more than half, yet the end is more than all; *finis coronat opus* [the end crowns the work]. The God of all perfections looks that our *ultimum vitae* [end of life] should be his *optimum gloriae* [highest glory], that our last works should be our best works; and that we should persevere in closet prayer to the end (*Rev.* 2:10).

8. My eighth advice and counsel is this, *In all your closet prayers, thirst and long after communion with God.*

In all your private retirements, take up in nothing below fellowship with God, in nothing below a sweet and spiritual enjoyment of God (*Song of Sol.* 3:1–3; *Psa.* 73:28);

---

[1] *Non progredi est regredi* [not to go forward is to go back].

Psa. 27:4, 'One thing have I desired of the LORD, that will I seek after, that I may dwell in the house of the LORD all the days of my life, to behold the beauty of the LORD, and to inquire in his temple.' The temple of the Lord, without communion with the Lord of the temple, will not satisfy David's soul: *Psa.* 42:1, 2, 'As the hart panteth after the water-brook, so panteth my soul after thee, O God. My soul thirsteth for God, for the living God; when shall I come and appear before God?'

The hart, as Aristotle and others observe, is of all creatures most hot and dry of itself; but especially when it is chased and hunted, then it is extremely thirsty. The female is here meant, as the Greek article, η ελαφος, makes clear. Now, in the females the passions of thirst are more strong, as the naturalists observe. By this David discovers what a vehement and inflamed thirst there was in his soul after communion with God; and as nothing could satisfy the hunted hart but the water brooks, so nothing could satisfy his soul but the enjoyments of God: *Psa.* 43:4, 'Then will I go unto the altar of God, unto God my exceeding joy.' The altar of God is here put for the worship of God. Now, it is not barely the worship of God, but communion with God in his worship, that was David's exceeding joy: *Psa.* 63:1-2, 'O God, thou art my God, early will I seek thee; my soul thirsteth for thee, my flesh longeth for thee in a dry and thirsty land, wherein no water is; to see thy power and thy glory, so as I have seen thee in the sanctuary.' David's soul did not thirst after a crown, a kingdom, or any worldly greatness or glory, but after a choice and sweet enjoyment of God in his wilderness estate. Never did any woman with child long more after this or that than David's soul did long to enjoy sensible communion with God in the midst of all his sorrows and sufferings: *Psa.* 84:2, 'My soul longeth, yea, even fainteth for the courts of the LORD: my heart and my flesh crieth out for the living God.' By the 'courts of the LORD', we are to understand the ordinances. Now, these without communion with God would never have satisfied David's soul.

I commend that speech of Bernard, *Nunquam abs te, absque te recedo,* 'I never come to you, but by you; I never come from you, without you.'[1]

Whenever you go into your closets, press hard after real and sensible communion with God, that so you may come out of your closets with some shines of God upon your spirits, as Moses came down from the mount with his face shining (*Exod.* 34:29–35). Oh, do not take up in your closet prayers, or tears, or joys, or enlargements; but labour and long to enjoy that inward and close fellowship with God in your closets, as may leave such a choice and sweet savour of God, both upon your hearts and lives, as others may be forced to say, Surely these have been with Jesus (*Acts* 4:13). It is sad when Christians return from their closets to their shops, their trades, their families, their commerce, etc., without the least visible rays of divine glory upon them.

O sirs! closet prayer will be found to be but a dry, sapless, lifeless, heartless, comfortless thing, if you do not enjoy communion with God in it. Communion with God

[1] Epist. 116.

is the very life, soul, and crown of all your closet duties; and therefore press after it as for life. When you go into your closets, let every thing go that may hinder your fruition of Christ, and let everything be embraced, that makes way for your enjoyment of Christ. Oh, let closet prayer be a golden bridge, a ferry-boat, a chariot to convey your souls over to God, and to bring you into a more intimate communion with God. Let no closet duty satisfy you or content you, wherein you have not conversed with God, as a child converses with his father, or as a wife converses with her husband, or as a friend converses with his friend, even face to face. Nothing speaks out more unsoundness, falseness, and baseness of heart than this, when men make duty the end of duty, prayer the end of prayer; than when men can begin a duty, and go on in a duty, and close up a duty, and bless and stroke themselves after a duty, and yet never enjoy the least communion with God in the duty.

QUESTION: *But how shall a man know whether he has a real communion with God in a duty or not?*

This is a very noble and necessary question, and accordingly it calls for a clear and satisfactory answer; and therefore, thus:

SOLUTION 1: *First, a man may have communion with God in sorrow and tears, when he has not communion with God in joy or delight (Psa. 51:17).* A man may have communion with God in a heart-humbling, heart-melting, and heart-abasing way, when he has not communion with God in a heart-reviving, a heart-cheering, and a heart-comforting way. It is a very great mistake among many tender-spirited Christians, to think that they have no communion with God in their closets, except they meet with God embracing and kissing (*Song of Sol.* 2:4–6), cheering and comforting their souls. When they find God raising the springs of joy and comfort in their souls; when they find God speaking peace to them; when they find the singular sensible presence of God cheering, refreshing, and enlarging them in their closets, oh, then they are willing to grant that they have had sweet communion with God in their closets. But if God meets with them in their closets, and only breaks their hearts for sin, and from sin, if he meets with them and only makes his power and his presence manifest in the debasing and casting down of their souls, upon the sight and sense of their strong corruptions and many imperfections, how unwilling are they to believe that they have had any communion with God!

Well, friends, remember this once for all, viz., that a Christian may have as real communion with God in a heart-humbling way, as he can have in a heart-comforting way. A Christian may have as choice communion with God when his eyes are full of tears as he can have when his heart is full of joy (*John* 20:11–19). Sometimes God meets with a poor Christian in his closet, and exceedingly breaks him and humbles him, and at other times he meets with the same Christian in his closet, and mightily cheers him, and comforts him; sometimes God meets with a poor soul in his closet, and there he sweetly quiets him and stills him, and at other times he meets with the same soul in his closet, and then he greatly revives him and quickens him. God does not always come upon the soul

one way, he does not always come in at one and the same
door (*John* 3:8). We sometimes look for a friend to come
in at the front-door, and then he comes in at the back-
door; and at other times, when we look for him at the
back-door, then he comes in at the front-door; and just so
it is with God's coming into his people's souls. Sometimes
they go into their closets, and expect that God will come
in at the front-door of joy and comfort, and then God
comes in at the back-door of sorrow and grief; and at
other times, when they look that God should come in at
the back-door of humiliation, breaking, and melting of
their hearts, then God comes in at the front-door of joy
and consolation, cheering and rejoicing their souls. But,

SOLUTION 2: *Secondly,* I answer, *that all do not enjoy a
like communion with God in their closets.* Some enjoy
much communion with God in their closets, and others
enjoy but little communion with God in their closets.
Moses had a more clear, glorious, and constant communion with God in his days than any others had in those
times in which he lived (*Exod.* 33:11; *Deut.* 5:4; *Num.*
12:7, 8). God spoke to none 'face to face' as he did to
Moses. And Abraham (*Gen.* 18), in his time, had a more
close, friendly, and intimate communion with God, than
holy Lot, or any others had in that day. And though all
the disciples, Judas excepted, had sweet communion with
Christ in the days of his flesh, yet Peter, James, and John
had a more clear, choice, and full communion with him
than the rest had (*Matt.* 17:1–4). Among all the disciples
John had most intimate communion with Christ, he was
the greatest favourite in Christ's court, he leaned on

Christ's bosom, he could say anything to Christ, and he could know anything of Christ, and he could have anything of Christ (*John* 13:23; 20:2; 21:20). Now that all Christians do not enjoy communion with God alike in their closets, may be thus made evident:

First, all Christians do not prepare alike to enjoy closet communion with God; and therefore all Christians do not enjoy communion with God alike in their closets (*Eccles.* 5:1; *Psa.* 10:17). Commonly he that prepares and fits himself most for closet communion with God is the man that enjoys most closet communion with God (2 *Chron.* 30:17–20).

Secondly, all Christians do not alike prize communion with God in their closets. Some prize communion with God in their closets before all and above all other things; as that noble marquis said, 'Cursed be he that prefers all the world to one hour's communion with God.'[1] They look upon it as that pearl of price, for the enjoyment of which they are ready to sell all and part with all; others prize it at a lower rate, and so enjoy less of it than those that set a richer price and value upon it (*Job* 23:12; *Psa.* 119:127; *Matt.* 13:45, 46).

Thirdly, all Christians do not alike press after communion with God in their closets. Some press after communion with God in their closets as a condemned man presses after a pardon, or as an incarcerated prisoner presses after his freedom, or as a poor beggar presses after an alms (*Psa.* 73:8; *Isa.* 26:8, 9). Now, you know these press on with the greatest earnestness, the greatest

---

[1] Galeacius Carraciolus. See Sibbes' *Works*, vol. 1, pp. 289–90.

fervency, and the greatest importunity imaginable. But others press after communion with God in their closets more coldly, more carelessly, more slightly, more lazily: 'I have put off my coat, how shall I put it on? I have washed my feet, how shall I defile them?' (*Song of Sol.* 5:3). Now they that press hardest after communion with God in their closets, are usually blessed with the highest degrees of closet communion with God.

Fourthly, all Christians do not alike improve their communion with God in their closets; and therefore all Christians do not enjoy communion with God alike in their closets. Some Christians make a more wise, a more humble, a more holy, a more faithful, a more fruitful, and a more constant improvement of their closet communion with God than others do; and therefore they are blessed with higher degrees of communion with God than others are. Some Christians do more improve their closet communion with God against the world, the flesh, and the devil than others do; and therefore no wonder if they do enjoy more communion with God in their closets than others do.

Fifthly, all Christians do not alike need communion with God in their closets; and therefore all Christians have not a like communion with God in their closets. All Christians have not a like place in the mystical body of Christ (*1 Cor.* 12:14–30); some rule, and others are ruled. Now, every man stands in more or less need of communion with God, according to the place that he bears in the body of Christ. Again, all Christians have not the same burdens to bear, nor the same difficulties to encounter, nor the same dangers to escape, nor the same temptations to wrestle with, nor the same passions and corruptions to mortify, nor the same mercies and experiences to improve, etc.; and therefore all Christians don't need alike communion with God in their closets. Now, commonly God lets himself out more or less in ways of communion according as the various necessities and conditions of his people require.

Sixthly and lastly, *all Christians do not alike meet with outward interruptions, nor inward interruptions;* and therefore all Christians have not alike communion with God in their closets. Some Christians meet with a world of outward and inward interruptions more than others do; some Christians' outward callings, relations, conditions, and stations, etc., do afford more plentiful matter and occasions to interrupt them in their closet communion with God than other Christians' callings, relations, conditions, and stations do, etc.

Besides, Satan is more busy with some Christians than he is with other Christians; and corruptions work more strongly and violently in some Christians than they do in other Christians, etc.; and let me add this to all the rest, that the very natural tempers of some Christians are more averse to closet duties than the natural tempers of other Christians are; and therefore all Christians have not alike communion with God in their closets, but some have more and some have less, according as God in his infinite wisdom sees best.

Now, let no Christian say, that he has no communion with God in closet prayer because he has not such a full, such a choice, such a sweet, such a sensible, and such a constant communion with God in closet prayer, as such and such saints have had, or as such and such saints now have; for all saints do not alike enjoy communion with God in their closets: some have more, some have less; some have a higher degree, others a lower; some are rapt up to the third heaven, when others are but rapt up to the clouds. What man is there so childish and babyish as to argue thus, that he has no wisdom, because he has not the wisdom of Solomon; or, that he has no strength, because he has not the strength of Samson; or, that he has no life, because he has not the swiftness of Ahimaaz; or, that he has no estate, because he has not the riches of Dives?

And yet so childish and babyish many weak Christians are, as to argue thus: viz., that they have no communion with God in their closets, because they have not such high, such comfortable, and such constant communion with God in their closets as such and such saints have had, or as such and such saints now have; whereas they should seriously consider, that though some saints have a great communion with God, yet other saints have but a small communion with God; and though some Christians have a strong communion with God, yet other Christians have but a weak communion with God; and though some of the people of God have a very close and near communion with God, yet others of the people of God have but a more remote communion with God; and though some of God's servants have a daily, constant, and uninterrupted communion with God, yet others of his servants have but a more transient and inconstant communion with God.

SOLUTION 3: *Thirdly*, I answer, *when a man acts grace in closet duties, then certainly he has communion with God in closet duties* (2 Tim. 1:17; 1 Tim. 2:8). When a man in closet-duties acts faith on God, or faith on the promises, or faith on the blood of Christ; or when a man in private duties acts repentance for sin, or love to Jesus Christ, or sets up God as the object of his fear, or as the object of his joy, etc., then he has communion with God, then he has fellowship with the Father, and with the Son (1 John 1:3).

An unregenerate man may act gifts and parts in a duty, but he cannot act grace in a duty; for no man can act grace in a duty, but he that has grace in his soul; and hence it comes to pass that unsanctified persons under the highest activity of their arts, parts, and gifts in religious duties, enjoy no communion with God at all; witness the scribes and Pharisees, Demas, Judas, Simon Magus, etc. (*Isa.* 1:11–13). As ever you would have an evidence of your communion with God in closet duties, carefully look to the activity of your graces, carefully stir up the grace of God which is in you (2 Tim. 1:6). But,

SOLUTION 4: *Fourthly*, I answer, *when a man has communion with God in his closet, then he gives God the glory of all his actings and activities* (Psa. 115:1). Communion with God always helps a man to set the crown of praise and honour upon the head of God. Witness that gracious and grateful doxology of David and his people, in *1 Chron.* 29:13, 'Now therefore, our God, we thank thee, and praise thy glorious name.' Men that enjoy no communion with God in religious duties, continue to sacrifice unto their own net, and burn incense unto their own drag (*Hab.* 1:16); they continue to bless themselves, and stroke themselves, and applaud themselves; they think the garland of praise, the crown of honour, suits no head but their own (*Luke* 18:11, 12). But now, men that enjoy communion with God in religious duties, will uncrown themselves to crown God, they will uncrown their duties to crown the God of their duties, they will uncrown their arts, parts, gifts, and enlargements, to set the crown of praise upon the head of God alone (*Acts* 3:11-13, 16; *Rev.* 4:10, 11; 5:11-12). You think that you have communion with God in closet duties, yes, you say that you have communion with God in closet duties; but on whose head do you put the garland of praise? (*Psa.* 148:13). If on God's head, you have communion with God; if on your own head, you have no communion with God. As all the rivers run into the sea, and all the lines meet in the centre, so, when all our closet duties terminate and centre in the advance of God's glory, then have we communion with God in them.

Constantine used to write the name of Christ over his door. When a man has communion with Christ in a duty, then he will write the name of Christ, the honour of Christ, upon his duty. Some say that the name of Jesus was engraved upon the heart of Ignatius; sure I am, when a man has communion with God in a duty, then you shall find the honour and glory of Jesus engraved upon that duty. But,

SOLUTION 5: *Fifthly,* I answer, *when the performance of closet duties leaves the soul in a better frame, then a man has communion with God in them.* When a man comes off from closet duties in a more holy frame, or in a more humble frame, or in a more spiritual frame, or in a more watchful frame, or in a more heavenly frame, or in a more broken frame, or in a more quickened and enlivened frame, then certainly he has had communion with God in those duties. When a man comes out of his closet, and finds the frame of his heart to be more strongly set against sin than ever, and to be more highly resolved to walk with God than ever, and to be more eminently crucified to the world then ever, and to be more divinely fixed against temptations than ever, then without all peradventure he has had communion with God in his closet.

SOLUTION 6: *Sixthly,* I answer, *when closet duties fit a man for those other duties that lie next to his hand, then doubtless he has had communion with God in them.* When private duties fit a man for public duties, or when private duties fit a man for the duties of his place, calling, and condition wherein God has set him, then certainly he has had fellowship with God in them (*Eccles.* 9:10). When a man in closet duties finds more spiritual strength and power to perform the duties that are next incumbent upon him, then assuredly he has met with God; when private prayer fits me more for family prayer, or public prayer, then I may safely conclude that God has drawn near to my soul in private prayer; or when one closet duty fits me for another closet duty, as when praying fits me for reading, or reading for praying; or when the more external duties in my closet, viz., reading or praying, fit me for those more spiritual and internal duties, viz., self-examination, holy meditation, soul-humiliation, etc., then

I may rest satisfied that there has been some choice intercourse between God and my soul. When the more I pray in my closet, the more fit I am to pray in my closet; and the more I read in my closet, the more fit I am to read in my closet; and the more I meditate in my closet, the more fit I am to meditate in my closet; and the more I search and examine my heart in my closet, the more fit I am to search and examine my heart in my closet; and the more I humble and abase my soul in my closet, the more fit I am to humble and abase my soul in my closet: then I may be confident that I have had communion with God in my closet.

SOLUTION 7: *Seventhly,* I answer, *that all private communion with God is very soul-humbling and soul-abasing.* Abraham was a man who had much private communion with God, and a man who was very vile and low in his own eyes: *Gen.* 18:27, 'And Abraham answered and said, Behold, now I have taken upon me to speak unto the Lord, which am but dust and ashes.' In respect of my original, says Abraham, 'I am but base dust and ashes'; and in respect of my deserts, I deserve to be burnt to ashes. There are none so humble as they that have nearest communion with God (*Gen.* 28:10–18). Jacob was a man that had much private communion with God, and a man that was very little in his own eyes: *Gen.* 32:10, 'I am not worthy of the least of all the mercies, and of all the truth, which thou hast shewed unto thy servant', or, as the Hebrew has it, 'I am less than all thy mercies.' When Jacob had to deal with Laban, he pleads his merit; but when he has to do with God, he debases himself below the least of his mercies (*Gen.* 31:38–41). Moses was a man who had much private communion with God, as I have formerly evidenced, and a man that was the meekest and humblest person in all the world: *Num.* 12:3, 'Now the man Moses was very meek, above all the men that were upon the face of the earth.'

Josephus, writing of Moses, says, if he may be believed, 'that he was so free from passions, that he knew no such thing in his own soul; he only knew passions by their names, and saw them in others, but felt them not in himself'. And so, when the glory of God appeared to him, he falls upon his face (*Num.* 16:22), in token of humility and self-abasing. David was a man that had much private communion with God, as is granted on all hands; and how greatly does he debase himself and vilify himself! 1 *Sam.* 26:20, 'The king of Israel is come out to seek a flea'; and what more weak and contemptible than a flea? So chapter 24:14, 'After whom is the king of Israel come out? after whom dost thou pursue? after a dead dog, after a flea?' As if David had said, 'It is not worth the while, the labour; it is below the dignity and honour of the king of Israel to take such pains and to pursue so violently after such a poor nothing as I am, who has no more strength nor power to bite or hurt than a dead dog or a poor flea has.' So *Psa.* 22:6, 'But I am a worm, and no man.' Now, what is more weak, what less regarded, what more despicable, what more trampled under foot than a poor worm?

The Hebrew word *tolagnath*, that is here rendered worm, signifies a very little worm, such as breed in scarlet, which are so little that a man can scarcely see them, or perceive them. Thus you see that holy David debases himself below a worm, yea, below the least of worms. No man sets so low a value upon himself as he does who has most private communion with God. The twenty-four elders throw down their crowns at the feet of Jesus Christ (*Rev.* 5:10–11). Their crowns note all their inward and outward dignities, excellencies, and glories; and the throwing down of their crowns notes their great humility and self-debasement. When Christians, in their closets and out of their closets, can throw down their crowns, their duties, their services, their graces, their enlargements, their enjoyments, etc., at the feet of Jesus Christ, and sit down debasing and lessening of themselves, then certainly they have had a very near and sweet communion with God.[1] Chrysostom has a remarkable saying about humility: 'Suppose that a man were defiled with all manner of sin and enormity, yet humble, and another man enriched with gifts, graces, and duties, yet proud, the humble sinner were in a safer condition than this proud saint.'

When a man can come off from closet duties, and say, as Ignatius once said of himself, *Non sum dignus dici minimus*, I am not worthy to be called the least, then certainly he has had fellowship with God in them. All the communion that the creature has with God in his closet is very soul-humbling and soul-abasing. In all a man's communion with God, some beams, some rays of the glory

---

[1] Augustine being once asked what was the first grace, answered, humility; what the second? Humility; what the third? Humility.

and majesty of God, will shine forth upon his soul. Now all divine manifestations are very humbling and abasing, as you may clearly see in those two great instances of Job and Isaiah: *Job* 42:5–6, 'I have heard of thee by the hearing of the ear, but now mine eye seeth thee: Wherefore I abhor myself, and repent in dust and ashes.' *Isa.* 6:1, 5, 'In the year that king Uzziah died, I saw also the Lord sitting upon a throne, high and lifted up, and his train filled the temple. Then said I, Woe is me! for I am undone; because I am a man of unclean lips, and I dwell in the midst of a people of unclean lips: for mine eyes have seen the King, the LORD of hosts.' What sweet communion Elijah had with God in the low cave!

There was a gentlewoman, of no ordinary quality or breeding, who, being much troubled in mind and sadly deserted by God, could not be drawn by her husband, or any other Christian friends, either to hear or read anything that might work for her spiritual advantage; at last her husband, by much importunity, prevailed so far with her that she was willing he should read one chapter in the Bible to her; so he read Isaiah 57; and when he came to the 15th verse, 'For thus saith the high and lofty One that inhabiteth eternity, whose name is Holy, I dwell in the high and holy place, with him also that is of a contrite and humble spirit, to revive the spirit of the humble, and to revive the heart of the contrite ones', 'Oh,' she said, 'is it so, that God dwells with a contrite and humble spirit? Then I am sure he dwells with me, for my heart is broken into a thousand pieces. Oh, happy text and happy time, that ever I should hear such comfort!', and with that she was recovered. The more communion any man has with God, the more humble and broken his heart will be.

Holy John Bradford was a man who had much private communion with God, and he would many times subscribe himself in his letters, 'John the hypocrite, and a very painted sepulchre.' Agur was one of the wisest and holiest men on the earth in his days, and he condemned himself for being more brutish than any man, and not having the understanding of a man (*Prov.* 30:2). How sweet is the smell of the lowly violet, that hides his head, above all the gaudy tulips that be in your garden.

The lowly Christian is the most amiable and the most lovely Christian. When a man can come out of his closet, and cry out with Augustine, 'I hate that which I am, and love and desire that which I am not. O wretched man that I am, in whom the cross of Christ has not yet eaten out the poisonous and the bitter taste of the first tree.' Or, as another says, 'Lord, I see, and yet am blind; I will, and yet rebel; I hate, and yet I love; I follow, and yet I fall; I press forward, yet I faint; I wrestle, yet I halt'; then he may be confident that he has had communion with God in his closet. He that comes off from closet duties in a self-debasing way, and in laying of himself low at the foot of God, he certainly has had communion with God; but when men come out of their closets with their hearts swelled and lifted up, as the hearts of the Pharisees were (*Luke* 18:11–12), it is evident that they have had no communion with God. God has not been near to their souls, who say, Stand by thyself, come not near to me; for I am holier than thou (*Isa.* 65:5). But,

Solution 8: Eighthly, and lastly, *when a man finds such a secret virtue and power running through his closet duties, as wounds and weakens his beloved corruption, as breaks the strength and the power of his special sin, and sets his heart more fully, resolutely, and constantly against his darling lust, as stirs up a greater rage, and a more bitter hatred, and a more fierce indignation against the toad in the bosom, then certainly he has had communion with God in his closet duties.* Consult these Scriptures: *Isa.* 2:20, 'In that day a man shall cast his idols of silver, and his idols of gold, which they have made each one for himself to worship, to the moles and to the bats.' In the day in which God should take these poor hearts into communion with himself, their hearts should be filled with such rage and indignation against their most delectable and desirable idols, that they should take not only those made of trees and stones, but even their most precious and costly idols, those that were made of silver and gold, and cast them to the moles and to the bats, to note their horrible hatred and indignation against them.

Idolatry was the darling sin of the Jews; their hearts were so exceedingly affected and delighted with their idols, that they did not care what they spent upon them: *Isa.* 46:6, 'They lavish gold out of the bag, and weigh silver in the balance, and hire a goldsmith, and he maketh it a god: they fall down, yea, they worship.' The word here used for *lavish,* in the Hebrew, signifies properly *to waste,* or spend riotously; they set so light by their treasure, that they cared not what they spent upon their idols. God gave them gold and silver as pledges of his favour and bounty, and they lavish it out upon their idols, as if God had hired them to be wicked. Oh, but when God should come and take these poor wretches into a close and near communion with himself, then you shall find their wrath and rage to rise against their idols, as you may see in *Isa.* 30:19–21. Their communion with God is more than hinted; but mark, verse 22, 'Ye shall defile also the covering of thy graven images of silver, and the ornament of thy molten images of gold; thou shalt cast them away as a menstruous cloth; thou shalt say unto it, Get thee hence.' None defile, deface, detest, and disgrace their idols like those that are taken into communion with God.

Fellowship with God will make a man cast away, as a menstruous cloth, those very idols, in which he had most delighted, and with which he had been most pleased and enamoured. Idols were Ephraim's bosom sin. *Hos.* 4:17, 'Ephraim is joined', or glued, as the Hebrew has it, 'to idols; let him alone.' Oh! but when you find Ephraim taken into close communion with God, as you do in *Hos.* 14:4–7, then you shall find another spirit upon him: verse 8, 'Ephraim shall say, what have I to do any more with idols?' I have had too much to do with them already, I will never have to do with them any more. Oh! how does my soul detest and abhor them, and rise up against them. Oh! how do I now more loathe and abominate them, than ever I have formerly loved them, or delighted in them. After the return of the Jews out of Babylon, they so hated and abhorred idols, that in the time of the Romans they chose rather to die, than suffer the eagle, which was the imperial arms, to be set up in their temple.

Though closet duties are weak in themselves, yet when a man has communion with God in them, then they prove exceeding powerful to the casting down of strongholds, and vain imaginations, and every high thing and thought, that exalts itself against the knowledge of God (2 *Cor.* 10:4–5). When a man comes out of his closet with a heart more fully and steadfastly set against every known sin, but especially against his bosom sin, his darling sin, his Delilah that he played and sported himself most with, and that he has hugged with pleasure and delight in his arms, then certainly he has had private communion with God.

After Moses had enjoyed forty days' private communion with God in the mount, how did his heart rise, and his anger grow hot against the molten calf that his people had made! *Exod.* 22:19–20, 'And it came to pass, as soon as he came nigh unto the camp that he saw the calf and the dancing; and Moses' anger waxed hot, and he cast the tables out of his hands, and brake them beneath the mount: and he took the calf which they had made, and burnt it in the fire, and ground it to powder, and strawed it upon the water, and made the children of Israel drink of it.' Moses had never more intimate fellowship with God than now, and he never discovered so much holy zeal, anger, and indignation against sin as now. When a man comes off from the mount of closet duties with a greater hatred, anger, wrath, and indignation against bosom sins, darling sins, complexion sins, that were once as dear to him as right hands or right eyes, or as Delilah was to Samson, or Herodias to Herod, or Isaac to Abraham, or Joseph to Jacob, then certainly he has had communion with God in those duties. When a man finds his beloved sins, his Delilahs, which, like the prince of devils, command all other sins, to fall before his closet duties, as Dagon fell before the ark, or as Goliath fell before David, then assuredly he has had fellowship with God in them. Pliny writes of some families that had marks on their bodies peculiar to those of that line. Certainly, there are no families, no persons, but have some sin or sins, some secret marks on their souls that may in a peculiar way be called theirs. Now when in private duties they find the bent of their hearts, and the purposes, resolutions, and inclinations of their souls more raised, inflamed, and set against these, they may safely and comfortably conclude, that they have had communion with God in them.

O sirs! there is no bosom sin so sweet or profitable that it is worth burning in hell for, or being shut out of heaven for; and therefore, in all your private duties and services, labour after that communion with God in them that may break the neck and heart of your most bosom sins. When Darius fled before Alexander, that he might run the faster out of danger, he threw away his heavy crown from his head. As ever you would be safe from eternal danger, throw away your golden and your silver idols, throw away your bosom sins, your darling lusts.

And this I have done with the answers to that noble and necessary question, that was last proposed.

9. My ninth advice and counsel is this, *In all your closet duties make sure that your aims are right, make sure that the glory of God is your ultimate end, the mark, the*

target, that you have in your eye. There is a great truth in that old saying, *Quod non actibus, sed finibus pensantur officia,* that duties are esteemed, not by their acts, but by their ends. As the shining sun puts out the light of the fire, so the glory of God must consume all other ends. A work may be bad, though materially good, as with Jehu's zeal. Two things make a good Christian, good actions and good aims. And though a good aim does not make a bad action good, as in Uzzah, yet a bad aim makes a good action bad, as in Jehu, whose justice was approved, but his policy punished. God writes a zero upon all those services in which men's ends are not right: *Jer.* 32:23, 'They obeyed not thy voice, neither walked in thy law; they have done nothing of all that thou hast commandedst them to do.'

So *Dan.* 9:13, 'All this evil is come upon us, yet made we not our prayer before the LORD our God.' The Jews were very much in religious duties and services; witness *Isa.* 1:11-15; *Isa.* 58:1-3; *Zech.* 7:5-6. I might produce a hundred more witnesses to confirm it, were it necessary; but because they did not aim at the glory of God in what they did, therefore the Lord writes a zero upon all their duties and services. It was Ephraim's folly, that he brought forth fruit unto himself (*Hos.* 10:1). And it was the Pharisees' hypocrisy that in all their duties and services they looked at the praise of men. *Matt.* 6:1-5, 'Verily', says Christ, 'you have your reward.' A poor, a pitiful reward indeed! Such men shall be sure to fall short of divine acceptance, and of a glorious recompense, that are not able to look above the praises of men. Woe to that man that, with Augustus, is ambitious to go off the stage of duty with a *plaudit*.[1] Peter was not himself when he denied his Lord, and cursed himself to get credit amongst a cursed crew. As ever you would ask and have, speak and speed, seek and find, look that the glory of the Lord be engraven upon all your closet duties. He shall be sure to speed best, whose heart is set most upon glorifying God in all his secret retirements. When God crowns us, he does but crown his own gifts in us; and when we give God the glory of all we do, we do but give him the glory that is due unto his name; for it is he, and he alone, that works all our works in us and for us. All closet duties are good or bad, as the mark is at which the soul aims. He that makes God the object of closet prayer, but not the end of closet prayer, loses his prayer, and takes pains to undo himself. God will be *Alexander or Nemo;* he will be all in all, or he will be nothing at all. Such prayers never reach the ear of God, nor delight the heart of God, nor shall ever be lodged in the bosom of God, that are not directed to the glory of God. The end must be as noble as the means, or else a man may be undone after all his doings. A man's most glorious actions will at last be found to be but glorious sins, if he has made himself, and not the glory of God, the end of those actions.

10. My tenth advice and counsel is this, *Be sure that you offer all your closet prayers in Christ's name, and in his alone. John* 14:13–14, 'And whatsoever ye shall ask in my name, that will I do, that the Father may be glorified in the Son. If ye shall ask anything in my name, I will do

[1] See *The Crown and Glory of Christianity* in Brooks' *Works*, vol. 4.

it.' *John* 15:16, 'That whatsoever ye shall ask of the Father in my name, he may give it you.' *John* 16:23–24, 26, 'Verily, verily, I say unto you, whatsoever ye shall ask the Father in my name, he will give it you. Hitherto have ye asked nothing in my name: ask, and ye shall receive, that your joy may be full. At that day ye shall ask in my name: and I say not unto you, that I will pray the Father for you.'

O sirs! this is your privilege as well as your comfort, that you never deal with God but by a mediator. When you appear before God, Jesus Christ appears with you, and he appears for you; when you *invocate*, then he *advocates*; when you put up your petitions, then he makes intercession for you. Christ gives you a commission to put his name upon all your requests; and whatsoever prayer comes up with this name upon it, he will procure it an answer. In the state of innocency, man might worship God without a mediator; but since sin has made so wide a breach between God and man, God will accept no worship from man but what is offered up by the hand of a mediator. Now this mediator is Christ alone; *1 Tim.* 2:5, 'For there is one God, and one mediator between God and men, the man Christ Jesus.' One mediator, not of redemption only, as the papists grant, but of intercession also, which they deny.

The papists make saints and angels co-mediators with Christ; but in this, as in other things, they fight against clear Scripture light. The apostle plainly tells us, that the office of intercession pertains to Christ, as part of his mediation (*Heb.* 7:25): and it is certain, that we need no other master of requests in heaven, but the man Christ Jesus; who being so near to the Father, and so dear to the Father, and so much in with the Father, can doubtless carry any thing with the Father, that makes for his glory and our good. This was typified in the law. The high-priest alone did enter into the sanctuary, and carry the names of the children of Israel before the Lord, whilst all the people stood outside; this pointed out Christ's mediation (*Exod.* 28:21).

In *Lev.* 16:13–14, you read of two things: first, of the cloud of incense that covered the mercy seat; secondly, of the blood of the bullock that was sprinkled before the mercy-seat. Now that blood typified Christ's satisfaction, and the cloud of incense his intercession.

Some of the learned think, that Christ intercedes only by virtue of his merits; others, that it is done only with his mouth. I conjecture it may be done both ways, the rather because Christ has a tongue, as also a whole body, but glorified, in heaven; and is it likely that that mouth which pleaded so much for us on earth, should be altogether silent for us in heaven?

There is no coming to the Father, but by the Son (*John* 14:6). Christ is the true Jacob's ladder, by which we must ascend to heaven. Joseph, you know, commanded his brethren, that as ever they looked for any good from him, or to see his face with joy, that they should be sure to bring their brother Benjamin along with them. O sirs! as ever you would be prevalent with God, as ever you would have sweet, choice, and comfortable returns from heaven to all your closet prayers, be sure that you bring your elder brother, the Lord Jesus Christ, in the arms of your faith, be sure that you treat and trade with God only in the name of the Lord Jesus.

It is a notable saying that Luther has on Psalm 130, 'Often and willingly', he says, 'do I inculcate this, that you should shut your eyes, and your ears, and say you know no God out of Christ, none but he that was in the lap of Mary, and sucked her breasts.' O sweet name of Christ! When you go to closet prayer, look that you pray not in your own names, but in the name of Christ; and that you believe and hope not in your own names, but in the name of Christ; and that you look not to speed in your own names, but in the name of Christ: *Col.* 3:17, 'And whatsoever ye do in word or deed, do all in the name of the Lord Jesus.' Whatever we do, we are to do it by the authority of Christ, and through the assistance of Christ, and in the name of Christ, and for the sake and glory of Christ. Christ's name is so precious and powerful with the Father, that it will, carry any suit, obtain any request at his hands. Jesus, in the Chinese language, signifies the rising sun. When a man writes the name of Jesus upon his closet prayers, then he shall be sure to speed. Though God will not give a man a drop, a sip, a crumb, a crust, for his own sake, yet for Jesus' sake he will give the best, the choicest, and the greatest blessings that heaven affords; that name is still mighty and powerful, prevalent and precious before the Lord.

The prayers that were offered up with the incense upon the altar were pleasing (*Rev.* 8:3); and came up with acceptance (8:4). Joseph's brothers were kindly treated for

Benjamin's sake. O sirs! all our duties and services are accepted of the Father, not for their own sakes, nor for our sakes, but for Christ's sake. There are no prayers that are either heard, owned, accepted, regarded, or rewarded, but such as Christ puts his hand to. If Christ does not mingle his blood with our sacrifices, our services, they will be lost, and never ascend as incense before the Lord. No coin is current that does not have Caesar's stamp upon it; and no prayers will be received in heaven that do not have the stamp of Christ upon them. There is nothing more pleasing to our heavenly Father, than to use the mediation of his Son. Such shall be sure to find most favour, and to speed best in the court of heaven, who present themselves before the Father with Christ in their arms. But,

11. My eleventh and last advice and counsel is this, *When you come out of your closets, carefully watch what happens to your private prayers.*

Look at what door, in what way, and by what hand the Lord shall please to give you an answer to the secret desires of your souls in a corner. It has been the custom of the people of God to look after their prayers, to see what success they have had, to observe what entertainment they have found in heaven: *Psa.* 5:3, 'My voice shalt thou hear in the morning, O LORD; in the morning will I direct my prayer unto thee, and will look up.' In the words you may observe two things: first, David's posture in prayer; secondly, his practice after prayer.

First, his posture, 'I will direct my prayer unto thee.'

Secondly, his practice after prayer, 'And I will look up.' The prophet, in these words, makes use of two military words. First, he would not only pray, but marshal up his prayers, he would put them in battle-array; so much the Hebrew word *gnarach* imports. Secondly, when he had done this, then he would be as a spy upon his watchtower, to see whether he prevailed, whether he got the day or not; and so much the Hebrew word *tsaphah* imports. When David had set his prayers, his petitions, in rank and file, in good array, then he was resolved he would look abroad, he would look about him, to see at what door God would send in an answer of prayer. He is either a fool or a madman, he is either very weak or very wicked, that prays and prays, but never looks after his prayers; that shoots many an arrow towards heaven, but never minds where his arrows alight: *Psa.* 85:8, 'I will hear what God the LORD will speak; for he will speak peace unto his people, and to his saints.'

If David would have God to hearken to his prayers, he must then hearken to what God will speak; and upon this point it seems he was fully resolved. The prophet's prayer you have in the first seven verses of this Psalm, and his gracious resolution you have in the eighth verse, 'I will hear what God the LORD will speak.' As if he had said, 'Certainly it will not be long before the Lord will give me a gracious answer, a seasonable and a suitable return to my present prayers'; *Psa.* 130:1-2, 5-6, 'Out of the depths have I cried unto thee, O LORD. Lord, hear my voice, let thine ears be attentive to the voice of my supplications . . . I wait for the LORD, my soul doth wait, and in his word do I hope. My soul waiteth for the Lord, more than they that watch for the morning; I say, more than they that watch for the morning.' Those that watch out in dangerous times and tedious weather look frequently after the peep of day. How does the weary sentinel that is wet with the rain of heaven, or with the dew of the night, wait and watch, look and long, for the morning light.

Now this was the frame and temper of David's spirit when he came off from praying; he falls into waiting for a gracious answer. Shall the husbandman wait for the precious fruits of the earth, and shall the merchantman wait for the return of his ships, and shall the wife wait for the return of her husband, that is gone on a long journey? (*James* 5:7–8), and shall not a Christian wait for the return of his prayers? Noah patiently waited for the return of the dove to the ark with an olive branch in his mouth, so must you patiently wait for the return of your prayers.

When children shoot their arrows, they never mind where they fall; but when prudent archers shoot their arrows up into the air, they stand and watch where they fall. You must deal by your prayers as prudent archers do by their arrows: *Hab.* 2:1, 'I will stand upon my watch, and set me upon the tower, and will watch to see what he will say unto me.' The prophet, in the former chapter, having been very earnest in his expostulations, and very fervent in his supplications, gets now upon his watchtower, to see what becomes of his prayer. He stands as a sentinel, and watches as vigilantly and as carefully as a spy, a scout, earnestly longing to hear and see the event, the issue, and success of his prayers. That Christian that in prayer has one eye upon a divine precept, and another upon a gracious promise, that Christian will be sure to look after his prayers. He that prays and waits, and waits and prays, shall be sure to speed; he shall never fail of rich returns (*Psa.* 40:1–4). He that can want as well as wait, and he that can be contented that God is glorified, though he be not gratified; he that dares not antedate God's promises, but patiently waits for the accomplishment of them, he may be confident that he shall have seasonable and suitable answers to all those prayers that he has posted away to heaven. Though God seldom comes at our time, yet he never fails to come at his own time: 'He that shall come, will come, and will not tarry' (*Heb.* 10:37). The mercies of God are not styled the *swift*, but the '*sure* mercies of David'.

He that makes as much conscience to look after his prayers as to pray, he shall shortly clap his hands for joy, and cry out with that blessed martyr, 'He is come, Austin, he is come, he is come.'[1] Certainly there is little worth in that man's heart, or in that man's prayers, who keeps up a trade of prayer, but never looks what becomes of his prayers. When you are in your closets, marshal your prayers; see that every prayer keeps his place and ground; and when you come out of your closets, then look up for an answer; only take heed that you be not too hasty and hot with God. Though mercy in the promise be yours, yet the time of giving it out is the Lord's; and therefore you must wait as well as pray. And thus much by way of counsel and advice, for the better carrying on of closet prayer.

[1] Robert Glover, see p. 140.

PART 6

MEANS, RULES, AND DIRECTIONS FOR FAITHFUL PRIVATE PRAYER

I HAVE NOW BUT ONE THING MORE to do before I shut up this discourse, and that is, to lay down some means, rules, or directions that may be of use to help you on in a faithful and conscientious discharge of this great duty, viz., closet prayer. And therefore thus,

1. First, as ever you would give up yourselves to private prayer, *beware of an idle and slothful spirit.*

If Adam, in the state of innocency, must work and dress the garden, and if, after his Fall, when he was monarch of all the world, he must yet labour, why should any be idle or slothful? Idleness is a sin against the law of creation. God creating man to labour, the idle person violates this law of creation; for by his idleness he casts off the authority of his Creator, who made him for labour. Idleness is a contradiction to the principles of our creation.[1] Man in innocency should have been freed from weariness, but not from employment; he was to dress the garden by divine appointment: 'And the LORD God took the man, and put

[1] Augustine on Genesis.

him into the garden of Eden, to dress it, and to keep it' (*Gen.* 2:15). All weariness in labour, and all vexing, tiring, and tormenting labour, came in by the Fall: 'In the sweat of thy face shalt thou eat bread' (*Gen.* 3:19). The bread of idleness is neither sweet nor sure: 'An idle person shall suffer hunger', Solomon says (*Prov.* 19:15). An idle life and an holy heart are far enough asunder. By doing nothing, says the heathen man, men learn to do evil things. It is easy slipping out of an idle life into an evil and wicked life; yes, an idle life is of itself evil, for man was made to be active, not to be idle.

The Cyclops thought man's happiness consisted in *nihil agendo*, in having nothing to do; but no excellent thing can be the child of idleness. Idleness is a mother-sin, a breeding-sin; it is *pulvinar diaboli*, the devil's cushion, on which he sits, and the devil's anvil, on which he frames very great and very many sins (*Eph.* 4:28; 2 *Thess.* 3: 10–12). Look, as toads and serpents breed most in standing waters, so sin thrives most in idle persons. Idleness is that which provokes the Lord to forsake men's bodies, and the devil to possess their souls.

No man has less means to preserve his body, and more temptations to infect his soul, than an idle person. Oh, shake off sloth! The sluggish Christian will be sleeping, or idling, or trifling, when he should be in his closet praying. Sloth is the green-sickness of the soul; get it cured, or it will be your eternal bane. Of all devils, it is the idle devil that keeps men most out of their closets. There is nothing that gives the devil so much advantage against us as idleness. It was good counsel that Jerome gave to his friend,

Facito aliquid operas, ut te semper diabolus inveniat occupatum, that when the devil comes with a temptation, you may answer him that you are not at leisure.[1]

It was the saying of Mr Greenham,[2] at one time a famous and painstaking preacher of this nation, that when the devil tempted a poor soul, she came to him for advice how she might resist the temptation, and he gave her this answer: 'Never be idle, but be always well employed, for in my own experience I have found it. When the devil came to tempt me, I told him that I was not at leisure to hearken to his temptations, and by this means I resisted all his assaults.' Idleness is the hour of temptation, and an idle person is the devil's tennis-ball, tossed by him at his pleasure.

'He that labours', said the old hermit, 'is tempted but by one devil, but he that is idle is assaulted by all.' Cupid complained that he could never fasten upon the Muses, because he could never find them idle. The fowler bends his bow and spreads his net for birds when they are sitting, not when they are upon the wing. So Satan shoots his most fiery darts at men, when they are most idle and slothful. And this the Sodomites found by woeful experience (*Ezek.* 16:49), when God rained hell out of heaven upon them, both for their idleness, and for those other sins of theirs, which their idleness did expose them to.

It was said of Rome, that during the time of their wars with Carthage and other enemies in Africa, they knew not what vice meant; but no sooner had they gained the

[1] Jerome, *Epist.* 4.
[2] Richard Greenham (1531–91).

conquest, but through idleness they came to ruin. Idleness is a sin, not only against the law of grace but also against the light of nature. You cannot look any way but every creature checks and upbraids your idleness and sloth; if you look up to the heavens, there you shall find all their glorious lights constant in their motions, 'The sun rejoiceth as a strong man to run a race' (*Psa.* 19:5; 104:23); the winds blow, the waters run, the earth brings forth her pleasant and delightful fruits, all the fish in the sea, fowls in the air, and beasts in the fields and on the mountains, have their motions and operations, all which call aloud upon man not to be idle, but active.

Solomon sends the sluggard to the ant to learn industry (*Prov.* 6:6). The ant is a very little creature, but exceedingly laborious. Nature has put an instinct into her to be very busy and active all the summer; she is early and late at it, and will not lose an hour unless the weather hinder. And the prophet Jeremiah sends the Jews to school to learn to wait, and observe of the stork, the turtle, the crane, and the swallow (*Jer.* 8:7). And our Saviour sends us to the sparrows and lilies, to learn attendance upon providence (*Matt.* 6:26, 28). And let me send you to the busy bee, to learn activity and industry; though the bee is little in bulk, yet it is great in service; she flies far, examines the fields, hedges, trees, orchards, gardens, and loads herself with honey and wax, and then returns to her hive. Now how should the activity of these creatures put the idle person to a blush.

O sirs! man is the most noble creature, into whom God has put principles of the greatest activity, as capable of the greatest and highest enjoyments; and therefore idleness is forgetting man's dignity, and forsaking that rank that God has set him in, and debasing him below the least and meanest creatures, who constantly in their order obediently serve the law of their creation. No, if you look up to the blessed angels above you, you shall still find them active and serviceable. 'Are they not all ministering spirits, sent forth to minister for them who shall be heirs of salvation?' (*Heb.* 1:14). And if you look down to the angels of darkness below you, oh, how laborious and industrious are they to destroy and damn your precious and immortal souls (*1 Pet.* 5:8)!

For a close, remember that idleness is so great an evil that it has been condemned and severely punished by the very worst of men. Among the Egyptians, idleness was a capital crime. Among the Lucanians, he that lent money to an idle person was to lose it. By Solon's law, idle persons were to suffer death; and Seneca had rather be sick than idle. The Lacedaemonians called men to an account for their idle hours. Among the Corinthians, idle persons were delivered to the *Carnifex* [public executioner]. Antoninus Pius, being emperor, caused the roofs and coverings of all such houses to be taken away as were known to receive in idle people, affirming that nothing was more uncomely or absurd to be suffered than such idle caterpillars and slow-worms to have their food and nourishment from that commonwealth, in the maintenance of which there was no supply from their industry and labour. All which should steel us and arm us against sloth and idleness.

I have the longer insisted on this because there is not a greater hindrance to closet prayer than sloth and idleness. Slothful and idle persons commonly lie so long in bed, and spend so much precious time between the comb and the glass, and in trifling, etc., that they can find no time for private prayer. Certainly, such as had rather go sleeping to hell than sweating to heaven will never care much for closet prayer. And therefore shun sloth and idleness as you would shun a lion in the way, or poison in your meat, or coals in your bosom, or else you will never find time to wait upon God in your closets.

2. Secondly, *beware of spending too much of your precious time in circumstantial matters,* in the little things of religion, as 'mint, anise, and cummin' (*Matt.* 23:23), or in searching into the circumstances of worship, or in standing stoutly for this or that ceremony, and meanwhile neglect the studying of the covenant of grace; or in inquiring what fruit that was that Adam ate in paradise, or in inquiring after the authors of such and such books, whose names God in his infinite wisdom has concealed, or in inquiring what God did before the world was made.

When one asked Augustine that question, he answered, that he was 'preparing hell for such busy questioners as he was'. It was a saying of Luther, 'From a vainglorious doctor, from a contentious pastor, and from unprofitable questions, the good Lord deliver his church.' It is one of Satan's great designs to hinder men in the great and weighty duties of religion by busying them most about the lowest and least matters of religion. Satan is never better pleased than when he sees Christians puzzled and perplexed about those things in religion that are of no great moment or importance (*Col.* 2:21). Such as negotiate and trade in religion more for a good name than a good life, for a good report than a good conscience, to humour others rather than to honour God, etc., such will take no pleasure in closet duties. Such as are more busied about ceremonies than substances, about the form of godliness than the power (*2 Tim.* 3:5), such will never make it their business to be much with God in their closets, as is evident in the scribes and Pharisees (*Matt.* 6:1–6).

Such as are more taken up with the outward dress and garb of religion than they are with the spirit, power, and life of religion: such will never affect to drive a secret trade heavenwards (*Luke* 11:34–40). There cannot be a surer nor a greater character of a hypocrite than to make a great deal of stir about little things in religion, and in the meanwhile neglect the great and main things in religion. Such as these have all along in the Scripture discovered a strangeness and a perfect carelessness as to closet duties. I never knew any man hot and zealous about circumstantials, about the little things of religion, that was ever famous for closet prayer. But,

3. Thirdly, *beware of curiosity*, and of spending too much of your precious time in searching into those dark, abstruse, mysterious and hidden truths and things of God and religion that lie most remote from the understanding of the best and wisest of men. Curiosity is the spiritual adultery of the soul. Curiosity is a spiritual drunkenness;

for look, as the drunkard is never satisfied unless he see the bottom of the cup, be it never so deep, so those that are troubled with the itch of curiosity will say they can never be satisfied till they come to the bottom of the most deep and profound things of God; they love to pry into God's secrets, and to scan the mysteries of religion by their weak, shallow reason, and to be wise above what is written. Curious searchers into the deep mysterious things of God will make all God's depths to be shallows, rather than they will be thought not able to fathom them by the short line of their own reason. Oh, that men would once learn to be contentedly ignorant, where God would not have them knowing! Oh, that men were once so humble, as to account it no disparagement to them, to acknowledge some depths in God, and in the blessed Scripture, which their shallow reason cannot fathom!

They are only a company of great fools that affect to know more than God would have them. Did not Adam's tree of knowledge make him, and his posterity mere fools? He who goes to school to his own reason has a fool for his schoolmaster. The ready way to grow stark blind is to be still prying and gazing upon the body of the sun: so the ready way to spiritual blindness is to be still prying into the most secret and hidden things of God (*Deut.* 29:29). Are there not many who, by prying long into the secrets of nature, are become arch-enemies to the grace of God? (*Rom.* 9:20). Oh, that we were wise to admire those deep mysteries which we cannot understand, and to adore those depths and counsels which we cannot reach (*Rom.* 11:33). Oh, let us check our curiosity in the things of

God, and sit down satisfied and contented to resolve many of God's actions into some hidden causes which lie secret in the abyss of his eternal knowledge and infallible will. Christ, when he was on earth, very frequently, severely, and sharply condemned curious inquirers, as is evident by *John* 21:22 and *Acts* 1:6-7, and the great reason why our Saviour did so frequently check this humour of curiosity was because the great indulgers of it were too frequent neglecters of the more great, necessary, and important points of religion.

Curiosity is one of Satan's most dangerous engines, by which he keeps many souls out of their closets, yea, out of heaven. When many a poor soul begins in good earnest to look towards heaven, and to apply himself to closet duties, then Satan begins to stir himself up, and to labour with all his might so as to busy the poor soul with futile inquiries, and curious speculations, and unprofitable curiosities, so that the soul has no time for closet prayer. Ah! how well might it have been with many a man, had he but spent one quarter of that time in closet prayer that he has spent in curious inquiries after things that have not been fundamental to his happiness.

The pagan priests affected curiosity; they had their mythologies, and strange canting expressions of their imaginary inaccessible deities, to amaze and amuse their blind superstitious followers, and thereby to hold up their popish and apish idolatries in greater veneration. Oh, that there were none of this heathen spirit among many in these days, who have their faces toward heaven! Ah! how many are there that busy themselves more in searching after the reasons of the irrecoverableness of man's Fall than they do to recover themselves out of *their* fallen estate! Ah, how many are there that busy themselves more about the apostasy of the angels than they do about securing their interest in Christ! And what a deal of precious time have some spent in discovering the natures, distinctions, properties, and orders of angels.[1]

That high-soaring counterfeit Dionysius[2] describes the hierachy of angels as exactly as if he had dwelt among them. He says there are nine orders of them, which he grounds upon nine words, which are found partly in the Old Testament, and partly in the New; as seraphim, cherubim, thrones, powers, hosts, dominions, principalities, archangels, and angels; and at large he describes their several natures, distinctions, and properties, as that the first three orders are for immediate attendance on the Almighty, and the next three orders for the general government of the creatures, and the last three orders for the particular good of God's elect; that the archangel surpasses the beauty of angels ten times, principalities surpass the archangels twenty times, and that powers surpass the principalities forty times, etc. How he came to this learning is not known, and yet this hierarchy in these nine several orders has been widely received through many ages of the church.

[1] Peter Martyr says that to inquire accurately and subtly of the angels is *magis ad curiositatem nostram, quam ad salutem* [tends more to curiosity than to salvation]; and he wishes that the schoolmen in their knotty, thorny, and unprofitable discourses had observed this.

[2] A neo-Platonic writer whose works probably date from around 500 AD and were long wrongly attributed to Dionysius the Areopagite (*Acts* 17:34).

The Platonics were the first that divided the angels into three orders, some above heaven, called *super-coelestes;* others in heaven, called, *coelestes;* and others under heaven, called *subcoelestes,* and accordingly they assign them several offices, namely:

First, Those above heaven, I mean this visible heaven, continually stand before God, as they say, praising, and lauding, and magnifying his name.

Secondly, They in heaven are there seated to move, and rule, and govern the stars.

Thirdly, They under heaven are, some to rule kingdoms, others provinces, others cities, others particular men.

Several Christian writers, who have written on the hierarchy of angels, follow these opinions. Now, if we should take these for real truths, then it will follow that the highest angels minister not to the saints, but only and immediately to God himself, which is expressly contrary to several Scriptures, as you may see by those below, among others.[1] When I spoke on the ministration of the blessed angels, I then proved in several exercises, as some of you may remember, 'that all the angels in heaven were commanded and commissioned by God to be serviceable and useful to the heirs of salvation. Are they not all ministering spirits, sent forth to minister for them who shall be heirs of salvation?'

The devil knows he is no loser, and the curious soul but a very little gainer, if he can but persuade him to spend most of his precious time in studying and poring over the most dark, mysterious, and hidden things of God. He

[1] *Jude* 9; *Luke* 1:19, 26; *Zech.* 4:1–10; *Rev.* 5:6; *Heb.* 1:14.

who affects to read the Revelation of John more than his plain epistles, or Daniel's prophecies more than David's Psalms, and is more busy about reconciling difficult Scriptures than he is about mortifying lusts, or that is set more upon vain speculations than upon things that make most for edification, he is not the man that is cut out for closet prayer. Such as affect sublime notions, obscure expressions, and abstracted conceits, are but a company of wise fools, that will never take any delight to be with God in a corner. Had many men spent but half that time in secret prayer that they have spent in seeking after the philosopher's stone, how happy might they have been! How holy, how happy, how heavenly, how humble, how wise, how knowing, might many men have been, had they spent but half that time in closet prayer, that they have spent in searching after things that are hard to be understood! (2 *Pet.* 3:16). But,

4. Fourthly, *beware of engaging yourselves in a crowd of worldly concerns.*

Many have so much to do on earth that they have no time to look up to heaven. As much earth puts out the fire, so much worldly business puts out the fire of heavenly affections. Look, as the earth swallowed up Korah, Dathan, and Abiram (*Num.* 16:32), so much worldly business swallows up so much precious time that many men have no leisure to be with God in their closets. This business is to be done, and that business cannot be omitted, and the other necessary occasion must be attended, so that I have no leisure to step out of my shop into my closet, says the earthly-minded man (*Phil.* 3:19). Thus a crowd of worldly businesses crowds closet prayer quite out of doors. Many drive so great a trade in their shops, that their private trade to heaven is quite laid by. There is nothing that has kept men more from Christ and closet prayer, than the shop, the exchange, the farm, and the oxen, etc. (*Luke* 14:16–22). The stars which have least circuit are nearest the pole; and men that are least perplexed with worldly businesses are commonly nearest to God, to Christ, to heaven, and so the fitter for closet prayer.

It is sad when men grasp so much business, that they can have no leisure for communion with God in a corner. The noise is such in a mill as hinders all private intercourse between man and man; and so a multitude of worldly businesses makes such a noise as that it hinders all private intercourse between God and the soul. If a man of much business should now and then slide into his closet, yet his head and his heart will be so filled and distracted with the thoughts of his employments that God shall have little of him but his bodily presence, or, at most, but bodily exercise, which profits little (*1 Tim.* 4:8). If Christ blamed Martha (*Luke* 10:40–42), for the multitude of her domestic employments, though they were undertaken for the immediate service and entertainment of himself, because they hindered her in her soul's concerns, oh, how will he one day blame all those who, by running themselves into a crowd of worldly businesses, do cut themselves off from all opportunities of pouring out their souls before him in secret. But,

5. Fifthly, *beware of secret sins.*

There is no greater hindrance to secret prayer in all the world than secret sins; and therefore stand upon your watchtower, and arm yourselves with all your might against them. There is an antipathy between secret sinning and secret praying, partly from guilt, which makes the soul shy of coming under God's secret eye; and partly from those fears, doubts, disputes, and disorders that secret sins raise in the heart. Light is not more opposite to darkness, Christ to Belial, nor heaven to hell, than secret prayer is to secret sins; and therefore, whatever you do, look that you keep clear of secret sins. To that purpose consider these four things :

i. *First, that God is privy to our most secret sins.*[1] His eye is as much upon secret sins, as it, is upon open sins: *Psa.* 90:8, 'Thou hast set our iniquities before thee, our secret sins in the light of thy countenance.' God has an eye upon our inmost evils, he sees all that is done in the dark: *Jer.* 23:24, 'Can any hide himself in secret places that I shall not see him? saith the LORD: do not I fill heaven and earth? saith the LORD.' *Prov.* 15:3, 'The eyes of the LORD are in every place, beholding the evil and the good.' To say that God does not see the most secret sins of the children of men, is not only derogatory to his omniscience, but also to his mercy; for how can God pardon those sins, which he does not see to be sins? There is no, cloud, nor curtain, nor moment of darkness, that can stand between the eyes of God and the ways of men: *Prov.* 5:21, 'The ways of men are before the eyes of the LORD,

[1] *Psa.* 139:1-4; *Jer.* 13:27; 29:23; *Psa.* 39:1; *1 Kings* 20:39; *Job* 10:12.

and he pondereth all his goings.' In this Scripture Solomon mainly speaks of the ways of the adulterer, which usually are plotted with the most cunning secrecy; yet God sees all those ways. Look, as no boldness can exempt the adulterer from the justice of God, so no secrecy can hide him from the eye of God. Though men labour to hide their ways from others, and from themselves, yet it is but labour in vain to endeavour to hide them from God. Men that labour to hide God from themselves, can never hide themselves from God.

I have read that Paphnutius converted Thais and Ephron, two famous harlots, from uncleanness, only with this argument, 'That God sees all things in the dark, when the doors are fast, the windows shut, and the curtains drawn.' *Heb.* 4:13, 'Neither is there any creature that is not manifest in his sight: but all things are naked and opened (or anatomised) even to the eyes of him with whom we have to do.' This is an allusion to the priests under the law, who, when they killed a beast, all things that were within the beast were laid open and naked before the priest, that he might see what was sound and what was corrupted. Though evil be done out of the eye of all the world, yet it is naked and manifest in his sight with whom we have to do.

Those sins which lie closest and are most secretly lurking in the heart, are as obvious and odious to God as those that are most openly written upon a man's forehead. God is πανοφθαλμος, *all eye*, so that he sees all, the most secret turnings and windings of our hearts. Our most secret sins are as plainly seen by him, as any thing done by us at noonday: *Psa.* 139:11–12, 'If I say, Surely the darkness shall cover me; even the night shall be light about me. Yea, the darkness hideth not from thee; but the night shineth as the day: the darkness and the light are both alike to thee.' Not the thickest clouds can bar out his observance, whose eyes fill heaven and earth. What is the curtain, or the darkest night, or the double lock, or the secret chamber, to him who clearly observes all things in a perfect nakedness. God has an eye upon the most inward intentions of the heart, and the most subtle motions of the spirit. Those philosophers were mistaken that held the eye and ear of God descended no lower than the heavens. Certainly there is not a creature, not a thought, not a thing, but lies open to the all-seeing eye of God. The Lord knows our secret sinnings as exactly as our visible sinnings: *Psa.* 44:21, 'He knoweth the secrets of our hearts.' Would not a malefactor speak truly at the bar, did he know, did he believe, that the judge had windows that looked into his heart?

Athenodorus, a heathen, could say, that all men ought to be careful in the actions of their life, because God was everywhere, and beheld all that was done. Zeno, a wise heathen, affirmed that God beheld even the thoughts.

It was an excellent saying of Ambrose, 'If you cannot hide yourself from the sun, which is God's minister of light, how impossible will it be to hide yourself from him, whose eyes are ten thousand times brighter than the sun.'[1] Though a sinner may baffle his conscience, yet he cannot baffle the eye of God's omnisciency. Oh! that poor souls

---

[1] Ambrose, *Offic.* lib. i. cap. xiv.

would remember, that as they are never out of the reach of God's hand, so they are never from under the view of his eye. God is all eye. *Jer.* 16:17, 'For mine eyes are upon all their ways; they are not hid from my face, neither is their iniquity hid from mine eyes.' *Job* 34:21–22, 'For his eyes are upon the ways of man, and he seeth all his goings. There is no darkness, nor shadow of death, where the workers of iniquity may hide themselves.' *Jer.* 32:19, 'For thine eyes are open upon all the ways of the sons of men, to give every one according to his ways, and the fruit of his doings.'

You know what Ahasuerus, that great monarch, said concerning Haman when, coming in, he found him cast upon the queen's bed on which she sat, 'What', he said, 'will he force the queen before me in the house?' (*Esther* 7:8). There was the killing emphasis in the words *before me*. 'Will he force the queen before me? What, will he dare to commit such villainy, and I stand and look on?' O sirs! to sin in the sight of God, to do wickedly under the eye of God, is a thing that he looks upon as the greatest affront, and as the highest indignity that can possibly be done unto him. What, he says, will you be drunk before me? Will you swear and blaspheme before me? Will you be wanton and unclean before me? Will you be unjust and unrighteous under mine eye? Will you profane my Sabbaths, and pollute my ordinances before my face? Will you despise and persecute my servants in my presence?

This, then, is the killing aggravation of all sin, that it is done before the face of God, that it is committed in the royal presence of the King of kings; whereas the very

THE SECRET KEY TO HEAVEN

consideration of God's omnipresence should bravely arm us against sin and Satan; the consideration of his all-seeing eye should make us shun all occasions of sin, and make us shy of all approaches of sin. Shall the eye of the master keep the scholar from blotting his copy? Shall the eye of the judge keep the malefactor from picking and stealing? Shall the eye of the master keep the servant from idling and trifling? Shall the eye of the father keep the child from wandering and gadding about? Shall the eye of the husband keep the wife from extravagancies and indecencies?

Shall the sharp eye of wise Cato, or the quick eye of a near neighbour, or the severe eye of a dear friend, keep you from many enormities and vanities? And shall not the strict, the pure, the jealous eye of an all-seeing God, keep you from sinning in the secret chamber, when all curtains are drawn, doors bolted, and every one in the house in bed or abroad but you and your Delilah? Oh! what dreadful atheism is bound up in that man's heart, who is more afraid of the eye of his father, his pastor, his child, his servant, than he is of the eye, the presence of the eternal God? Oh! that all whom this concerns, would take such serious notice of it, as to judge themselves severely for it, as to mourn bitterly over it, as to strive mightily in prayer with God both for the pardon of it, and for power against it.

The apostle sadly complains of some in his time who wallowed in secret sins. *Eph.* 5:12, 'For it is a shame even to speak of those things which are done of them in secret.' He speaks of such as lived in secret fornications and uncleanness. There were many that had put on a form of godliness who yet did allow themselves in the secret acting of abominable wickedness and filthiness, as if there were no God to behold them, nor conscience to accuse them, nor judgment-day to arraign them, nor justice to condemn them, nor hell to torment them. Oh! how infinitely odious must they be in the eyes of a holy God, who can highly court and compliment him in public, and yet are so bold as to provoke him to his face in private. These are like those whores who pretend a great deal of affection and respect to their husbands in public, and yet at home will play the harlots before their husbands' eyes.

Such as perform religious duties only to cloak and colour over their secret filthinesses, their secret wickednesses; such as pretend to pay their vows, and yet wait for the twilight (*Prov.* 7:13–15; *Job* 24:15); such as commit wickedness in a corner, and yet with the harlot wipe their mouths, and say, What have we done? Such shall at last find the chambers, the stones out of the wall, the beam out of the timber, the seats they sit on, and the beds they lie on, to witness against all their wanton dalliances, and lascivious carriages in secret (*Hab.* 2:11). *Heb.* 13:4, 'Whoremongers and adulterers God will judge.' He will sentence them himself; and why? but because such sinners carry it so closely and craftily, that oftentimes none but God can find them out. Magistrates often neglect the punishing of such sinners, when secret wickedness is made known; and therefore God himself will sit in judgment upon them. Though they may escape the eyes of men, yet they shall never escape the judgment of God.

Heart iniquities do not fall under any human sentence. Usually whoremongers and adulterers are marvellously furtive and secret and subtle to conceal their abominable filthiness; therefore the harlot is said to be subtle of heart (*Prov.* 7:10). The Hebrew is translated by Rabbi Solomon *munito corde,* having her heart fenced; 'For', he says, 'as a city is environed with fortifications, so her heart is fortified round about with subtlety.' Or else it may be rendered *occlusa corde,* 'fast shut up in the heart, even as closed as a besieged city', that is, 'most secret in the subtlety of her heart, however open she be in the boldness of her outward carriage.' So the prophet Agur reckons the way of a man with a maid, and the way of an adulterous woman, among those things which neither himself nor any other man was possibly able to discover and find out, and compares it to the way of three things which no intelligence nor industry of man is able to discover; but yet God sees all, and will bring them to the bar (*Prov.* 30:19–20). But,

ii. *Secondly,* consider *that secret sins shall be revealed.*[1] The most hidden works of darkness shall be openly manifested; for though the actings of sin be in the dark, yet the judgings of sin shall be in the light; *Luke* 8:17, 'For nothing is secret that shall not be made manifest; neither anything hid, that shall not be known, and come abroad.' The slanders of the Jews concerning the magical arts of

[1] In my treatise 'Apples of Gold' [Brooks' *Works,* vol. 1], I have proved by many arguments that the sins of the saints shall not be brought into the judgment of discussion and discovery in the great day, and therefore understand this second particular of such who live and die in their secret sins without repentance and faith in the blood of Christ.

Christ and his apostles, the horrible lies of the pagans concerning the incestuous copulations of the Christians, and their drinking man's blood, were in time discovered what they were: *Eccles.* 12:14, 'God shall bring every work into judgment, with every secret thing, whether it be good or whether it be evil.' Mark, he does not say some work, but *every* work; and not only works, but *secrets;* and not only secrets, but *every* secret; and not only secret good things but *evil* too; whether good works or evil works, whether secret or open, all must be brought to judgment. The books of God's omniscience, and man's conscience, shall then be opened, and then secret sins shall be as legible in your forehead, as if they were written with the most glittering sun-beams upon a wall of crystal. All men's secret sins are printed in heaven, and God will at last read them aloud in the ears of all the world: *1 Cor.* 4:5, 'Judge nothing before the time, until the Lord come, who both will bring to light the hidden things of darkness, and will make manifest the counsels of the heart.'

Look, as there is a world of flies and motes in the air, which we never see till the sun shines, so there are many thousand thousands of proud thoughts, and unclean thoughts, and worldly thoughts, and malicious thoughts, and envious thoughts, and bloody thoughts, etc., which the world does not see, does not know; but in the great day, when the counsels of all hearts shall be manifest, then all shall out, then all shall appear, both to the upper and the lower world. In the great day all masks, visors, and hoods shall be pulled off, and then all shall come out;

all that ever you have done in the secret chamber, in the dark corner, shall be made known to men and angels, yes, to the whole court of heaven, and to all the world beside. *Rom.* 2:16, 'In the day when God shall judge the secrets of men by Jesus Christ.'

In this great day, God will judge not only our words but our works, not only our open works, but also our secret works and ways. When Jehoiakim was dead, there were found the characters, superstitious marks, and prints of his sorcery upon his body (2 *Chron.* 36:8); which shows how deeply idolatry was rooted in his heart, seeing he bare the marks in his flesh during his life. He being a king bore it out bravely, and kept all hidden; but when he was dead, then all came out, then the marks of his abominable idolatry appeared upon his body. Though sinners, though the greatest of sinners, may hide and keep close their horrid abominations for a time, yet there will come a time when all shall out, when all their secret marks and secret abominations shall be obvious to all the world.

But sinners may be ready to object and say, 'Let us but alone in our secrets sins till that day, and then we shall do well enough.'

iii. And therefore in the third place, consider that *God many times does, even in this life, discover and make known to the world men's secret sins* (*Isa.* 41:21–23). God loves to act suitable to his own names. Now, to be a revealer of secrets, is one of his names (*Dan.* 2:47); and accordingly, even in this world, he often brings to light the most hidden things of darkness. Of all the glorious attributes of God, there is none that suffers so deeply by secret sins, as the attribute of his omniscience; and therefore in this world God often stands up to vindicate the honour of that attribute, by unmasking sinners, and by bringing to the light all those secret paths and ways of wickedness in which they have long walked undiscovered.

It was for the honour of this blessed attribute of God, that the secretly plotted sin of Ananias and Sapphira (*Acts* 5:1–12), was so openly discovered; 'And great fear came upon all the church, and upon as many as heard these things.' Joseph's brethren for a long time hid their malice, their craft, their cruelty, their envy, their treachery, in selling their brother into Egypt; but at last by amazing and thought-provoking providences, all was brought to light (*Gen.* 42:21–22; 50:15–22).

Conscience, that for a time may seem to be asleep, yet will in time awake, and make the sinner know, that he is as faithful in recording, as he is fearful in accusing; and this Joseph's brethren found by sad experience. As with Gehazi: he sins secretly, he lies fearfully, and after all he defends it stoutly; but at last all comes out, and instead of being clothed richly, he and his posterity were clothed with a leprosy for ever; and instead of two changes of garments, God hangs them up in chains, as a monument of his wrath to all generations (2 *Kings* 5:20–27). So Achan secretly and sacrilegiously steals a fine Babylonian garment, and two hundred shekels of silver, and a wedge of gold of fifty shekels' weight, and hides them in the earth in the midst of his tent, and by reason of this, Israel flees before their enemies; but at last Achan is taken, and all comes out, and his golden wedge proved a wedge to

cleave him, and his Babylonian garment a garment to
shroud him. Joshua makes a bonfire of all that he had
secretly and sinfully stolen, and burns him, and his children, and all that he had, in it. Oh, how openly, how
severely does God sometimes punish men for their most
secret iniquity!

The same you may see in that great instance of David;
2 *Sam.* 12:9–12, 'Wherefore hast thou despised the commandment of the Lord, to do evil in his sight? thou hast
killed Uriah the Hittite with the sword' (this was done in
a secret letter), 'and hast taken his wife to be thy wife.
Now, therefore, the sword shall never depart from thy
house, because thou hast despised me, and hast taken the
wife of Uriah the Hittite to be thy wife. Thus saith the
Lord, Behold, I will raise up evil against thee out of thine
own house, and I will take thy wives before thy eyes and
give them to thy neighbour, and he shall lie with thy wives
in the sight of the sun. For thou didst it secretly, but I will
do this thing before all Israel, and before the sun' (see
2 *Sam.* 16:22). David was very studious and very industrious to hide his sin, and to save his credit; but the
covering made of Uriah's blood was too short, and too
narrow to hide his folly with Bathsheba, and therefore
when he had done all he could, his sin was tossed like a
ball, from man to man, through court, city, and country.

I have read of one Parthenius, treasurer to Theodobert,
king of France, who, having traitorously slain a special
friend of his called Ausonius, with his wife Papianillae,
when no man suspected or accused him of it, he detected
and accused himself after this strange manner: as he slept

in his bed, suddenly he roared out most pitifully, crying for help, or else he perished; and being asked what troubled him, he, half asleep, answered, 'That his friend Ausonius and his wife, whom he had slain long ago, summoned him to judgment before God.' Upon which confession he was apprehended; and, after due examination, stoned to death.[1] Thus the terrors and horrors of his own conscience discovered that secret wickedness which none could prove against him.

I have read[2] how Sultan Muhammad II, the great Turk, had with great rewards procured two Turks to undertake to kill Scanderbeg [an Albanian national hero, c. 1404–68]. These traitors came to Scanderbeg, making such a show of their detestation of Muhammad's tyrannical government and vain superstition that they were both by Scanderbeg and others reputed to be indeed the men they desired to be accounted; and so after they had learned the principles of the Christian religion, they were both, by their own desire, baptized. Soon after, by a providence, it so fell out that these two traitors fell at variance between themselves, by which means the plot came to be discovered; and after due examination and confession of the fact, they were presently condemned and executed. Conscience is God's spy in the bosom.[3] Conscience, as a

[1] Thomas Beard, *Theatre of God's Judgments,* 1597.

[2] Richard Knolles, *General History of the Turks,* 1603.

[3] Conscience, says Philo, is the little consistory of the soul. Conscience is *mille testes,* a thousand witnesses, for or against a man. Conscience is a court of record, and whatever it sees it writes down; and conscience is always as quick in writing as the sinner can be in sinning. The very heathen could say that conscience was a god to every man.

scribe, a register, sits in the closet of your hearts, with pen in hand, and makes a daily record of all your secret ways and secret crimes, which are above the cognizance of men. It sets down the time when, the place where, the manner how, and the persons with whom such and such secret wickednesses have been committed; and that so clear and evident, that, go where you will, and do what you can, the characters of them shall never be cancelled or razed out till God appear in judgment. Let a man sin in the closest retirement that human policy can contrive, let him take all the ways he can to hide his sins, to cloak and cover his sin, as Adam did, yet conscience will so play the judge, that it will bring in the evidence, produce the law, urge the penalty, and pass the sentence of condemnation upon him.

There is many a man who makes a fair profession, and who has a great name in the world, who yet is αυτο-κατακριτος, self-condemned, for those secret sins which are not obvious to the eyes of man, nor punishable by the hands of men; yes, many times in this life God raises such a hell of horror and terror in many men's consciences, by reason of their secret sins, that they can have no rest nor quiet, neither at bed nor at board, neither lying down nor rising up. Happily would they conceal their sins, they are unwilling that the world should know how vile they have been in secret; but conscience being upon the rack, and continuing to gnaw, accusing, and condemning them, they can hold no longer. Now all must out; and now those sins that were most secret and concealed, come to be published upon the housetop.

Some who have been in anguish of conscience, others that have been smitten with a frenzy, and many in their very sleep, have been often the blazers and proclaimers of their own secret filthiness and wickedness. In those cases God has made many a secret sinner cry out with the leper, 'Unclean, unclean' (*Lev.* 13:45); and with Judas, before all present, 'I have sinned, I have sinned' (*Matt.* 27:4). Many times in this life God very strangely and wonderfully discovers those secret works of darkness in which persons have lived long undiscovered.

A Pythagorean bought a pair of shoes upon trust; the shoemaker dies, he is glad, thinks them gained; but a while later his conscience flies at him, and becomes a continual chider and tormentor of him. He hereupon repairs to the house of the dead, casts in his money with these words, 'There, take your due; you live to me, though dead to all besides.' But,

iv *Fourthly,* consider that *secret sins are in some respects more dangerous than open sins.* Many a man bleeds to death inwardly and no man perceives it. The more inward and secret the disease is, the more the man is in danger to lose his life. There are no fevers so dangerous as those that prey upon the spirits and inward parts; so there are no sins so dangerous and pernicious to the souls of men as those that are most inward and secret. Secret sins often reign in the souls of men most powerfully when least apparently.

First, consider that *he that sins secretly deprives himself of those helps and remedies which, by a divine blessing, might arm him against, yes, make him victorious over sin;*

THE SECRET KEY TO HEAVEN

namely, the prayers, counsels, reproofs, examples, and encouragements of friends, relations, etc. A man's house may be on fire, but whilst it is all inward, help comes not in; but when the fire flames out, when it catches the outside of the house, then help runs in, then help on all hands is ready. He that sins in secret debars himself of all public remedy, and takes great pains to damn his soul in a corner, and to go to hell in the dark. But,

Secondly, secret sins will make way for public sins. He that makes no conscience of sinning in the secret chamber, will before long, with Absalom, be ready to spread a tent upon the top of the house, and to go in to his concubines in the sight of all Israel (2 *Sam.* 16:22). Such as have made no conscience of stealing a few pins or pence or a few shillings in private, have in time come to be so bold as to take the road at high noon. The cockatrice must be crushed in the egg, else it will soon become a serpent. The very thought of sin, if but thought on, will break forth into action, action into custom, custom habit, and then both body and soul are irrecoverably lost to all eternity.

If Satan can but wound our heel, as the poets say of Achilles, he will make a hard shift but he will send death from the heel to the heart. If this subtle serpent can but wriggle in his tail by an ill thought, he will soon get in his head by a worse action.

Hence it is that Christ calls hatred murder, and a wanton eye adultery. Secret hatred often issues in open murder, and secret wanton glances of the eye often issue in visible adultery. If Amnon be sick with the sinful conception of incestuous lust, how will his soul be in pain and travail till he has brought forth! And how many are there that in secret have now and then but one cup more than enough, who now may be seen at high noon reclining against every post. As secret diseases in the body, if not cured, will in time openly break forth, so secret sins in the soul, if not pardoned and purged, will in time be openly revealed. Covetousness was Judas' secret sin; and no sooner does an occasion or a temptation present itself, but he is very ready and forward to betray and sell his Lord and Master for thirty pieces of silver before all the world: 'Lust having conceived, brings forth sin' (*James* 1:15); and that thus, first, sin has its conception, and that is delight; and then its formation, and that is design; and then its birth, and that is action; and then its growth, and that is custom; and then its end, and that is damnation.

Thirdly, secret sinning puts far more respect and fear upon men than upon God. You will be unjust in secret, and wanton in secret, and unclean in secret, and treacherous in secret, etc., and why, but because you are afraid that such or such men should know it, or that such and such friends should know it, or that such and such relations should know it? Ah! poor wretch, are you afraid of the eye of a man, of a man that shall die, and of the son of man, which shall be made as grass? (*Isa.* 51:12), and yet not tremble under his eye, 'whose eyes are as a flame of fire, sharp and terrible, such as pierce into the inward parts?' (*Rev.* 1:14; *Heb.* 4:13). Ah! how full of atheism is that man's heart that tacitly says, 'If my sins be but hid from the eyes of the world, I do not care though the Lord knows them, though the Lord strictly observes them, though the Lord sets a mark, a memorandum upon them.' What is this, O man, but to brave it out with God, and to tempt him, and provoke him to his very face, who is 'light, and in whom there is no darkness at all'? (1 *John* 1:5–6). Ah! sinner, sinner, can man damn you? Can man disinherit you? Can man fill your conscience with horrors and terrors? Can man make your life a very hell? Can man bar the gates of glory against you? Can man speak you into the grave by a word of his mouth? And after all, can man cast you into endless, easeless, and remediless torments? Oh, no! Can God do all this? Oh, yes! Why, then, does your heart not stand more in awe of the eye of the great God, than it does of the eye of a poor, weak, mortal man?

I have insisted the longer on this particular, because there is not any one thing in all the world that more hinders secret communion with God and secret prayer than secret sins. And oh, that you would all make it your great business to watch against secret sins, and to pray against secret sins, and to mourn over secret sins, and deeply to judge and condemn yourselves for secret sins, and carefully and conscientiously to shun and avoid all occasions and provocations that may be as fuel to secret sins.

Certainly there are no men or women that are so sincere and serious in closet prayer, or that are so frequent, so fervent, so constant in closet prayer, or that are so delightful, so resolute, so undaunted, or so unwearied in closet prayer, as those that keep themselves most clear and free from secret sins. For a close, remember this, that though secret sins are in some respects more dangerous than other sins are, yet in three respects they are not so bad nor so dangerous as other sins are:

First, In that they do not so scandalize religion as open sins do.

Secondly, In that they do not shame, grieve, and wound the hearts of the saints as open sins do.

Thirdly, In that they are not so infectious to others, nor such provocations to others to sin against the Lord as open sins are.

And thus you may see what those things are that you must carefully take heed of, if you would addict yourselves to closet prayer.

And as you must take heed of these five things, so there are several other things that you must carefully and conscientiously apply yourselves to, if you would be found faithful and constant in this great duty, viz. closet prayer. Now they are these:

1. First, *lament greatly and mourn bitterly over the neglect of this choice duty.*

He that does not make conscience of mourning over the neglect of this duty, will never make conscience of performing this duty. Oh, that your heads were waters, and your eyes a fountain of tears, that you might weep day and night for the great neglect of closet prayer (*Jer.* 9:1). He that mourns most for the neglect of this duty will be found most in the practice of this duty. He that makes most conscience to accuse, arraign, and condemn himself for neglecting closet prayer, will make most conscience of giving himself up to closet prayer. It is said of Adam that he turned his face towards the garden of Eden, and from his heart bitterly lamented his great Fall. Oh, that you would turn your faces towards your closets, and bitterly lament your rare going into them. But,

2. Secondly, *cultivate the habit and accustom yourselves to closet prayer.*

Make private prayer your constant trade. Frequency begets familiarity, and familiarity confidence. We can go freely and boldly into that friend's house whom we often visit. What we are in the habit of doing, we do with ease and delight. A man who is in the habit or accustomed to write, to read, to ride, to run, or to play on this or that musical instrument, etc., does it all with delight and ease; and so does a man who is in the habit of closet prayer; he will manage it with delight and ease. But,

3. Thirdly, *keep a diary of all your closet experiences* (*Deut.* 7:18–19; *Psa.* 66:12).

Oh, carefully record and note down all your closet mercies! Oh, be often in reading over your closet experiences, and be often in meditating and in pondering upon your closet experiences! There is no way like this, to inflame your love to closet prayer, and engage your hearts in this secret trade of private prayer.

Oh, remember that at such a time you went into your closets with hard hearts, and dry eyes; but before you came out of your closets, how sweetly, how evangelically, how powerfully were you melted, humbled before the Lord (*Psa.* 6:6; 39:12; 56:8)! Oh, remember how that at another time you went into your closets clouded and benighted, but came out of your closets with as glorious a shine of God upon your souls, as Moses had upon his face, when he came down from the mount from communing with God (*Exod.* 34:28-29)! Oh, remember how often you have gone into your closets with cold, frozen spirits, but before you came out of your closets what a fire has God kindled in your souls, what a spirit of burning have you found in your hearts (*Luke* 24:31-32; *Isa.* 4:4)! Oh, remember how often you have gone into your closets straitened and shut up, but before you have come out, how have your souls been like the chariots of Amminadib (*Song of Sol.* 6:12)! Oh, remember what power God has given you against corruptions in your closets, and what strength God has given you against temptations in your closets! Oh, remember the sweet discoveries of divine love that you have had when in your closets! Oh, remember the secret visits, the secret kisses, the secret embraces, the secret whispers, the secret love tokens that Christ has given you in your closets! Oh, seriously ponder upon these things, and then closet duties will be sweet unto you!

It was a sweet saying of Bernard, 'O saint, do you not know that your husband Christ is bashful, and will not be familiar in company; retire yourself by meditation into your closet, or into the fields, and there you shall have Christ's embraces' (see *Song of Sol.* 7:11-12). *Meditatio nutrix orationis*, meditation is the nurse of prayer. Oh, the more any man meditates upon his closet experiences, the more he shall find his heart engaged to closet duties; the

THE SECRET KEY TO HEAVEN

more you ponder upon closet experiences, the sweeter will closet experiences be to your souls; and the sweeter closet experiences are to your souls, the more your souls will delight to be with God in your closets.

Pliny tells us of one Messalla Corvinus, whose memory was so bad, that he forgot his own name.[1] And I am afraid that many of your memories are so bad, that you forget your closet mercies, your closet experiences.

I have read of such a pestilential disease once at Athens, as took away the memories of those that were infected with it, so that they forgot their own names. Oh, that I had not cause to fear that some pestilential disease or other has so taken away the memories of many that they have quite forgotten their closet experiences. Well, friends, remember this, though stony hearts are bad, yet iron memories are good; and oh, that you would all labour after iron memories, that so you may remember and ponder upon your closet experiences. I have read of the heathens, how they made use of white and black stones, for these two ends: first, they gave them to persons at their arraignment before the judges; if they were condemned to death, they gave him a black stone, but if absolved and set free, a white stone, to which custom the Holy Ghost seems to allude in *Rev.* 2:17, 'To him that overcometh will I give a white stone.' A second use of those stones was this, that by them they might keep an account of all the good days or evil days they had met with in their lives. Hence Giacopo Senzaro having been long in love, and much crossed about his match, he filled

[1] Lib. vii., cap. 24.

a pot full of black stones, putting only one white stone among them, and being asked the reason, answered, 'There will come one white day', meaning his marriage day, 'which will make amends for all my black days.'

Ah, friends! how often has God given you the white stone in your closets! Certainly you have had more white stones than black stones: your closet mercies and experiences have been more than your public losses and miseries. O sirs! did you but reckon your good days according to the white stones you have had in your closets, it would make you more in love with closet prayer than ever. But,

4. Fourthly, *be sure that you do not spend so much of your precious time in public duties and ordinances as that you can spare none for private duties, for secret services.*

Though Pharaoh's cattle ate up one another, yet our duties must not eat up one another (*Gen.* 41:4). Public duties must not eat up family duties, nor family duties eat up public duties, nor either of them eat up closet duties. The wisdom of a Christian most eminently sparkles and shines, in giving every duty its proper time and place; I was going to say, that either he was no Christian, or at least no excellent Christian, that is all eye to read, or all ear to hear, or all tongue to speak, or all knee to bow, to kneel, to pray (*Eccles.* 8:5). Ah! how many are there that spend so much time in hearing of this man and that, and in running up and down from meeting to meeting, that they have no time to meet with God in their closets. O sirs! your duties are never so amiable and lovely, they are never so radiant and beautiful, as when they are season-ably and orderly performed.

Oh, how wise are the men of this world so to order all their civil affairs that no one business shall interfere with another. They set apart for each business a convenient proportion of time; they allot an hour for one business, two for another, three for another, etc. Oh, that we were as wise for our souls, as wise for eternity, as they are for this world. Oh, that our hearts would so consult with our heads, that we may never want a convenient time to seek God in a corner! That devil that loves to set one man against another, and one nation against another, and one Christian against another, loves to set one ordinance against another, and one duty against another. Hence it is that on the one hand he works some to cry up public prayers in opposition to secret prayer; and on the other hand he works others to cry up private duties in opposi-tion to all public duties; whereas all Christians stand obliged by God so to manage one sort of duties as not to shut out another sort of duties. Every Christian must find time and room for every duty incumbent upon him. But,

5. Fifthly, *love Christ with a more inflamed love.*

Oh, strengthen your love to Christ, and your love to closet duties. Lovers love much to be alone, to be in a cor-ner together (*Song of Sol.* 7:10–12). Certainly the more any man loves the Lord Jesus, the more he will delight to be with Christ in a corner. There was a great deal of love between Jonathan and David (*1 Sam.* 18, 19, and 20 compared), and according to their love, so was their private converse, their secret communion one with another; they were always best when in the field together, or when in a corner together, or when behind the door together, or when locked up together; and just so would it be with you, did you but love the Lord Jesus Christ with a more raised and a more inflamed love; you would be always best when you were most with Christ in a corner.

Divine love is like a rod of myrtle, which, as Pliny reports, makes the traveller that carries it in his hand so lively and cheerful, that he never faints or grows weary.[1] Ah! friends, did you but love the Lord Jesus with a more strong, with a more raised love, you would never faint in closet duties, nor you would never grow weary of closet duties. Look, as the Israelites removed their tents from Mithcah to Hashmonah, from *sweetness* to *swiftness,* as the words import (*Num.* 33:29), so the sweetness of divine love will make a man move swiftly on in a way of closet duties. Divine love will make all closet duties more easy to the soul, and more pleasant and delightful to the soul; and therefore do all you can to strengthen your love to Christ, and your love to closet work.

It was observed among the first Christians, that they were so full of love one to another that they could be acquainted one with another as well in half an hour as in half a year. O sirs! if your hearts were but more full of love to Christ, and closet duties, you would quickly be better acquainted with them, you would quickly know what secret communion with Christ behind the door means. But,

[1] *Natural History*, Lib. xv. cap. 35–39.

6. Sixthly, *be highly, thoroughly, and fixedly resolved, in the strength of Christ, to keep close to closet duties*, in the face of all difficulties and discouragements that you may meet withal (*Psa.* 44:17–20).

A man of no resolution, or of weak resolution, will be won with a nut, and lost with an apple. Satan, and the world, and carnal relations, and your own hearts, will cast in many things to discourage you, and take you off from closet prayer; but be nobly and firmly resolved to keep close to your closets, let the world, the flesh, and the devil, do and say what they can.

Daniel was a man of an invincible resolution; rather than he would omit praying in his chamber, he would be cast into the den of lions.

Of all the duties of religion, Satan is the most deadly enemy to this of secret prayer; partly because secret prayer spoils him in his most secret designs, plots, and contrivances against the soul, partly because secret prayer is so musical and delightful to God, partly because secret prayer is of such rare use and advantage to the soul, and partly because it lays not the soul so open to pride, vain glory, and worldly applause as prayer in the synagogue does; and therefore he would rather that a man should pray a thousand times in the synagogues, or in the corner of the streets, or behind a pillar, than that he should pray once in his closet; and therefore you have need to steel your hearts with holy courage and resolution, that whatever suggestions, temptations, oppositions, or objections you may encounter, that yet you will keep close to closet prayer.

There is not any better bulwark in the day of battle than a heroic resolution of heart before the day of battle. Sanctified resolutions do exceedingly weaken and discourage Satan in his assaults, they do greatly daunt and dishearten him in all his undertakings against the soul. That man will never long be quiet in his closet who is not steadfastly resolved to seek the Lord in a corner, though all the powers of darkness should make head against him. O sirs! divine fortitude, holy resolutions, will make you like a wall of brass that no arrows can pierce; they will make you like armour of proof, that no shot can hurt; they will make you like that angel who rolled away the stone from before the door of the sepulchre (*Matt.*28:2); they will either enable you to remove the greatest mountains of oppositions that lie between you and closet prayer, or else they will enable you to step over them.

Luther was a man of great resolution, and a man that spent much time in closet prayer. And such another was Nehemiah, who met with such opposition that, had he not been steeled by a strong and obstinate resolution, he could never have rebuilt the temple, but would have sunk in the midst of his works. Now, he was a man for private prayer, as I have shown in the beginning of this treatise. Who more resolute than David? And who more for secret prayer than David? The same I might say of Paul, Basil, and many others, who have been famous in their generations.

O sirs! sanctified resolutions for closet prayer, will chain you faster to closet prayer than ever Ulysses' resolutions did chain him to the mast of the ship.

It was a noble resolution that kept Ruth close to her mother-in-law when her sister Orpah only complimented her, kissed her, and took her leave of her (*Ruth* 1:10–20). Be but nobly resolved for closet prayer, and then you will keep close to it, when others only court it, and take their leave of it.

In the Sallentine country, there is mention made of a lake that is always brimful: if you put in never so much, it never runs over; if you draw out never so much, it is still full.[1] The resolution of every Christian for closet prayer, should be like this lake, still brimful. Tide life, tide death,[2] come honour or reproach, come loss or gain, come liberty or bonds, come what can come, the true-bred Christian must be fully and constantly resolved to keep close to his closet. But,

7. Seventhly, *strive for a greater effusion of the Holy Spirit*; for the greater measure any man has of the Spirit of God, the more that man will delight to be with God in secret: *Zech.* 12:10, 'And I will pour upon the house of David, and upon the inhabitants of Jerusalem, the spirit of grace and of supplications'; verses 12–14, 'And the land shall mourn, every family apart; the family of the house of David apart, and their wives apart; the family of the house of Nathan apart, and their wives apart; the family of the house of Levi apart, and their wives apart; the family of the house of Shimei apart, and their wives

[1] Pliny, *Natural History*, Lib. ii. cap. 106. 226.
[2] This expression occurs in Shakespeare, *Midsummer-Night's Dream*, Act 5, Scene 1.

apart; all the families that remain, every family apart, and their wives apart' (see also *Joel* 2:28–29; *Isa.* 44:3); mark, in the last of the last days, when men shall be generally under a greater effusion of the Holy Spirit than ever, then they shall be more given up to secret prayer than ever. There will never be such praying apart, and such mourning apart, as there will be when the Lord shall pour out most richly, gloriously, abundantly, of his Spirit upon his poor people. Now, every one shall pour out his tears and his soul before God in a corner, to show the soundness of their sorrow, and to show their sincerity by their secrecy; for *ille dolet vere, qui sine teste dolet,* he grieves with a witness [truly] that grieves without a witness [observer].

Certainly, the more any man is now under the blessed pouring out of the Spirit of Christ, the more that man gives himself up to secret communion with Christ. Every man is more or less with Christ in his closet, as he is more or less under the anointings of the Spirit of Christ. The more any man has of the Spirit of Christ, the more he loves Christ, and the more any man loves Christ, the more he delights to be with Christ alone. Lovers love to be alone. The more any man has of the Spirit of Christ, the more his heart will be set to please Christ.

Now, nothing pleases Christ more than the secret prayers of his people: *Song of Sol.* 2:14, 'O my dove that art in the clefts of the rock, in the secret places of the stairs, let me see thy countenance, let me hear thy voice; for sweet is thy voice, and thy countenance is comely.' And therefore such a one will be much in secret prayer. The more any man has of the Spirit of Christ, the more his heart will be set upon glorifying and exalting Christ. Now, nothing glorifies Christ more, nor exalts him more, than secret prayer; and therefore the more any man has of the Spirit of Christ, the more that man will be found in secret prayer.

There are many persons who say they would be more in their closets than they are, but that they meet with many hindrances, many occasions, many diversions, many temptations, many oppositions, many difficulties, many discouragements, which prevent them. Ah, friends! had you a greater measure of the Holy Spirit upon you, none of these things would ever be able to hinder your secret trade heaven-ward. Had you a more rich anointing of the Spirit upon you, you would never plead, there is a lion in the way, a lion is in the streets (*Prov.* 26:13); but were there a thousand lions between you and your closets, you would either step over them, or make your way through them, that so you might enjoy communion with Christ in your closets. But,

8. Eighthly and lastly, as ever you would keep close to private prayer, *be frequent in the serious consideration of eternity.*

Oh, see eternity standing at the end of every closet prayer, and this will make you pray to purpose in your closets.

O sirs! every work you do is a step to a blessed or to a cursed eternity. Every motion, every action in this life, is a step toward eternity. As every step that a traveller takes brings him forward to his journey's end, so every step that a man takes in the secret ways of righteousness and holiness, such as closet duties are, they bring him nearer to his journey's end, they bring him nearer to a blessed eternity. Look, as every step the sinner takes in a way of wickedness brings him nearer to hell, so every step that a saint takes in a way of holiness brings him nearer to heaven. Look, as every step that a wicked man takes in the ways of unrighteousness brings him nearer to a cursed eternity, so every step that a godly man takes in a way of righteousness brings him nearer to a blessed eternity.

Zeuxis, the famous painter, was so exceedingly careful and cautious in drawing all his lines, that he would let no piece of his go abroad into the world to be seen of men, till he had turned it over and over, and viewed it on this side and that side again and again, to see if he could spy any fault in it; and being asked the reason why he was so curious, and so long in drawing his lines, answered, *Æternitati pingo*, I paint for eternity. O sirs! we all pray for eternity, we fast for eternity, we read for eternity, we hear for eternity, we wait for eternity, we weep for eternity; and therefore, oh, how curious, how exact, how wise, how faithful, how careful, how diligent, how unwearied should we be in all our closet duties and services, seeing that all we do is in order to eternity! Friends! you must all before long be eternally blessed, or eternally cursed; eternally happy, or eternally miserable; eternally saved, or eternally damned; eternally accepted, or eternally rejected. And therefore what infinite cause have you frequently to shut your closet doors, and to plead mightily with God in a corner, for the lives of your poor, precious, and immortal souls, that they may be eternally saved in the great day of our Lord Jesus. O sirs! when any hindrances to closet prayer present themselves to you, seriously remember eternity, and that will remove them.

It is related of one Pachomius that whenever he felt any unlawful desires to arise in his mind, he used to drive them away with the remembrance of eternity.[1]

The same author relates a story out of *Benedictus Rhexanus*,[2] of an ungodly fellow who, on a certain night could not sleep, and, upon the serious consideration of death and eternity, and the damned lying in hell, could not be at rest, but eternity did still run in his mind; gladly would he have shaken off the thoughts thereof, as gnawing worms; therefore he followed sports, and pastimes, and merry meetings, and sought out companions like himself, and sat on many occasions so long at his cups that he laid his conscience asleep, and so seemed to take some rest; but when he was awakened, his conscience flew in his face, and would continually suggest thoughts of eternity to him. Of all things in the world he could not bear to be kept awake in the night; but so it happened that, being sick, he was kept awake one night, and could not sleep at all, whereupon these thoughts rose in him: 'What, is it so tedious, then, to be kept from sleep one night, and to lie a few hours in the dark? Oh, what is it then to be kept in torments and everlasting darkness! I am here in my own house upon a soft bed in the dark, kept from sleep but one night; but to lie in flames and endless

[1] Jeremias Drexel (1581–1638), *Considerations on Eternity*, 8.
[2] ibid., 5

misery, how dreadful must that needs be!' These and such like meditations were the happy means of this young man's conversion.

I have read a notable story of one Theodorus, a Christian young man in Egypt who, when there was a great deal of feasting, mirth, and music in his father's house, withdrew himself from all the company, and being got alone, he thus thought with himself, 'Here is content and delight enough for the flesh, I may have what I desire, but how long will this last? This will not hold out long'; then falling down upon his knees before the Lord in secret, he said, 'O Lord, my heart is open to thee, I indeed know not what to ask, but only this: Lord, let me not die eternally; O Lord, thou knowest I love thee, O let me live eternally to praise thee.'

If there be any way or means on earth to bring us upon our knees before God in secret, it is the serious and solemn thoughts of eternity. Oh, that the fear of eternity might fall upon all your souls! Oh, that you would all seriously consider that, after a short time is expired, you must all enter upon an eternal estate! Oh, consider that eternity is an infinite, endless, bottomless gulf, which no line can fathom, no time can reach, no age can extend to, no tongue can express. It is a duration always present, a being always in being; it is *unum perpetuum hodie*, one perpetual day, which shall never see night. O sirs! This is and must be for a lamentation, viz., that eternity is a thing that most men never think of, or else very slenderly; a snatch and away, as dogs are said to lap and away at the river Nile. But as ever you would have your hearts chained to your closets and to closet duties, as the men of Tyre chained their god Apollo to a post, that they might be sure of him; then seriously and frequently ponder upon eternity, and with those forty valiant martyrs, continually cry out ω αιδιοτης, ω αιδιοτης, 'O eternity, eternity!'[1]

Mr Wood,[2] after some holy discourse, fell into deep thought, and cried out before all present, for near half a quarter of an hour together, 'For ever, for ever, for ever.' Augustine's prayer was, 'Hack me, hew me, burn me here, but spare me hereafter, spare me hereafter.' Certainly, if Christians would but spare one quarter of an hour every day in the solemn thoughts of eternity, it would make them more in love with closet prayer than ever, yea, it would make them more fearful of omitting closet prayer than ever, and more careful and conscientious in the discharge of all closet-duties than ever.

And thus, according to my weak measure, I have given out all that at present the Lord has graciously given in to my poor soul, concerning this most necessary, most glorious, and most useful point of points, viz., closet prayer.

I shall, by assisting grace, follow this poor piece with my prayers, that it may be so blessed from on high as that it may work mightily to the internal and eternal welfare of reader, hearer, and writer.

[1] Basil, *Homily on the Feast of the Forty Martyrs*.
[2] Probably the Mr Wood whose funeral sermon was the first form of 'Apples of Gold'. See Brooks' *Works*, vol. 1.